EXPLORER

2.0

EXPLORE GOD AND THE NATIONS

Books may be ordered by writing:

usa@movida-net.com

Movida USA Inc.
PO Box 472
Alliance, NE 69301

Or by logging onto
www.movida-net.com

This book was published in 2014 and was printed by Publication Printers Corp. 2001 S. Platte River Drive • Denver, Colorado 80223

Designed by: Ana Alarcon, (Paraguay)
Edited by: Scott Langemeier and Geoff House (USA)

Translated from the original Spanish version Explorer 2.0

Scripture references are taken from THE HOLY BIBLE, NEW INTERNATIONAL VERSION®, NIV® Copyright © 1973, 1978, 1984, 2011 by Biblica, Inc.®

Printed in USA

ISBN
978-0-692-02880-3

Experience "MISSIONS" In A New Way With Explorer 2.0!

1. **Imagine,** people would understand the verb "go" always involves a geographical relocation.

2. **Imagine,** from this understanding, thousands of young Christians from Europe and the United States would "go" to the mission field.

3. **Imagine,** sending missionaries would become something normal, a daily service of the church and not just an exception.

4. **Imagine**, in church services, world missions would be talked about, prayed for, and given to.

5. **Imagine,** more young people would be motivated to study at Bible schools with the goal of being trained to serve the unreached.

6. **Imagine,** more Christian bookstores would present more literature about World Missions and not just gifts, calendars, and novels.

If these dreams become a reality, we would once again become a generation of Christians who rewrite history. Explorer 2.0 desires to be a tool to make these goals come true! To make Jesus known - worldwide - is the most beautiful and most important task of His Church, but sadly this responsibility is not a burden to many Christians. We must understand that missions and the Church have unity in the heart of God. Jesus' Church is not a place where you go, but it is who you are. The Word of God should help you "go," and prayer should prepare the ground for it. It is known worldwide that Christians of the so-called "third world" now understand this responsibility! They are an example to the rest of the world and are overtaking the "first world" on the fast track. This is something we need to notice!

Exactly 24 years ago, we started our first mission training camp in Chile, in an old tent, with 20 young people. Today, God is using our camps to mobilize thousands to spread the Gospel around the world!

Are you willing to be influenced by Explorer 2.0? If you are, then you are ready to experience missions in a new way!

Thomas Vögelin

Swiss. Founder and director of MOVIDA. Served 25 years as a missionary in South America and is now serving in Weingarten, Germany at MOVIDA's international headquarters.

Defining Decisions

As I look back on my life, I recognize certain key decisions have had a major influence in affecting where I stand today. As a 15-year-old, when God changed my life, I never dreamed I would be used to influence the lives of thousands of people around the world. I am sure young David had similar thoughts as he stood before Goliath with just a sling and stone. I can only imagine the young virgin girl, Mary, doubted she could impact the world carrying the Messiah. I also believe Jesus' group of young disciples did not understand their decision to follow him would change the world forever.

The Bible is full of stories about young people taking God at his word. Today, you have two choices before you: 1) You can live by succumbing to the lie your day is guaranteed and has little impact in the Kingdom. 2) You can live recklessly abandoned in faith and believe your day is a responsibility to be treasured.

Accept the challenge to live in faith. The decisions you make today will define your future. You have a tool in your hands that can play an instrumental role in affecting both your life and the Kingdom of God. Explorer 2.0 will challenge you at your core. It will connect you to the heart of God and will allow you to hear his beautiful voice.

Over 2,000 years ago, Jesus gave us the greatest command in the history of the world when he said, "All authority in heaven and on earth has been given to me. Therefore go and make disciples of all nations, baptizing them in the name of the Father and of the Son and of the Holy Spirit." By putting the words of Explorer 2.0 into action in your life, you are making the choice to be obedient to Christ in His command to reach the nations!

Scott Langemeier
MOVIDA USA Founder

A Special Thanks

From the depths of our heart, we thank our Lord and Savior, Jesus Christ, for providing the passion, resources, and opportunity to produce this devotional book. For the first time, Explorer 2.0 has been produced in the English language. Understanding how this book started leaves one standing in awe of the grace of God. The work of this devotional began in Paraguay, but the book has now been distributed throughout Europe and the United States. In his mighty ways, God is using this devotional to reach the unreached people groups of the world.

A special thanks goes to Felix and Maria Rodriguez (Paraguay). Their excitement to reach the world with the Gospel of Christ has been a driving force of the Explorer project over the past ten years. Through faith and dedication, they began this work and have since affected the lives of thousands of people around the world.

Thank you to the numerous authors for investing time and energy in writing the devotions. Their life experience and revelations from God are part of what makes this devotional so unique.

The MOVIDA International team has also played an instrumental role in the production of this devotional. A special thanks goes to Scott Langemeier and Geoff House (United States) for their enthusiastic work on the English translation of Explorer 2.0. Without their commitment, the dream of translating this devotional into the English language would not have become a reality. The MOVIDA USA team of translators and editors is deserving of a warm thanks for their dedicated hard work. They have personified self-sacrifice and commitment.

A final thanks is extended to Ana Alarcón (Paraguay) for her creative graphic design work. Her work is easily overlooked, but has been fundamental to the production of this devotional. Ana designed the cover and pages of this incredible devotional.

May God carry this devotional into the hands of faithful disciples, may their prayers be heard, and may they forever change the eternal density of this lost world.

Thanks!

JANUARY

Olympic Competitors

> *Do you not know that in a race all the runners run, but only one gets the prize? Run in such a way as to get the prize. 1 Corinthians 9:24*

The swimmer who has won the most Olympic medals in the history of the games, Michael Phelps, decided to become a professional athlete at the young age of fourteen. After his decision was made, he had to adjust many things in his life, in his thinking, and in his daily habits. These adjustments helped him achieve his goals.

The Olympic events are not a present day invention; they were also popular in the time of Paul. He saw the effort and sacrifice needed to be an Olympic athlete was similar to the sacrifices needed in order to follow Christ. Paul understood this sacrifice well. In his own life, he had to pay a high price to be faithful to his calling of taking the Gospel to many nations. This meant hardship, rejection, danger, and even death.

Despite all these problems, Paul was not discouraged. Like a true athlete, he had determination. In the middle of adversity, Paul said, "Run to win." We must decide what we want to achieve in life and to what purpose. Paul knew exactly why he "ran" and what his purpose in life was. He wanted to fulfill his mission and to be able to receive the award that lasts forever.

God calls you to take His message to others and to be willing to pay the price. But be encouraged; this price is not in vain. God has promised to love and care for those who trust in Him and obey His call.

A. Betancur

Let us run to win!

Adyghe - Syria

Population: 31,000
The Adyghe are a subgroup of the Circassians who live in the north of Syria. They have a good economy, and many are members of the government and army. Their language is Adyghe, which has a translation of the New Testament and a film about Jesus. It is estimated that 0.4% are Christians.

Pray: For the church to be strengthened and to be a powerful testimony about Jesus.

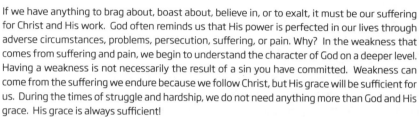

Suffering For Christ

> But he said to me, "My grace is sufficient for you, for my power is made perfect in weakness." Therefore I will boast all the more gladly about my weaknesses, so that Christ's power may rest on me. 2 Corinthians 12:9

If we have anything to brag about, boast about, believe in, or to exalt, it must be our suffering for Christ and His work. God often reminds us that His power is perfected in our lives through adverse circumstances, problems, persecution, suffering, or pain. Why? In the weakness that comes from suffering and pain, we begin to understand the character of God on a deeper level. Having a weakness is not necessarily the result of a sin you have committed. Weakness can come from the suffering we endure because we follow Christ, but His grace will be sufficient for us. During the times of struggle and hardship, we do not need anything more than God and His grace. His grace is always sufficient!

Often we will feel weak. We compare ourselves to other people who we believe are more capable, and we become discouraged. It is in that moment we should seek the power of God. God's plan is perfect. He longs to show us how powerful He is. He is capable of showing His power in our lives during the times of suffering and pain. To be used by God, you do not need to be strong and self-sufficient. He uses ordinary people who recognize and rest in His grace. No matter what circumstances you are going through, remember to trust God and His grace!

A. Gulard

God uses the weak to perfect His power.

Abai Sungai - Malaysia

Population: 1,400
The Abai Sungai live near the coast on Sabah Island. Although they have many animistic traits in their daily life, they are considered Muslims. They speak Abai, and there is no translation of the Bible available. It is estimated that no Christians live among them.

Pray: For Bible translators to live among the Abai Sungai and to provide them with the Word of God in their language.

All Things New

> "He who was seated on the throne said, "I am making everything new!" Then he said, "Write this down, for these words are trustworthy and true." Read Revelation 21:5-7

Last year, you may have had many stressful and intense moments, but hopefully you recognized God's favor during both the good and the bad times. God in His glory created what you have today: life. You are here, and you are alive.

Jeremiah 29:11 says, "God has clear thoughts and purposes for your life, for good and not for evil. Therefore, let every situation you experience, good or bad, lead to a new level of growth and achievement in your spiritual life." This year, make a commitment to walk in faith. Stop doing things that hinder your walk with Jesus and start celebrating the life God has given you. Your future is full of new opportunities. Do not forget, you live in God's hands!

Part of accepting this exciting life is also realizing that suffering is a part of our earthly life. God did not promise our days would be only happy, but He did promise He would always be with us until the end of the world.

When we are able to understand His love, through the power of the Holy Spirit, we will begin to understand that He is always with us. God is with us, in our lives, to make all things new. Start this new year fresh... Allow God to make it new!

D. Duk

Are you ready for a new start?

Achagua - Colombia

Population: 300
The Achagua have portions of the Bible in their Achagu language, but the younger generation is bilingual and speaks Spanish as well. Twelve percent are believers, and most of them live in the cities.

Pray: For God to strengthen the church among the Achagua.

Bible in a year: Luke 4-5 / Genesis 6-7 / Psalm 3

Everybody vs. Nobody

> Therefore go and make disciples of all nations, baptizing them in the name of the Father and of the Son and of the Holy Spirit.
> Matthew 28:19

In a missionary newsletter I read recently, there was an interesting story about four people named Everybody, Somebody, Anybody, and Nobody:

"There was once a very important job that should be done by Everybody, and Everybody was sure that Somebody would do it. Anybody could have done it, but Nobody did. Somebody got angry because it was a job for Everybody. Everybody thought that Anybody could do it, but Nobody imagined he would prevent Everybody from doing it. In the end, Somebody blamed Everybody when Nobody did what Anybody could do."

The command in Matthew 28:19 is a job that everyone can and should do. However, we often believe someone else is going to do it, and in the end we complain that no one is doing it. How many people in your church are involved in the Great Commission? Is everyone doing their part? Anyone in your church can be engaged in missionary work. Are you part of the group who believes that anyone can do it, but in the end no one does it? Do not let this story be a reality in your life or your church.

F. Rodriguez

Everybody is included in the work!

Alsatian - France

Population: 1,701,000
The Alsatian people live on the border of Switzerland. They speak Swiss German and French. Although they have the Bible in their language, 40% are non-religious, and only 1.5% of Alsatians follow Jesus. They live immersed in secularism.

Pray: : For spiritual awakening in their lives and for a desire in their hearts to seek God.

Right To Doubt

{ *The Lord said to Abram, "Leave your country, your people and your father's household and go to the land I will show you ." Genesis 12:1*

As I write this, I am crossing the Andes, as I have done many times. However, this time is different. I, along with my family, have decided to leave the comfort and security we had in Chile, a beautiful country where we have many good friends. In Chile, we served as youth pastors and were the leaders of a missions organization. We are now moving to Argentina where we do not know many people. We have no close friends there, and we know little about our new ministry. In almost every aspect, we are starting completely new.

While looking out my window at the falling snow, many questions come to my mind. Did I understand the voice of God correctly? What if this is not the correct plan for my family? What if we cannot adapt to the new environment? Is it wrong to have so many doubts?

I believe it is clear that many biblical characters had to move, leave things behind, change lands, and start from scratch. The Bible tells us their stories, and we are able to see the characters weaknesses and realize they were as human as we are. I'm sure when they experienced obstacles, they too had many questions. I'm so thankful their doubts didn't stop them from doing what God wanted them to do. In the same way, God himself will respond to every doubt and obstacle we think is in our way.

If you are in a time of transition, you have the right to question. But do not let your doubts prevent you from moving to where God wants you to be!

W. Nuñez

Have courage!

Acheron - Sudan

Population: 10,000
The Acheron are located in the southern part of Sudan. The entire family lives together, and they farm and breed barnyard animals. The predominant religion is Islam, and 30% have retained their animist beliefs. There are very few Christians among these ten thousand.

Pray: For the Word of God to impact the Acheron's hearts.

The Owner Of The Mission

{ *God is love. 1 John 4:16*

When we think about God and world missions, it is essential to understand the mission to reach the world with the Gospel of Jesus is not our own idea or private project. The mission was given to us from God. God is a missionary God. World missions are ordained from God, and He uses the church as His instrument for His mission. Therefore, we need to mobilize our local churches. God desires to use the church as an instrument, and that is why the church must show God's universal love for all people!

World missions rests in the heart of God who is a fountain of love. The true meaning of missions is that we have an assignment simply because God loves people. In other words, it is through the church God wants to show everyone His universal love. The church as the Body of Christ is the physical presence of Jesus in this world for the blessing and transformation of the world. So why do we participate in the mission of God?

•Because God is a God of love, God's mission is love, and sending that love into the world is the purpose of God.

•Because it is who we are - we are elected to serve, and we are the instruments God uses to bless the nations.

How is your life and the life of the church affected when you participate in the mission of God? C. Scott

Become part of the mission!

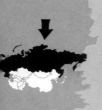

Abaza - Russia

Population: 38,000

The Abaza people live in the Caucasus Mountains near the border of Georgia. They are devoted to raising animals and cultivating tobacco, and are well known for their hospitality. Their language is Abaza, which has no translation of the Bible. The majority of them profess the Islamic faith.

Pray: For the Word of God to be translated into their language.

We Will Not Be Silent

> For if you remain silent at this time, relief and deliverance for the Jews will arise from another place, but you and your father's family will perish. And who knows but that you have come to your position for such a time as this? ... Esther 4:14

Often we believe the task of sharing the love of Christ with others is only for pastors, missionaries, or for those who can articulate biblical knowledge with ease. We also often believe our actions alone are enough to convey the message of salvation, so we remain silent and do not speak about Christ. However, God expects something very different than this passive mindset. In this world, no one is accidentally created. God has a purpose for every life, and the main purpose of our lives is to talk with others about what Jesus did on the cross. We talk with others so they can know how to be reconciled with God. God puts us in specific places, at specific times, for a purpose. If we fail to do what He has called us to accomplish, God is capable of using another person. When God uses another person, however, we miss out on the opportunity to be blessed as a useful tool in the hands of God. Queen Esther knew what God wanted her to do, and she took steps needed to fulfill that mission. She served God and His people in her obedient desire to fulfill the task God had given her, even though she also knew severe consequences were possible.

Now is the time to be obedient to His divine appointments. Today, you have the opportunity to bring relief and deliverance to others.

W. Bello

Let us not remain silent!

Ache - Paraguay

Population: 1,500
The Ache people live in the area of Alto Parana. Their mother tongue is Ache, which has a complete Bible translation. They face many territorial problems with other people groups. Their belief is a mix of Christianity and animism.

Pray: For missionaries to boldly speak with the Aches. Pray for their hearts to be opened to the Gospel.

The Endorsement Of A Missionary

> { *Paul, an apostle of Christ Jesus by the will of God, To God's holy people in Ephesus, the faithful in Christ Jesus... Ephesians 1:1*

Paul defends his calling as an apostle with two very important points. His first defense of his calling is by stating that his church had commissioned him to be sent. Secondly, he claims his apostleship is the will of God for his life.

It is important for missionaries to know that Jesus Christ was "sent." In Hebrew and Greek, Christ, or Messiah, means "the anointed one". This is important because the Jewish people had been waiting for God to send the Messiah. Jews believed the Messiah was to come and adopt the Gentiles as part of the people of God. The name Jesus in Hebrew means "God Saves." It is encouraging for those who share the Gospel to know they are messengers of Jesus and that God is the one who saves. The name of Jesus guarantees it!

Paul was a man who was at complete peace with God's will for his life. He knew his ministry was God's will. He did not base his calling on his high educational qualifications or on his ability to theologically articulate ideas. Paul's local church in Antioch had commissioned him to serve. In doing this, they took the responsibility to stand beside him and support him in his service as a missionary. Although this was important, Paul knew the real support and comfort he received was in the assurance that he was doing the will of God. In a pastoral or missionary ministry, it is important to have a divine calling, and it is equally important for the church to be the one sending. This means the main question is: are your ears open to hear His call?

There is no greater honor than to be a servant sent by Jesus Christ, by the will of God, and through His church.

A. Neufeld

Will you answer the call?

Aghu - Indonesia

Population: 4,400
The Aghu live on the bank of a river near the border of Papua New Guinea. They spend their time fishing, gathering sago, hunting, and deforesting the lowlands. They have seen the influence of the Gospel on their neighbors in Papua New Guinea; however, they do not have a translation of the Bible.

Pray: For the Aghu to be able to hear the Gospel in their language.

We Are Ambassadors

> We are therefore Christ's ambassadors, as though God were making his appeal through us. We implore you on Christ's behalf: Be reconciled to God. 2 Corinthians 5:20

Every Christian is considered an ambassador of God, and every ambassador has a specific mission to fulfill. The apostle Paul proposes evangelism as being such a mission. Being an ambassador of Christ can be compared to being an ambassador of a government. As an ambassador of a government, you do not make decisions or act on your own accord. Ambassadors never proclaim their own message but rather the message of their government or kingdom. Ambassadors remain faithful to the orders entrusted to them. As ambassadors of Christ, we must understand God has sent us with a mission to complete. God will protect us as we powerfully proclaim to the world the truth about His glorious Kingdom.

Usually, ambassadors do not live in their home country. If you are going to be an ambassador to the world, you cannot hide in the comfort of your home. You need to go where people have not heard the Word of God. In doing this, do not expect unbelievers to have an overwhelming interest in your service. It is not their responsibility to be interested in you, but rather it is the church's responsibility to be interested in unbelievers!

Being an ambassador can be a dangerous task, but that in and of itself is not a reason to back away from your calling. We can expect anguish and pain when living a life in Christ, but there is nothing more glorious than sharing in His work! As ambassadors of Christ, preaching the gospel is our responsibility!

O. Simari

Are you willing to fulfill your mission as an ambassador of Christ?

Agaria - India

Population: 222,500

Traditionally, the Agaria are Hindu. Their native language is Agariya. Around 14,000 Agarias have now embraced Islam. They often face discrimination and have therefore adopted Urdu as their language, in which the Gospel is available.

Pray: For God to use His Word in Urdu for the salvation of the Agarias.

Know It Well!

> *...That you may know the certainty of the things you have been taught. Read Luke 1:1-4*

The Gospel of Luke was written to effectively order the life events of Jesus and to give testimony to His work. Luke originally wrote this Gospel to enlighten others so they "may know the certainty of the things they have been taught." Luke knew the importance of sound truth and longed for others to understand it.

In the world today, many people claim to be "new age pastors" or "enlightened speakers." A danger within this emerging group is that their messages often distort the uncompromising Word of God. When someone claims to have a "new view," it is important to make sure the view is rooted in Scripture and not based on personal ideas. Professing a "fresh view" must support truth conveyed in the Bible!

Being rooted in Biblical truth is highly important. Do not be deceived into thinking only pastors and Bible teachers have the responsibility to study the Scriptures. Every believer has a responsibility to know God's Word. Acts 17:11 says, "Now the Berean Jews were of more noble character than those in Thessalonica, for they received the message with great eagerness and examined the Scriptures every day to see if what Paul said was true."

Paul honors the nobility and wisdom of the Berean Christians because they were relentless in studying the Word of God. Follow their example and study the Bible!

M. de Rodriguez

Know your Bible!

Akhdam - Yemen

Population: 272,000
The Akhdam are a group of black Arabs living in the slums. They speak Arabic Taizzi-Aden and have no translation of the Bible. They are strict followers of Islam.

Pray: For the Akhdams to receive a Bible in their language. Pray for their hearts to be open to receive Jesus.

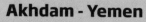

How Far Will You Go?

*{ If anyone forces you to go one mile, go with them two miles.
Matthew 5:41*

Thomas A. Edison was an American inventor who patented over one thousand inventions. Some of his inventions included the light bulb, phonograph, and motion picture machine. At age seven, he enrolled in a public school, but after only three months, his teacher expelled him. She claimed he was disinterested, clumsy, and deaf. His mother, Nancy Elliot, ignored the teacher's claims and began to educate the young boy.

Although Thomas was criticized, he continued to press on. His mother was motivated and accepted the double role she would have to play. She became not only his mother, but also his teacher. Her selfless actions were beyond her responsibilities as a mother.

Doing more than what is expected of you is our responsibility as Christians. Our goal is to be a blessing in the lives of others. Having a mindset of blessing others and doing more than what is expected of you prepares you to "go the extra mile."

The true meaning of serving is found when you "go the extra mile." It is in this extra mile that you experience the love, power, and majesty of God. Doing more than what is expected forces you to rely on God and leaves you dependent on His power, mercy, presence, and provision. Doing this frees you of selfishness and allows you to become the person God wants you to be. When you face adversity, serve beyond what is expected!

M. Inciarte

Go the extra mile!

Adyghe - United States

Population: 3,300
The Adyghe are a group of Caucasian origin, and they have preserved their language, Adyghe. The New Testament was translated into their language in 1992, but they still profess the Islamic faith. Despite evangelistic efforts, there are no known Christians among them.

Pray: For the Word of God to touch their hearts and for them to surrender to Christ.

Bible in a year: Luke 10:21-42 / Genesis 18 / Psalm 11

Are You A Friend of God?

> And the scripture was fulfilled that says, "Abraham believed God, and it was credited to him as righteousness," and he was called God's friend. James 2:23

Have you ever wondered if God has friends? In the book of James, God recognizes Abraham's belief and calls him a friend. Like Abraham, we should desire to have a deep friendship with our Heavenly Father. There is no greater honor than to be known as a friend of God.

Having a friendship with anyone requires trust, and it is no different with God. He will keep His promises; He will fulfill the things He vowed to do. If God has made you a promise, you can trust it will be fulfilled. We are sinful and disloyal, but God always remains faithful. He will fulfill everything without exceptions. The majority of people find believing and trusting God difficult, but God is patient and gives all believers the wonderful privilege to be known as His friend.

In order to trust God, you must believe in His faithfulness. When you believe in God and in the promises He has given, the next step is to obey and walk forward in faith. God gives friendship to those who desire it. If you want to live passionately for Jesus and desire to live the adventure of being friends with God, then obey and believe His word. Having a friendship with God will change your life!

What promises has He made you? Where has He called you?

G. Vergara

Be a friend of God!

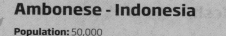

Ambonese - Indonesia

Population: 50,000
The Ambonese of Indonesia speak Malay Ambos. Eighty percent have embraced Protestant Christianity, but secularism and the desire for a comfortable life have resulted in a weak and nominal faith. They desperately need to be reminded of the most basic doctrines of Christianity.

Pray: For the filling of the Holy Spirit in the life of the Ambonese.

Seven Perceptions Of A Man

> But the Lord said to Samuel, "Do not consider his appearance or his height, for I have rejected him. The Lord does not look at the things people look at. Man looks at the outward appearance, but the Lord looks at the heart." 1 Samuel 16:7

In 1 Samuel 16 and 17, David is perceived in seven different ways:

1. David is perceived by God as the right person to rule Israel because of the characteristics of his heart.

2. David was perceived by Samuel as the one to be anointed, but Samuel would not have had this perception if not for the leading of God.

3. David was initially perceived by King Saul as one who "speaks well and is a fine looking man" (1 Samuel 16:18).

4. David was perceived by his father Jesse as a responsible man because he had served his brothers during a time of war (1 Samuel 17:17).

5. David was perceived by his brother Eliab as "conceited" and "wicked-hearted" (1 Samuel 17:28).

6. Later, David was perceived by King Saul as a small boy unable to defeat the giant Goliath (1 Samuel 17:33).

7. David was perceived by Goliath as a "little boy" who confronted him (1 Samuel 17:42). Little did Goliath know that just minutes later this "little boy" would be killing him, with a small stone, and cutting off his head with his own sword.

Do you know how others look at you? How do your parents, siblings, friends, teachers, bosses, and employees perceive you?

F. Chinatti

What is the perception God has of you?

Aguri - Bangladesh

Population: 1,000

The Aguris are found in the district of West Bengal. They consist of two main social castes: superior farmers and lower livestock laborers. Their language is Bengali. It is estimated that almost 100% are Hindu.

Pray: For missionaries working among the Aguri. Pray that they can present the message of salvation with boldness.

My Facebook Account

> *"I have the right to do anything," you say– but not everything is beneficial. "I have the right to do anything"– but I will not be mastered by anything. 1 Corinthians 6:12*

If the title of this devotion caught your eye, then you are probably one of the millions of people on earth who have a Facebook account. It amazes me the amount of people who are connected to a social network. I personally do not have a Facebook account because I know if I did, I would spend too much of my time following the lives of friends.

Instead of investing time into Facebook, I have decided to invest time into a "spiritual network," my Bible. I am convinced that those who invest time in God's spiritual network will grow in their walk with Christ. Investing time in reading the Bible will cause you to be more like Jesus. I find it difficult to start the day by posting a comment on the wall of a friend if the day has not been started by first posting, through prayer, on the wall of God.

We live in a world full of social media. Our virtual connection to others produces a misconception that our relationships are improving because we are constantly "connected" with one another. The constant distraction of social media has begun to weaken both our relationships and our spiritual lives. Do not let your Facebook account get more attention than your spiritual network. Today I invite you to post a message to your Heavenly Father. When Jesus comes back, what will your "posts" on his "wall" say? Will it be full of your gratitude, praise, worship, and genuine requests?

G. Galindo

How will you spend your time today?

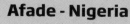

Afade - Nigeria

Population: 37,000

The Afade are known for being musicians and singers. Islam is a popular religion within their villages. Their society permits polygamy, but having a single wife is highly respected. Their language is Afade, which has some audio Bible stories. It is estimated only two percent are Christian.

Pray: For the church to grow in maturity and in number.

He's Sending Me?!

> { *Do you not know that in a race all the runners run, but only one gets the prize? Run in such a way as to get the prize. 1 Corinthians 9:24*

The mission God has entrusted to us is a comprehensive mission that includes every person on earth and embraces every aspect of people's lives. The church does not exist to please itself, but to serve humanity and fulfill the mission entrusted to it.

The local and global mission of God is carried out by His people when they intentionally cross barriers and leave their church to serve those with no church. It refers to bringing the message of salvation, which recognizes no boundaries, to every human being. It is accomplished with both word and deed. It is accomplished when others are invited to be reconciled with God, themselves, other people, and the world. In the words of Charles Van Engen, "Mission involves integrating those without a church into the dynamic life of living with other believers."

God calls all believers to participate in this incredible mission. What does it mean to you to share the Gospel with all people? What are the barriers the church must cross to transform the world?

C. Scott

What part will you have in the mission?

Kurmi - India

Population: 17,410,000

Kurmis live throughout India. Their lifestyle involves farming and trading. Although many have a comfortable life, prosperous and educated, they are seen as one of the lower castes. They majority of Kurmis are Hindus, but some are Buddhists and Jains. No known Christians live among them. Their main language is Hindi, but the entire group speaks over 60 languages.

Pray: The Kurmi would realize Jesus is their only hope for salvation.

With Passion And Compassion

> Suppose one of you has a hundred sheep and loses one of them. Doesn't he leave the ninety-nine in the open country and go after the lost sheep until he finds it? Luke 15:4

Jesus exhibited both passion and compassion very clearly in His life. Passion and compassion are attitudes of the heart. They do not contradict one another, but rather compliment each other perfectly.

Passion is an attitude that drives and motivates. Passion can cause unexpected actions that do not agree with logic or predictability. In our eyes, it seems impulsive to leave ninety-nine sheep to search for one that is lost, but when a shepherd is motivated by passion, this response is not unexpected.

Compassion is an attitude that causes us to be sensitive. Sensitivity allows us to stop, see, and feel what others are experiencing. It allows us to identify with those who are hurting. Compassion means willingly suffering for sheep, although the suffering is not earned.

If passion and compassion were not working in harmony, the world would have very few adventures to tell. These attitudes of the heart are contagious. If you are near a passionate or compassionate person, odds are, you will develop these attitudes.

If passion and compassion are contagious, why are there so many lost sheep? The desire to live comfortably quenches the power of passion. Often we believe being passionate is not worth the effort. In the Bible this is called quenching the Spirit (1 Thess. 5:19). Selfishness hinders having compassion. It is easier to blame our situation on others than to be compassionate and understanding. In the Bible, this refers to closing our hearts (1 John 3:17).

W. Altare

Will you have passion and compassion to find the lost sheep?

Aimele - Papua New Guinea

Population: 200

The Aimele people live in the area of Wawoi Falls. Their religion is animistic and their language is Aimele. The New Testament is in the process of being translated. They are desperate for missionaries to work among them.

Pray: For the completion of the New Testament in their language and for Biblical teaching.

Taking The Initiative In Reconciliation

> Therefore, if you are offering your gift at the altar and there remember your brother or sister has something against you, leave your gift there in front of the altar. First go and be reconciled to them; then come and offer your gift. Matthew 5:23-24

Sometimes I dream about how nice it would be to never fight with anyone, but when I upset my wife, children, friends, or colleagues, I am quickly brought back to reality.

Often when a person dreams about becoming a missionary, they envision a life without conflict. They dream about working with pure imitators of Christ who are mature and stable in their faith. When this dreamer reaches the mission field, he is instantly brought back into reality!

The majority of missionaries who are "serving the Lord" are very persistent in their actions (How else could you overcome all of the obstacles in the mission field?). The challenges a missionary faces when working with other cultures, languages, and personalities can be an enriching experience. Although the constant challenges can be enriching, it can also be very stressful.

Jesus knows the hearts of people. He knows their struggles and desires, which have not changed since the beginning of time. Prepare your hearts for intercultural relationships. Learn to humble yourself and learn not to insist on always being right. Take the initiative in reconciliation by beginning to appreciate others more than yourself!

T. Sandvig

Be like Jesus, the great Reconciler!

Ahar - India

Population: 1,488,500

The people of Ahar are some of India's wealthiest. They own large amounts of land. They follow Hinduism. Ahars are hard to reach with the Gospel because of their high social position. Their language is Hindi, which has many resources for evangelism.

Pray: They are reached with the Gospel, despite the barriers.

Ambassador Of God

> *Rabbi, we know that you are a teacher who has come from God...*
> *Read John 3:1-15*

In the passage above, Jesus is approached and asked a spiritual question. Surprisingly, Jesus answers the question before it is fully asked, "Unless one is born again, he can not enter the kingdom of God." After reading this passage, I have come to believe that we, as Christians, should anticipate questions from the people with whom we come into contact. This is particularly important when communicating with people with whom we already have a relationship. When you have a relationship with someone, it gives you the authority to speak truth and wisdom into their life.

When having a conversation, it is important to speak with purpose. Speaking with purpose can mean speaking about the things of eternity. Doing so will create a mission-minded lifestyle. When people know you speak with a purpose, they will begin to see you differently. When you take time to listen and invest in their lives, it creates possibilities to share biblical truth. This idea of speaking with a purpose and listening is what Jesus did when He met Nicodemus.

How do people see you? Are you seen as a messenger of God? Are you seen as an ambassador of Christ? People will come and talk to you when they see you are living a life obedient to God. Many may be afraid to ask questions, but you can anticipate their questions and speak about your Savior, Jesus Christ!

N. Rivas

Take the initiative!

Anfillo - Ethiopia

Population: 4,200

The majority are farmers or herders of goats and sheep. Marriages are common between clans. They profess Islam, but are very nominal in their beliefs. It is estimated only four percent believe in the Gospel of Jesus. They speak Anfillo, which has a few translated Bible stories.

Pray: For the Bible to be translated into their language.

Bible in a year: Luke 14:1-24 / Genesis 25 / Psalm 18

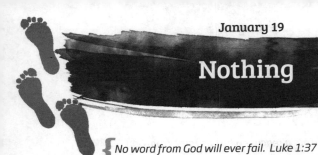

Nothing

{ *No word from God will ever fail. Luke 1:37*

A few years ago, a Muslim friend came to my house. While he was visiting, God moved in his heart and we began to discuss differences between the Bible and the Qur'an. My friend, Hamidu, said, "I know that your Jesus says the Bible is the Word of God. I understand. However, my family is Muslim. Unless I hear directly from God Himself, I do not know what direction I should be heading."

The Islam religion has deeply penetrated Hamidu's culture (Sooninkes in Africa) because it has been influencing them for over a thousand years. Many Sooninkes are Muslims and follow the five pillars of Islam.

As we continued to speak, Hamidu said, "I want God to speak to me through a dream tonight." As I heard this, my heart raced with excitement. I wonder how you would have reacted if Hamidu said this to you? Would you have the faith to say God, who is extremely interested in the salvation of mankind, could speak through a dream?

The Word of God clearly says, "With God nothing is impossible." When Hamidu said this, I was so convinced of God's love for him that I passionately prayed God would respond. When we woke up the next morning, I received the news God did respond!

In the following weeks, God continued to show Hamidu what direction he should be heading. God can do anything to bring someone to repentance!

Pescador

Do you believe God can do anything?

Ansari - Afghanistan

Population: 2,100
Most Ansaris are poor and illiterate. Many men and women work in silk fabrics. Their primary language is Urdu, which the Gospel has been translated into. Very few Ansaris are interested in Christianity. Those who are Christians struggle to connect with other believers.

Pray: The Bible would speak to the Ansaris with power.

Friend Of God

{ *And in you all the families of the earth will be blessed.*
Genesis 12:1-4

If you hear the words "Friend of God", or "Father of Faith", do you automatically think of Abraham? Throughout Abraham's life, he obeyed God and was an example of faith, but do you remember what happened "on the way to reaching his goal?"

Abraham received five major promises from God when he was commanded to leave his country. God promised Abraham:

1) I will make you into a great nation.
2) I will make your name great.
3) I will bless you.
4) I will bless those who bless you.
5) Through you, all people on earth will be blessed.

Despite these great promises, Abraham was a man who had weaknesses and sinned. In Genesis chapter 12 we see Abraham was fearful (v. 12), he was a liar (v.13), he was an opportunist, (v.13) and because of his fear, he was an irresponsible husband (v.16).

So why did God use Abraham, a man with so many weaknesses, as His channel of incredible blessing?

God is gracious and patient and therefore chose to use Abraham to bring His blessing to all people on earth. Today you and I, as a living part of the church, are "chosen" to bring God's blessing to the world. We all have weaknesses, but God still desires to use us!

H. Ziefle

You can be a blessing to this world!

Aragon - Spain

Population: 2,313,000

The Aragon people of Spain live mainly in the province of Zaragoza. Their native language is Aragonese, but the official language is Castilian. The majority are Roman Catholic. Very few believe in the God of the Bible.

Pray: For the Aragonese people to find salvation in Jesus Christ.

Endless Supply Of Love

> You have heard that it was said, "You shall love your neighbor and hate your enemy." But I say to you, love your enemies and pray for those who persecute you. Matthew 5:43-48

These verses are commands spoken by Jesus. A command is not subject to negotiation, which means we are called to love all people. Before Jesus came to earth, nothing like this had been said.

As Jesus proclaims, it is your responsibility to love your enemies and declare God's blessing over them. These commands can be difficult to fulfill because the human heart often desires retaliation against those who have wronged you. Refusing this behavior is one of the first steps in transforming your selfish mind. A transformation of the mind results in thinking as God does, which is contrary to our human nature.

In our human nature we create conflict. As a consequence, we have divided friendships, hardened hearts, and desires for revenge. Loving and praying for all people, including your enemies, will bring you closer to the heart of God. God wants you to love as He loves. When you understand you are infinitely loved, you are enabled to love both your friends and enemies. Understanding His infinite love transforms your heart. God will use your transformed heart to reach the world. Do you want to be a part of bringing salvation to the nations? If so, love everyone as God does!

D. Travis

Love everyone!

Akawaios - Guyana

Population: 4,500
The Akawaios have heard the Gospel. It is estimated that two thousand Akawaias are believers, but discipleship is urgently needed! They have the New Testament in their language.

Pray: : The Akawaia church will grow in the knowledge of Christ and reach more of their own people.

Selected

> Paul, was called to be an apostle of Christ Jesus by the will of God, and our brother Sosthenes,... 1 Corinthians 1:1

In our country, the coaches of the national football team selects the best players to play on the team. The selection of players is important because those who are selected will be representing the entire nation.

Paul was selected to be an apostle, which means he was sent by Jesus to go and share the message of salvation with the world. By the will of the Trinity, Paul was selected for his role as an Apostle. Through the working of the Holy Spirit, he was selected and was then sent by Jesus Christ, which was the will of God. The Trinity does not desire to call only Paul, but the Trinity also desires to call you! Jesus is holy. He desires those He calls to live a life of holiness, just as He does.

Every part of the body of Christ has its own calling. Some are called to be missionaries and others are called to play a role on the sending team. No matter what your role is, all Christians are called to be a part of the mission of Christ.

G. Rivas

What is your role?

Alak - Laos

Population: 4,900
The Alak people of Laos grow coffee beans, rubber trees, and bananas. Their language, Alak, has over 20 dialects. Each of the 20 dialects are unique and are not understandable by others. There are audio Bible stories in five dialects. Their religion is animistic.

Pray: The Word of God would touch their hearts and transform their lives.

The Holy Spirit Is A Missionary

> But you will receive power when the Holy Spirit comes on you; and you will be my witnesses in Jerusalem, and in all Judea and Samaria, and to the ends of the earth. Acts 1:8

The New Testament shows a clear relationship between the Holy Spirit and mission work. In Luke 4:18-19, Jesus speaks about the "mission" or "sending" nature of the Holy Spirit: "The Spirit of the Lord is upon me, because he has anointed me to preach good news to the poor. He has sent me to proclaim freedom for the prisoners and recovery of sight to the blind, to set the oppressed free, to proclaim the year of our Lord's favor". Jesus fulfilled his mission by the power of the Holy Spirit.

On another occasion Jesus said to His disciples: "Peace be with you! As the Father has sent me, I am sending you," and He immediately breathed on them and said to them, "Receive the Holy Spirit " (John 20:21-22). This is another passage in which the Holy Spirit shows a mission nature.

Some say the book "Acts of the Apostles" should be called "Acts of the Holy Spirit through the Apostles" because on every page, the Holy Spirit is taking the lead in advancing the mission of God. Acts 1:8 declares the Holy Spirit is in us is to be witnesses to the ends of the earth!

F. Rodriguez

Is the Holy Spirit leading you in missions?

Anii - Benin

Population: 64,000

The Anii people live in the province of Arácora. They work with agriculture and raise animals. Many of them follow Islam, while others are animistic. Their language, Anii, has a few Biblical audio translations. It is estimated only 4% of this people group are Christians.

Pray: For the Gospel to have a bigger impact in their lives.

Take Care Of Your Heart

> Above all else, guard your heart, for it is the wellspring of life.
> Proverbs 4:23

In the Bible, the words "heart" and "mind" refer to things within us. What is in our heart and mind determines what we do or how we act. Jeremiah 17:9 says, "The heart is deceitful above all things and desperately wicked. Who can know it?"

The sinful nature of men, which takes place in the heart, is what gives birth to evil thoughts, sexual immorality, theft, murder, adultery, greed, malice, deceit, lewdness, envy, slander, arrogance and folly. Within our mind, we manufacture ideas and thoughts against others. Often the sinful nature leads us into situations where these thoughts are brought into the light and exposed.

God is the only one who knows the secrets of the heart (Psalm 44: 20-21), but when you meditate on the word of God, walk in holiness, and strive for a pure heart, you can know your walk with Jesus is being built on solid ground.

Your prayer should be: "Search me, O God, and know my heart: try me and know my anxious thoughts. See if there is an evil way in me, and lead me in the everlasting way" (Psalms 139:23-24).

D. Duk

Will you do it?

Algonquin - Canada

Population: 5,700
The Algonquin live northwest of Ottawa, near Maniwaki. Their religion is Roman Catholic. The Anglican Church is working among them. It is estimated six percent have surrendered to Christ. They have had a New Testament translation in their native language since 1998.

Pray: For Algonquin believers and that God will strengthen the church.

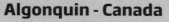

Obedient Servant

> *"I am the Lord's servant," Mary answered. "May your word to me be fulfilled." Luke 1:37-38*

The Virgin Mary is worthy of imitation, not worship. She led a righteous life, dependent upon the Lord, and was used for a great purpose in the Kingdom of God. That purpose was being the mother of our Savior, Jesus Christ.

When the angel told Mary she would be the mother of Jesus, it must have been very surprising. Although she was a virgin, Mary was called to bear a son. This situation must have been terrifying for Mary. During that time in that particular culture, a single mother was deserving of contempt or even sentenced to death. Despite this, Mary knew God would take care of everything. She knew God would carry out His Word faithfully. Sometimes I ask myself, would I have had the same attitude?

Mary possessed two attitudes that are very admirable. The first attitude is that of a servant who was is willing to carry out any calling given by God. The second attitude is one of obedience, regardless of the fact that God's calling could have cost her life.

Mary's example challenges us to depend on God, to put our will in His divine hands, and to be willing to be used by Him at all costs. Your decision to trust Him must be a conscious decision, not an impulsive act.

When have you had to trust God? Are you willing to put your life in God's hands and let His will be done? How has God used you as part of His plan? Have you shared it with others?

M. de Rodríguez

Follow the example of Mary!

Aji - Indonesia

Population: 16,000

The Aji people group is located south of Sumatra and professes the Islamic faith. Their language is predominantly Haji, but they are also multilingual and are able to speak the majority of languages in southern Sumatra. They have the Bible in their own language.

Pray: For the Aji people to share the Gospel in the other languages they can speak.

In All Areas

> You will be my witnesses in Jerusalem and in all Judea and Samaria, and to the ends of the earth. Acts 1:8

Often people create a conflict between "global" and "local" missions. It is important to unite both "global" and "local" missions as expressed in Acts 1:8. The line "Jerusalem, Judea, Samaria, and to the ends of the earth" describes the areas where the local and global levels of missions are united. Jesus speaks of witnessing as being done simultaneously, not sequentially. No area of missions should be more important than the other. They must be balanced and not ranked. The same amount of attention and energy should be given to each area.

The mission to reach others with the Gospel is a responsibility of all Christians. Christians are to remain faithful to completing this mission throughout their entire life. In the pursuit of fulfilling the mission, there should be a morality of faith that involves listening to the cries of the poor, the oppressed, and the lost.

The Bible shows God's plan to reconcile all people through Christ, and gives us the mandate for missions and evangelism (Colossians 1:15-20). The world is the center of God's activity and we must not retreat from it. Service in the world is a service to God.

How are you exercising your responsibility to local and global missions?

C. Scott

Should you do more?

Alu - Vietnam

Population: 3,600

The Alu people of Vietnam live in the northeast part of the country, on the border of China and Laos. Their religion is animistic, which includes ancestor worship and magic spells. Their language is Nisu. They have no translation of the Bible. It is unknown if Christians live among them.

Pray: The love of God reaches the Alu in their own language.

Light

{ *The light shines in the darkness, and the darkness has not overcome it. John 1:5*

Often times, we leave the house early in the morning when it is still dark. We turn on our headlights and we travel to our destination. When the sun comes up, our headlights lose their brightness and eventually we no longer realize they're still on. Sometimes, I accidentally leave my headlights on so long that I forget to turn them off. When this happens I usually come back the next morning and find my battery is dead.

Jesus told his followers, "You are the light of the world" (Matthew 5:14). When we only let our light shine in joyful times, with other Christians, our light begins to lose its power. We must remember light is not needed where there is already light.

God has called us to be light in the darkness. He desires our light to be helpful for others. Our lights brings hope to the lost, comfort to the afflicted, and peace to the tormented.

Jesus said, "Let your light shine before men" (Matthew 5:16). Shining your light before men includes your relatives, neighbors, friends, people in your city, people in your country, and people around the world.

Where are you shining your light? Is your light only shining by other Christians or in good circumstances? Is your light shining where it is needed the most, in the darkness? What changes can you make to fulfill this command?

F. Rodríguez

Let your light shine in the darkness!

Anufo - Togo

Population: 65,000
Anufos come from the Ivory Coast. They live on the border of Sierra Leone. Their religion is Islam, mixed with animistic practices. Their language, Anufo, has a translation of the New Testament. Christianity faces much opposition. It is estimated less than two percent of Anufos are believers.

Pray: The Word of God would speak with power among the Anufo people.

Only Obedience

> And the Lord God commanded the man, "You are free to eat from any tree in the garden; but you must not eat from the tree of the knowledge of good and evil, for when you eat from it you will certainly die." Genesis 2:16-17

Why was the tree of knowledge of good and evil created? If it had not been created, would man have sinned? Someday, if I am allowed, these are two questions I would love to ask God.

One thing is clear regarding Genesis 2:16-17: God gave a command, and because God gave the command, it was reason enough for the command to be obeyed.

The disobedience of Adam and Eve was very costly. The root of their disobedience is the same problem that continues to challenge people today. People don't want to be under authority, but rather be the authority. They don't want to be managers; they want to be owners.

The serpent offered Adam and Eve the opportunity to be like God, but their desire to be like God led them to be separated from Him. In the world today we see how a problem of feeling a sense of entitlement is causing families and societies to form habits of selfishness and rebellion. Selfishness and rebellion are two things that prevent many from following Jesus. Sadly, when someone decides to follow Jesus, the feeling of entitlement continues to cause problems. Feeling entitled to honor, glory, or authority hinders the growth necessary to become a mature child of God.

How is the Lordship of Christ represented your life? Are you modeling to the world what it looks like to surrender control to the Lord? If obedience were an exercise you did every day, it would make your life much easier!

H. Bascur

Practice obedience!

Syrian Arabic - Palestine

Population: 22,000
The Syrian Arabic people live in fertile regions in Palestine. The majority of Syrian Arabs make a living by working with agriculture. They follow Islam very strictly, practicing the five pillars. Evangelism is a challenge due to restrictions in the country. Their language is Arabic Levantine.

Pray: For an opening for the Gospel to be shared in Palestine.

Send Me, Help Me, Break Me

> *I want to know Christ—yes, to know the power of his resurrection and participation in his sufferings, becoming like him in his death, ...*
> *Philippians 3:10*

Harmon Schelzenbach is one of the most famous missionaries of the church of the Nazarene. His passion, love, and desire to serve God are reflected in the thousands of people who have accepted Christ during his service in Africa. At the top of his Bible, written in his own writing, is the most beautiful and inspirational quote I have ever read.

I want to share it with you, but before I do, I must warn you: This quote needs no explanation or study. It was written to be used and applied in life. The quote is not something to be taken lightly. Each of the three lines contains self-denial, dedication, sacrifice, and even pain.

Write this quote on your heart!

W. Nuñez

"Lay any burden upon me; only sustain me. Send me anywhere; only go with me. Sever any tie, but that one which binds me to Thy service and to Thy heart."

Harmon Schmelzenbach (1882-1929)

Do you dare?

Auvergne - France

Population: 1,385,000

The Auvergne is an ethnic group originally from France. Their native language is Occitan. Half of the population has no interest in religion and the other half follows Roman Catholicism. It is estimated only one percent are born-again believers.

Pray: The Auvergne people group will see the void in their hearts and fill it with God.

Bible in a year: Luke 21 / Genesis 38 / Psalm 29

The Majesty Of God

> "Woe to me!" I cried. "I am ruined! For I am a man of unclean lips, and I live among a people of unclean lips, and my eyes have seen the King, the Lord Almighty." Isaiah 6:5

In this passage, Isaiah is reacting to the Lord, who allowed him to appreciate His beauty and glory. Are you lacking appreciation of God's glory? If so, I assume you are also lacking motivation to serve Him. Often our motivation to serve is a reflection of our understanding and admiration of God in His glory. When you see God in His majesty, worship will begin to overflow from your heart and you begin to fall in love with Him. Can a person see God and not fall on their knees in worship? Are you overjoyed to serve Him?

God, in His mercy and grace, allowed Isaiah to catch a glimpse of His holiness and presence. Through this experience, Isaiah recognized the need to be sanctified.

When we are sanctified and in His presence of holiness, we are able to hear the voice of God. In His mercy and patience, God shares His longings, desires, and will with us.

In the life of Isaiah, God shared His heartache for the sinful and stubborn people who did not worship Him. How do you believe God feels about the people who cannot worship Jesus because they have not even heard of Him?

The goodness of God moves our soul to say, "Here I Am!" We say this not as if our service is a gift to God, but as if it is a privilege to serve! After seeing a glimpse of His majesty and splendor, how can you not adore Him? After seeing His holiness, how can you not desire purity? After knowing His heart, how can you not long to serve Him?

A. Gulard

Be in awe of His majesty!

Amahuaca - Brazil

Population: 840

The Amahuaca people live on the border of Peru. Their language is Amahuaca, which has a translation of the New Testament. They are animistic and are strongly influenced by witchcraft, drunkenness, and immorality. It is estimated only a few have given their lives to Jesus.

Pray: They will be set free from the influence of evil.

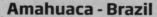

Bible in a year: Luke 22:1-38 / Genesis 39 / Psalm 30

Help Me See With Your Eyes

> "Don't be afraid," the prophet answered. "Those who are with us are more than those who are with them." And Elisha prayed, "Open his eyes, Lord, so that he may see." Then the Lord opened the servant's eyes, and he looked and saw the hills full of horses and chariots of fire all around Elisha. 2 Kings 6:16-17

Often we receive a promise from God or understand that He has called us to do something, but we find the promise or calling difficult to believe due to unfavorable circumstances. When bad news or something unexpected happens, it can stir up feelings of uncertainty, fear, and distrust. This causes a resistance to believing what God has said is true.

Elisha and his servant Gehazi woke up one morning and received terrible news: the King of Syria had commanded a troop of chariots to capture them. Their reaction to this horrible news was amazing. While Gehazi panicked, Elisha saw that God's provision and protection was greater than their problems. Elisha saw God had an army around them that would protect them. The story is fascinating, but Elisha's trust is something we can learn from. Elisha was fulfilling a purpose God had given him. He saw beyond the bad news and adversity. He knew God would protect them and defeat the enemies.

Are you struggling to trust God? Ask God to give you His holy perspective. The perspective of God allows you to see beyond present circumstances. His perspective allows you to believe and live your life with purpose and meaning. It's time to live an extraordinary life believing in God, regardless of your circumstances!

G. Vergara

Do you trust God, regardless of your circumstances?

Amami Oshima - Japan

Population: 11,700

The Adyghe are a subgroup of the Circassians who live in the north of Syria. They have a good economy, and many are members of the government and army. Their language is Adyghe, which has a translation of the New Testament and a film about Jesus. It is estimated that 0.4% are Christians.

Pray: For the Bible translation in their language to give life.

FEBRUARY

Used By God In A New Context

{ *May the LORD deal with me, be it ever so severely, if even death separates you and me. Read Ruth 1:16-17, 20-21*

In the book of Ruth chapter 1 verses 16 and 17, Ruth promised Naomi five things: 1) "I will go wherever you go," 2) "I will live wherever you live," 3) "your people will be my people," 4) "your God will be my God," and 5) "wherever you die, I will die." Ruth decided to leave her people, her religion, her comfort, and her personal identity to be a useful servant for the glory of the Lord in a new context! In Ruth 1:20-21, they had finally reached Naomi's town, but Naomi didn't express gratitude for her daughter-in-law Ruth. In the midst of Naomi's anguish she said, "The Lord has brought me back empty." I cannot imagine how Ruth felt in this moment! Ruth had left everything behind to go with Naomi and now Naomi seemed so ungrateful. If I were in Ruth's position, I think my attitude would have changed drastically toward Naomi! For that reason, I see in the life of Ruth, a woman who was dedicated, humble, self-sacrificing, loving, obedient, and very patient. Thinking about my own life, I wonder: Am I ready to obey God at all costs? During the difficult times of my life, will I be willing to walk in obedience to the image of Christ? Am I willing to leave behind all comforts and friends so that God may be glorified in my life? I desire to be committed to my Lord despite walking down a path full of challenges and ungrateful people. Therefore I declare, "Lord, you are with me and may use me in any context!"

MyT. Goddard

Imitate Ruth!

Arab - Gabon

Population: 3,100
They are an ethnic minority in their country. They live in large cities and live within the middle to upper social class. Males perform circumcision. Their language is Arabic, which has several audiovisual resources for evangelism. Approximately 0.5% of the population believes the Gospel.

Pray: The church will continue to grow. Pray for strength and courage throughout the Arab world.

Bible in a year: Luke 23:1-25 / Genesis 41 / Psalm 32

Tomorrow Could Be A Day Too Late

{ *So be careful how you live. Not as unwise but as wise, making the most of every opportunity, because the days are evil.*
Ephesians 5:15-16

One day, I was going to visit a friend who was sick, but my day was very busy so I decided I would go the next day at three in the afternoon. The following day I arranged the visit. I thought I would take my Bible to read a few lines to soothe her in the midst of her distress, but suddenly my phone rang and I received news she had already passed away. She did not "wait" until three in the afternoon when I had made time in my tight schedule.

God is the one who dictates time and the very moment He will call each one of us. Therefore, we do not own time or our own agenda. I had missed the opportunity God had given me the day before, when I felt I should go sit next to her and pray.

Tomorrow might be a day too late for someone who has departed without having heard His word, or tomorrow might be too late for the apology you owed your brother and now his heart is hurting more than yesterday because you had missed the opportunity. Tomorrow might be a day too late for a thirsty brother who is in need of a word of encouragement. Today though, he is seeking comfort in some dark addiction because you didn't find time to share with him the God who always has time to speak.

Today, give a word of comfort to the one next to you, apologize to those you have had a misunderstanding with, go and share your faith to others who are lost and insecure. Every day has responsibilities, to love our neighbors and our Heavenly Father. Do not let the days pass without doing His work. Do not let your routine remove yourself from His work. Let His work change your routine!

G. Galindo

Do not let this day pass!

Arem - Vietnam

Population: 100
They are a very poor ethnic group living in the mountains of northern Vietnam. Their language is Arem, but only about 20 elderly people speak it fluently. The Chut language is used most commonly but has no written knowledge regarding the Bible.

Pray: The mercy of God would reach the Arem and that they would have a chance to hear the gospel!

Just As Antioch Did

Now in the church at Antioch there were prophets and teachers: Barnabas, Simeon called Niger, Lucius of Cyrene, Manaen (who had been brought up with Herod the tetrarch) and Saul. While they were worshipping the Lord and fasting, the Holy Spirit said, "Set apart for me Barnabas and Saul for the work to which I have called them." So after they had fasted and prayed, they placed their hands on them and sent them off. Acts 13:1-3

The church of Antioch's first mission was meeting the needs of their local people. However, the church of Antioch also played a major role in the life of the global church. It was a church that crossed social barriers (Acts 11:19-20), rebuilt broken lives (Acts 11:21-24), encouraged spiritual growth (Acts 11:25-26), met the physical and spiritual needs of others (Acts 11:27-30), resolved doctrinal conflicts (Acts 15), had a shared leadership consisting of a pastoral team (Acts 13:1), and were willing to extend the boundaries of the Kingdom of God to the ends of the earth (Acts 13:2 -3).

Antioch had a vision of being an open door for world evangelism. We are challenged to follow this model.

What does it mean for your life and the church to follow the model of the church at Antioch?

C. Scott

Are you ready?

Alas - Indonesia

Population: 83,000

They live in the mountains, grow rice to eat, and trade with the neighboring villages. They profess Islam, but look to the Shaman for performing religious rituals concerning their harvest. Their language is Batak, which does not possess a translation of the Bible in their own language.

Pray: For their salvation and for a translation of the Bible.

To All The People

> *For my eyes have seen your salvation, which you have prepared in the sight of all nations: a light for revelation to the Gentiles, and the glory of your people Israel. Luke 2:30-32*

Simeon was a man of God in Jesus' time. He waited for God's promise to send a Savior to the world. Many Jews believed the Savior would be a political liberator, someone who would deliver them from the yoke of the Romans and would direct them to social freedom. However, Simeon understood God's plan. The salvation that God offered was spiritual because it was a freedom from the yoke of sin. Salvation is a promise not just for Israel, but also for every person, tongue, and nation on the planet.

Have you taken time to think about this? Have you felt excitement and gratitude to receive salvation from God?

The gift of salvation is not just for you, but for all people on earth! Did you know millions of people have not yet heard the message of Salvation? This is not because people have a lack of love for God, but because the church has not yet brought the message of salvation to all unreached people. The church has yet to fulfill the Great Commission left by Jesus (Matthew 28:19-20)! The truth is that you and I must take part in this task. We can participate by going to these people or mobilizing others to go.

You can go, give, or pray for the Gospel to be known to every person, tongue, and nation. If you have rejoiced in receiving salvation, strive for others to receive it as well!

M. de Rodríguez

Be a part of the Great Commission!

Amish - United States

Population: 17,000

The majority of Amish come from Pennsylvania. They are a very closed people group who profess Christianity, but they are very legalistic. It is estimated only 3% are born again Christians. The Amish speak their own German dialect and have a translated New Testament.

Pray: For a biblical renewal of their belief in Christianity. Pray they may have the strength to be freed from legalism and be touched by Jesus.

Character Of A Christian

> Therefore, since we are surrounded by such a great cloud of witnesses, let us throw off everything that hinders and the sin that so easily entangles. And let us run with perseverance the race marked out for us, fixing our eyes on Jesus, the pioneer and perfecter of faith. For the joy set before him he endured the cross, scorning its shame, and sat down at the right hand of the throne of God. Hebrews 12:1-2

To remove everything that hinders and the sin that so easily entangles means to remove all things so that the only thing which remains is that which is necessary for living a life of service and ministry for Him.

Running the race of faith requires concentration. God will test us, but He has our hearts in His hands because our daily circumstances are intimately known by Him.

By saying our eyes should be fixed on Jesus, we are encouraged to place our trust in Him because He will be the one renewing our strength. Jesus is the perfect trainer of our faith. It should be our goal to carry His cross with joy and rejoice in the results to come.

You must disregard the shame you feel when enduring trails. Jesus Himself received a lot of embarrassment through the circumstances He lived in, but He ultimately sat down at the right hand of God! When you are living through high pressures and difficulties, take heart! You will one day see a rewarding end result! Even Jesus suffered before sitting on the throne!

 D. Duk

Run the race!

Arleng - Bangladesh

Population: 800

The Arlengs live near the border of Myanmar. Their religion is Hindu and they speak the Karbi language. They possess an entire Bible in their own language. Recently evangelistic efforts have been made through an audio of the New Testament, but spiritual fruit has yet to be seen.

Pray: For the Word, which has been sown in their hearts. Pray God would cause seeds to grow!

Legalism Or Freedom

> The Pharisees said to him, "Look, why are they doing what is unlawful on the Sabbath?" Read Mark 2:23-27

The religious people of Jesus' time exaggerated the meaning of the law of God. They criticized Jesus' disciples for picking kernels of wheat to eat during the day of rest (the Sabbath). God's law did not prohibit such actions, but the religious people used God's law to control the lives of others.

While religious legalism presents the commandments of God as something heavy or impossible to keep, Jesus teaches us that God's laws exist to meet human needs. Then he said to them, "The Sabbath was made for man, not man for the Sabbath" (Mark 2:27).

Everything exists for the glory of God, but God is love and has made all things for our well being. We do not follow a religion, but a person who is the Lord and King of the universe. We follow a person who came to this world and humbled himself by dying to save us from our sins so we may be reconciled with God. "The Son of Man is Lord of the Sabbath," said God. We do not live to fulfill a set of codes and rules; we live for the Lord! The result of this is not to enslave us, but to live in authentic freedom.

God desires for you to share your message of love and freedom. Enjoy the freedom you have in Christ and proclaim it to others!

A. Betancur

Experience freedom in Christ!

Tihami Arabic - Saudi Arabia

Population: 129,000
They live on the shores of the Red Sea and the surrounding lands. Their language is Arabic Hijazi, which has some portions of the Bible translated. There are no known Christians among them. Many passionately profess Islam.

Pray: God would break any obstruction, which hinders the Gospel from coming into their lives.

Entropy vs. Negentropy

> For this is what the Lord has commanded us: "I have made you a light for the Gentiles, that you may bring salvation to the ends of the earth." Acts 13:47

I want to clarify that the title words are not insults, nor are they the names of my family members, nor names of two Nigerian boxers. Rather, they are the names that define two natural processes typical of any organism. Entropy is the natural tendency that consumes any weak, exhausted, and/or disordered system.

Negentropy is the opposite of Entropy and is the antidote to entropic effects. Today, the trend in the world is to say all things are going from bad to worse. We can see entropy manifested when we see people worried, anxious, or stressed. We see entropy when no solution is proposed to life's everyday overwhelming problems. In this precise moment, we as Christians are to come in.

Has anyone ever told you you're a "negentropic" agent?

Probably not! Or at least not in those words, but let me remind you that we are called to put things in order, to not let the system fall. We are called to be salt and light because we are God's agents here on earth! Christians are the antidote to the entropic effects of the world, the flesh, and the devil.

W. Núñez

Let's get to work!

Austrians- Austria

Population: 7,001,000
They are the majority population of Austria. They are concentrated in the Bavarian Alps and Lower Austria. They speak Bavarian German. They are mostly nominal Christians. It is estimated 1% have given their lives to Christ.

Pray: For an awakening in those who are nominal in their faith!

The First Missionary

{ *The Word became flesh and made his dwelling among us...*
John 1:14

Was Paul the first missionary? No! The first missionary was God. Isn't that wonderful? God became human, dressed Himself in flesh, and identified Himself with His people. In missionary vocabulary that is called "contextualization" or "transcultural missions." It is when a missionary goes to a place, dresses like the people, talks like the people, and eats what the people eat. Jesus did this so that the Gospel may be clearly conveyed. Because of His love, God did the same thing for us!

"Dwelt among us" literally means "set your tent among us," which means God decided to live as a human being among human beings, specifically the Jews. When Jesus lived among the Jews, he became a Jew. He shared the same customs and even dressed like the Jews. That is being a cultural missionary. It is imitating Jesus instead of being rigid in traditions. We must imitate Paul who said, "To the weak I became weak, to win the weak. I have become all things to all people so that by all possible means I might save some" (1 Corinthians 9:22).

F. Rodriguez

What are you willing to do so someone may be saved?

Anambé - Brazil

Population: 130

They live in the State of Pará, along the Rio Cairari. They are bilingual, speaking Anambé and Portuguese. Since 2004, they have a translated Bible in Anambé, but the Bible has yet to be widely distributed. Their main religion is animistic.

Pray: For the Bible to be distributed so the Gospel may be read and understood!

Eternal Decisions

> By faith Moses, when he had grown up, refused to be known as the
> son of Pharaoh's daughter. He chose to be mistreated along with
> the people of God rather than to enjoy the fleeting pleasures of sin.
> He regarded disgrace for the sake of Christ as of greater value than
> the treasures of Egypt, because he was looking ahead to his reward.
> Hebrews 11:24-26

The world offers us many things and often teaches us that the ultimate goal in this life is money, power, and fame. People such as Hollywood stars, athletes, music stars, wealthy businessmen, and politicians are admired because they can have anything they desire and often live a life of extravagance and luxury. Millions of people dream of living this sort of life, but they often inadvertently find themselves living empty lives to achieve these wordly goals. Very few people realize the value and meaning in life is in seeking God's eternal treasures. Moses is a wonderful example because he was someone who decided to disregard everything to seek heavenly treasures, although he was a prince of the powerful Egyptian empire.

Moses won the freedom of his people because he was not satisfied with the abuse they suffered at the hands of the Egyptians. He faced the uncertainty of walking in the desert because he preferred to believe God. It is important to understand: In order to believe in God you must know who God is because you cannot trust those whom you do not know.

Moses trusted God because he had known God since childhood. Moses understood the reward God has prepared for those who believe in Him and for those who live a life of loving obedience to Him. Moses saw the importance of challenging the values of this fallen world!

Remember the decisions you make today have eternal consequences.

G. Vergara

**Are you living a
life of meaning?**

Aweer - Kenya

Population: 8,000
They are a group of hunter-gatherers living in Lamu District. They live where most of the violence took place during the Kenya-Somalia Conflic in 2012. Their religion is Islam. Only 2% of the population is Christian. Their language is Aweer, which has some audio Bible translations available.

Pray: The Gospel will speak powerfully into their lives.

Got The Power?

> The Lord's hand was with them, and a great number of people believed and turned to the Lord. Acts 11:21

Every Christian is called to participate in the ministry of priesthood. The mission takes place everywhere and is driven by faith. Christians constantly interact among believers and unbelievers while testifying about their faith. Since God is a missionary God, the people of God are a missionary people. The Spirit of God has been poured out upon all the people of God, not only a select few.

In Jürgen Moltmann's thesis on the theology of the future he writes, "Service to God is directed not only to the divine service within the church, but also to the divine service in the daily world. This service takes place in the ordinary life of the Christian. It takes place in their community, in tents, villages, farms, cities, classrooms, homes, legal offices, clinics, in politics, governments, and in recreation."

There are billions of people who do not know the Lord. The church must, without delay, fullfil their responsibility in world evangelism.

What does it mean to exercise the priesthood of all believers? Is the mission only for some or for all? I believe it is for all!

C. Scott

God has given his power to all!

Ath Pahariya Rai - Nepal

Population: 2,700
They are dedicated to agriculture, but lack technology and must drink water of very poor quality. They are known warriors in the Nepal Army. Their religion is Buddhism. They have no Bible in their own language.

Pray: People will take the Gospel to them and that the love of God will be seen!

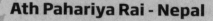

I Will Play!

> The kingdom of heaven is like treasure hidden in a field. When a man found it, he hid it again, and then in his joy went and sold all he had and bought that field. Matthew 13:44

Humans usually tend to minimize risk. That is why a decision is weighed. We desire to know that all possible consequences have been evaluated. We are used to securing everything and playing it safe. This man, however, did not think twice. Instead, he took a chance on what he had discovered.

Is it worth it to sell everything you own and leave nothing on the side for a new discovery? What if it was for something very valuable? Or would it still be too crazy?

When you find Jesus, the best thing you can do is give everything for Him! If you are not willing to risk it all, it is likely you have not discovered the value of the "hidden treasure." There is a decision that is worth risking everything. It is to follow and serve Jesus!

J. Segnitz

Take a risk!

Ambelau - Indonesia

Population: 6,000

They live in the Maluku islands. The predominant religion is Islam, but it is mixed with their traditional animistic religion. Their language, Ambelau does not have a translation of the Bible.

Pray: For God to touch their hearts with the Gospel. Pray for a Bible translation.

Three Priorities

> Jesus answered, "It is written: 'Man shall not live on bread alone, but on every word that comes from the mouth of God.'"
> Read Matthew 4:1-11

In this passage, Jesus is confronted with the direct temptation of Satan, but even in His struggle He lets us see three priorities every Child of God must have...

The first priority Jesus shows is: Communion with God is more important than food (v.3-4). Jesus had just been introduced as the Son of God, so The Holy Spirit led Him into the wilderness to show what the priorities of the Son of God are. To have a lot of food is worthless without communion with God. It is worthless to have a full stomach and an empty spirit. It is through our fellowship with God and not our satisfied needs that we show others who our Father is.

The second priority is: Having fear in God is more important than physical protection (v.6-7). At the start of His ministry, Satan asked Jesus to prove who He is. At the end of His ministry, Jesus had proven who He was when He was with the thief on the cross. Jesus had proven that God is shown as our Father in not just what we say, but also in how we live!

The third priority is: Integrity is more important than power (v.8-10). Satan wanted to form a partnership with Jesus. "You will be the manager... even better, and I'll be your assistant." Satan offered power, which did not include Jesus having to go to the cross. Our priority is not "having", it is "being."

L. Díaz

> The priority of the Son of God is not to be blessed; it is to be obedient and faithful.

Andoque - Colombia

Population: 600
They are an indigenous group living in the Amazon. Christian witnesses arrived decades ago and 20% responded to the Gospel. Sadly, Andoques continue to struggle with their pagan customs and beliefs.

Pray: The Andoque believers will receive effective discipleship and will strive for holiness.

The Pure Gospel

> *And so it was with me, brothers and sisters. When I came to you, I did not come with eloquence or human wisdom as I proclaimed to you the testimony about God. For I resolved to know nothing while I was with you except Jesus Christ and him crucified. 1 Corinthians 2:1-2*

All too often the success of evangelism is measured by the number of people who are standing, have their hand raised, or have made a decision at the end of worship. At the time of the apostles, the key to evangelism was to ensure preaching was faithful to the Word of God. The apostles strived to ensure the message was not a worldly man-made message, but rather the Word of the living God, which transforms those who are spiritually dead in this world (1 Thessalonians 2:13).

The problem is: We as Christians sometimes get carried away by fads and trends of this world. Often we imagine we are acting biblically, when in fact we are highly influenced by the demands of human opinion. The triumph in evangelism for Paul did not depend on the approval of men, lost or saved, but the conviction that he preached the Gospel in its purity (2 Corinthians 4:5). To express this knowledge is the primary task of every Christian. Preach the pure Gospel!
O. Simari

Do not mix Biblical truth with worldly ideas!

Ati - China

Population: 16,000
They live in the mountains of the Yunnan province. They are animists and polytheists. They revere and worship the dragon god. Every village has a "dragon tree" for this purpose. Their language is Sani, which has no translation of the Bible.

Pray: The Gospel will speak in the lives of the Ati and will free them from spiritual darkness.

Bible in one year: Hebrews 9:23-10:18 / Exodus 9-10 / Proverbs 3

Death - Life

> { *While they were stoning him, Stephen prayed, "Lord Jesus, receive my spirit." Acts 7:59*

Did Stephen know at the moment of death a book would be written concerning the Acts of the Apostles? Do you think he knew his death would be part of a book? Do you think he knew his testimony would be used by the Holy Spirit to transform lives for the glory of God? Do you think he knew his death would not be in vain? I assume not. Stephen probably had no idea his story would be recorded in history. 1 Corinthians 2:9 says, "For no eye has seen, no ear has heard, no mind has conceived what God has prepared for those who love him." I'm sure Stephen never imagined the impact of his life and death.

Many people would question Stephen: Is it worth it to die so young? Why did you not shut up so you could continue to preach later? It is likely if someone would tell the story of Stephen, as a current event, we would think..."Close your mouth, and leave those old religious people alone. It is not worth you dying so young; God can use you in other ways."

Is it worth dying for Christ? Stephen's story shows us the answer is yes!

When we look at his story (and many others) we are left with no excuse! We know the power of the Gospel, but the question is: How are you responding? In Philippians, Paul says whether he dies or lives, his greatest desire is for Christ to be glorified in his body.

Do your desires resemble those of Paul?

Someone once said there are no "closed fields" for the Gospel, just not enough people who are willing to shed their blood to open them.

A. Gulard

> **It is better to die sharing the Gospel than to live a life seeking comfort.**

Belgian Fleming - Belgium

Population: 5,943,000
It is the national majority group living in Flanders. On paper, they are Roman Catholics, but 30% are tired of religion and prefer a prosperous and cultured life. The true Christian Church has been reduced to approximately 1.2%. Their primary languages are Dutch and French.

Pray: For a spiritual awakening in Belgium!

Bible in one year: Hebrews 10:19-39 / Exodus 11-12 / Proverbs 4

Two Groups Made Into One

> For he himself is our peace, who has made the two groups one and has destroyed the barrier, the dividing wall of hostility. Ephesians 2:14

The separation of Jews and Gentiles is described as a dividing wall. A wall may be protective, but in this passage it played a dividing role and was a symbol of hatred. It may be when Paul wrote this passage, he had in mind the dividing wall placed in the temple of Jerusalem. This wall separated the court of the Gentiles from the court of the Jews. The wall had a sign, which communicated in three languages: Any Gentile who entered the courtyard of the Jews would be in danger of death.

Paul's imprisonment in Jerusalem was due to the fact he was accused of leading Trophimus, an Ephesian Gentile believer, to the temple. The wall Christ destroyed was much more than a sign of a distant Jerusalem. The wall was also a sign of the hatred that divided people who said: "us and you" and "near and far." Peace was possible because Christ removed hate, thus merging together two different human groups.

Jesus died not only to save, but also to break down the walls, which separate people. Jesus desires unified people of all nationalities and cultures.

If Jesus gave His life for this purpose, are you willing to fulfill God's desire that every nation should become part of His people?

A. Neufeld

What are we willing to give?

Jordanian Arab - Palestine

Population: 985,500

Jordanian Arabs are very hospitable. They profess Islam. Within their people group live several extremist groups who often carry out terrorist acts against Christians. It is estimated only 0.3% of the population are believers.

Pray: God would protect the lives of believers and that their testimony would remain powerful!

To Be Or Not To Be

> The Lord is not slow in keeping his promise, as some understand slowness. Instead, he is patient with you, not wanting anyone to perish, but everyone to come to repentance. 2 Peter 3:9

We have been sent into the world to love, serve, preach, teach, heal, and release. Every person has the right to hear the message of the Gospel. The mission is universal and comprehensive.

The mission is to be done in both word and deed. Actions without words are silent; words without actions are empty. John Stott said, "Discipleship includes a call to work with God in the service of His Kingdom. Discipleship will direct your attention to the aspirations of ordinary men and women in society. It will direct your attention to their dreams of: justice, security, full-lives, and human dignity." God calls people to missions and evangelism. It is a call to service. Winning people to Jesus is showing your loyalty to God's priorities.

The church comes together to praise God, to enjoy mutual fellowship, and to receive spiritual nourishment. The church departs to serve God in the mission field. The work of the church must involve justice, mercy, and truth.

What does being a missionary church in the world today look like? Can a church be full of missionaries?

C. Scott

Are you playing your part in the mission?

Angaité - Paraguay

Population: 2,200
Their native language is Angaite, but they can understand Guarani and Sanapaná, which has a Bible translation. New believers are having strong opposition from their community.

Pray: For young believers, to be salt and light in their community!

57

In A Good Way

> *...All peoples on earth will be blessed through you.*
> *Read Genesis 12:1-16*

Abraham was declared "the way" for the blessing of God to be given to the world. He was obedient to leave his land and his people, just as God had asked.

During his obedience, he was traveling to the Promised Land when "there was famine in the land." It is interesting that Abraham came to the Promised Land by obeying God's command, but on his way to the Promised Land he was guided by circumstances. Famine is what dictated his steps to Egypt, but Egypt was not the land God had intended for him.

In verse 16, we see Abraham receiving a material blessing, but we know the blessing was not from God but from the world. The blessing was based on selfishness, lies and deception. Abraham's first missionary journey resulted in failure due to his inability to be honest and bless the people of Egypt (v.16).

Although he made mistakes, his "call" remained the same. Abraham's lies, fear, and disobedience did not remove his call from God. The hand of God continued to be on his life. Despite his disobedience, God did not reject him. Abraham risked his mission because he was selfish, saw only his own interests, and did not let the hand of God guide him.

And you? Has God given you a mission? Who are you guided by?

H. Ziefle

Be guided by the Word of God!

Ambrak - Papua New Guinea

Population: 400

They are an animist group living in the province of Sandaun. Their language is Ambrak, which urgently needs a translation of the Bible. It is estimated only 2% have responded to the Gospel, but most do not have a full understanding of Biblical truths.

Pray: For Bible translators, and for the discipleship of new believers among the Ambrak.

The Perfect Perspective

> David said to the Philistine, "You come against me with sword and spear and javelin, but I come against you in the name of the LORD Almighty, the God of the armies of Israel, whom you have defied. This day the LORD will deliver you into my hands, and I'll strike you down and cut off your head. This very day I will give the carcasses of the Philistine army to the birds and the wild animals, and the whole world will know that there is a God in Israel." 1 Samuel 17:45-46

When David looked at Goliath and the Philistine army, he saw a very different picture than the soldiers in Saul's army saw. In faith, David believed there were no undefeatable enemies. David did not fight against what he saw with his own eyes, but by what he saw through the eyes of God. This is why David was confident to fight against Goliath with a simple sling!

David's heart was what appealed to God and what led God to choose him as king. A similar heart is what God is looking for today. God is not searching for faultless men, but rather men of faith. The size of your enemy is always subjective. This subjectivity varies according to the size of your God and the state of your heart, which is why Solomon wrote: "Above all else, guard your heart, for everything you do flows from it" (Proverbs 4:23). The prophet Jeremiah said, "The heart is deceitful above all things and beyond cure. Who can understand it?" (Jeremiah 17:9)

How can you care for your heart? Praying every day and taking time to read the Bible is a great start. You should search for friends who have the same values and convictions as you do. Search for friends who live in holiness and fight to obey Jesus' commandments. Serve at home, in your community, in your church, and share the message of salvation to the ends of the earth!
F. Chinatti

So you may have the perfect perspective!

Baha'i - Bangladesh

Population: 9,900
The Baha'is believe all religions are acceptable to God. They believe God is revealed through prophets such as Moses, Muhammad, Jesus, and others. They speak Bengali and have had some contact with the Gospel, but it is estimated that no Christians exist among them.

Pray: For the Baha'is to recognize the only way to please God and to be in a relationship with Him is through Jesus.

The Re-Integration

> From Attalia they sailed back to Antioch, where they had been committed to the grace of God for the work they had now completed. On arriving there, they gathered the church together and reported all that God had done through them and how he had opened a door of faith to the Gentiles. And they stayed there a long time with the disciples. Acts 14:26-28

Before missionaries are sent out they are usually aware they will experience many cultural and linguistic changes when they arrive in their new surroundings. Often this process results in expected frustration, anger, and judgment for the missionaries. It is important for those who support the missionary to understand this reality called "culture shock."

When Paul and Barnabas returned to their church in Antioch after their first missionary journey to Asia Minor, they gathered at the church and informed everyone what God had done during their trip.

Have you considered the important roles missionaries and their support team play? Missionaries can also have unpleasant and disheartening experiences when they come back to their homeland, congregation, or even their own family.

Missionaries may begin to feel they have two homes, which results in a difficult transition to their original "home." If you are supporting missionaries, you need to be taking care of them not only during their time abroad, but also when they return. They need your help to "re-locate." This is important in all aspects of life: materially, emotionally, spiritually, and culturally. Missionaries need you to listen and to support them!

Are you or your church supporting a missionary who is serving abroad? Get ready to welcome and support them at home!

T. Sandvig

Re-integrate your missionaries!

Awjilah - Libya

Population: 3,700
The Awjilah are a nomadic tribe in the Sahara desert. They travel in caravans with their livestock and belongings, selling various products throughout the country. There is no Bible translation in their language (also called Awjilah), and they profess Islam as their religion.

Pray: For missionaries who are willing to come and reach them with Christ!

Paralytic?

> { Then Jesus said to him, "Get up! Pick up your mat and walk." John 5:8

During our first year serving on the mission field, we faced the harsh reality of what serving as missionaries truly meant. This experience caused a wide range of emotions, which all missionaries encounter at some point during their service.

I remember one day, we were called and informed my mother had just died. I was confused and did not know what to do, so I began to pray. Earlier that day I had been meditating on a passage and in this moment the passage came to mind. It said, "Get up! Pick up your mat and walk." Jesus' words of power began to comfort me and show me the path I was to take.

As events continued to unfold, God performed a miracle and allowed my wife and I to fly to Lima, Peru, which was almost impossible in our given circumstances. When we arrived at the airport that night, I was told we would have to wait. I then decided to take out my Bible and share the Word of God. Through my mother's death, the Gospel of Jesus was presented seven times. Her death was used to help lead others to a new life in Christ.

The words of Jesus are to live within us each day, because every day brings new challenges we must face in Jesus' strength.

It is easy for missionaries who are serving abroad in a new culture to think, "no one understands me." The Word of God leads us to action. It leads us to rise above challenges and live a life of faith, knowing God is in control of everything.

G. Rivas

Get up and go!

Awa Cuaiquer - Colombia

Population: 25,800

The Awa Cuaiquer live in scattered settlements along a flowing river. They are dedicated hunters and fishers. It is estimated only 6% of the population is Christian, but a Christian influence has been present in their population since the 1980s.

Pray: For spiritual growth and understanding for the Awa Cuaiquer.

I Am A Priest?

> But you are a chosen people, a royal priesthood, a holy nation, God's special possession, that you may declare the praises of him who called you out of darkness into his wonderful light. 1 Peter 2:9

A church that shares the message of salvation and the fellowship of the Kingdom fulfills the commitment God has made to the world. This commitment is fulfilled through the universal priesthood of all believers and through sending missionaries.

Your mission field is the world. God has entrusted the gift of priesthood to all of His believers. Therefore we can say, "Through him we received grace and apostleship to call all the Gentiles to the obedience that comes from faith for his name's sake" (Romans 1:5). The Bible clearly teaches the role given to the church is meant for all believers. Every believer is both a priest and a missionary. Christians are created to work in unity with the Body of Christ throughout the world. It is crucial to recognize the global church has been entrusted to complete the task of sharing the message of salvation.

What is the work the Lord has called you to? What new challenges has He put in your hands?

C. Scott

If you do not know, ask about it in prayer!

Ampanang - Indonesia

Population: 36,000

The Ampanang live in a tribe along a river. They eat wild animals they have hunted, fish they have caught, and berries they have gathered. Their religion is deeply animistic, with specific rituals dedicated to their dead. No Bible translation exists in the Ampanang language.

Pray: For God to free them from their darkness and for workers to begin translating the Bible into their language.

Heralds Of Salvation

Every valley shall be filled in, every mountain and hill made low. The crooked roads shall become straight, the rough ways smooth. And all people will see God's salvation. Luke 3:5-6

John the Baptist was a servant who prepared the way for Jesus. He announced repentance for the forgiveness of sins and was the voice of God after 400 years of silence. His service was the fulfillment of prophecy, uttered by Isaiah over 500 years earlier.

John's ministry was centered on the banks of the Jordan River. He proclaimed salvation and the coming of the Messiah to Israel. Prophecy said "all men" would see the salvation of God, but John's ministry was short-lived. Following his death, God has continued to call others to carry on his work. People have continued to proclaim salvation and the name of Jesus to the nations. Some who have been called have won thousands of souls for the Lord; others, maybe only one. Each, however, has done his or her part in the ministry John began; a ministry centered on proclaiming repentance and salvation from the punishment of sin.

As a child of God, you are to preach righteousness. Your mission must be to bring God's salvation to the people of this earth. Your mission begins in your city, transitions to your country, and ends with the entire earth.

Are you playing your role? How are you contributing so others may hear the Gospel? Pray and ask for direction.

M. de Rodriguez

Get to work!

Walloons - Belgium

Population: 3,533,000

Walloons are French-speaking Belgians who are immersed in an atmosphere of prosperity. They often believe they have no need for religion. It is estimated only 1% of the population is following Jesus.

Pray: The Belgian church's faith would be strengthened.

Brokenhearted

> The Lord is close to the brokenhearted and saves those who are crushed in spirit. Psalm 34:18

We live in a time when showing weakness, being honest, and displaying humility are seen as "old-fashioned." We often think we have to be strong and have everything together to be considered normal, but the truth is everyone has difficulties, problems, and struggles they are affected by.

Over time, problems often combine with other problems and become more drastic. Our procrastination in addressing problems ultimately causes more difficulties and leaves us having to admit our brokenness.

A kiss is not the answer to a broken marriage, nor does time heal all wounds. We experience moments in life where God allows us to be broken, but we often do not know why. The difficulties we experience remind us of how dependent we are on the Lord. Difficulties bring us an awareness of our helplessness and inability to solve our own problems. Sometimes when we reach the bottom, or are overwhelmed from the consequence of sin, we begin to better understand that something within us is broken.

Having a broken heart can end our selfish plans and make a way for God's perfect plan. Heartbreak opens our narrow perspective and allows us to see God in his magnificent plan. A broken heart is part of a process; it is not a reason to quit. It allows you to leave a good life and transform it into something better!

The valuable combination of being hurt, weak, incapable, and humble in spirit allows you to receive God's strength. In the moments of a broken heart, we realize the Lord is near and are enabled to show compassion to others who are suffering.

W. Altare

With a broken heart you are in a place to receive the blessing of God!

Bahelia - Nepal

Population: 100
The Bahelia profess Hinduism as their religion. They are often poor, discriminated against, and illiterate. They speak Nepali. The Bahelia posses the New Testament and other resources that explain the Gospel, but it is believed no one as accepted the Bible as truth.

Pray: Their hearts would be broken for God and that they would look to Jesus.

Living For Christ

> For to me, to live is Christ and to die is gain. Philippians 1:21

The Apostle Paul wrote this amazing passage, which showed his firm decision to live by serving the Lord Jesus Christ at all costs. Serving whole-heartedly was his conviction as a servant of Christ, even if it meant death. We as human beings usually fear death above all else, but because Paul had his eyes on eternity, he had the perspective to see death as something positive. Paul was ready to go to heaven so he could be with the Lord, but he wanted to live each day surrendered to Christ while making a difference in the world. Paul had to make the decision to surrender his entire life to the service of Christ. In making this decision Paul left an impressive legacy. Through his death he became an example of complete loyalty and love for the Lord.

Being a Christian means accepting Jesus Christ as your Savior. Often in our prayers we call Him Lord, but rarely do we live as if He is truly the Lord of our lives. It is rare for people to live with the goal of influencing others to question a future beyond this earthly life. We must look ahead to eternity, but in this life we are to bring glory to Jesus so others can recognize He is the Lord of our lives.

G. Vergara

Does your life reflect Christ is Lord?

Laba - China

Population: 286,000
They live in the province of Guizhou. Their religion is animistic and is influenced by the Miao and Han cultures. Many Labas worship their ancestors. Their main language is Mandarin Chinese. Despite evangelistic efforts, it is estimated only 0.7% have responded to Jesus.

Pray: Every Laba has the opportunity to hear the message of salvation again.

When You Fear, Look Through The Rear View Mirror

> So do not fear, for I am with you; do not be dismayed, for I am your God. I will strengthen you and help you; I will uphold you with my righteous right hand. Isaiah 41:10

At one point in my life I became overwhelmed by fear. I had fear of getting hurt and fear for how my plans would alter the future without me knowing the end result. During my fear attack, a friend whispered in my ear: "Do not just look through the front window, you need to look in the rear view mirror and acknowledge what God has done for you so far."

His words halted my fear and allowed me to see through the perspective of my past. Through this perspective I could see the hand of God in every step of my life. I then knew everything was within His perfect plan and purpose. Feeling fear is something we often experience, but when we take time to look back and see how God has remained faithful we begin to understand that the things we cannot see are not a reason to have fear!

Do not despair and be fearful. God knows the path before you. God knows where you have been and where you are going. You must allow Him to guide you, even when you cannot see what is ahead. Remember when fear begins to overcome you, look through the rear view mirror.

In your fear, come to God in prayer and remember all He has done for you. Some events you may have thought of as "coincidences" could actually be evidence of God actively working in your life according to His good plan! Always remember, fear is not from God! God is light and not darkness, He made us to be victorious and not defeated. Where God is, you have everything you could ever need!

G. Galindo

Keep going!

Babalia - Chad

Population: 8,100
The Babalia live in Chad's Boroko region, which includes 23 villages. Their diet typically consists of minimal grains, as well as poultry that they breed. They speak Creole Babalia, into which some portions of the Bible have been translated. It is estimated that 100% of the Babalia are Muslim.

Pray: For God's word to be distributed and for spiritual fruit to grow in the Babalia people.

Fellowship

> *Join together in following my example, brothers and sisters, and just as you have us as a model, keep your eyes on those who live as we do. Philippians 3:17*

In this passage, the Apostle Paul gives us the mission to follow his model and work as a team. Paul is defining the role of teamwork. Teamwork has a strong connection with the word fellowship.

From Paul's perspective, the Philippians are part of his team (Philippians 1:5, Philippians 4:14-16). Paul often spoke about the fellowship he shared with people who were on his team. Fellowship is an important word, but it is a word we often overlook. To be in fellowship with your team means to be in "communion", to "share", or to "contribute" to one another's work. The idea of fellowship knows no boundaries. It is the idea of sharing and partnering in work, service, ideas, success, and even failures. Everything must be shared. The most important thing to share and have fellowship in is faith. When we have fellowship in our faith we begin to have a deeper communion with those serving on our team. Fellowship in faith is what defines teamwork.

Are you open to fellowship? Are you willing to begin sharing and participating in service with other churches and people in your town, city or region?

C. Scott

What does this mean for my life?

Lodha - India

Population: 6,630,000
The men cultivate the land and the women make clothes. Their religion is Hindu (99%). Their primary language is Hindi, which has many resources for evangelization. It is estimated 0.26% are Christians. Sadly, nominal Christianity has caused many Lodhas to misunderstand what it means to follow Christ.

Pray: For missionaries to take the Gospel message to the Lodhas, with both their mouths and Biblical translations.

Just Numbers?

> *After this I looked, and there before me was a great multitude that no one could count, from every nation, tribe, people and language, standing before the throne and before the Lamb. They were wearing white robes and were holding palm branches in their hands. Revelation 7:9*

Do you ever wonder if God cares about statistics and numbers? In Matthew 18:20 it says, "For where two or three gather in my name, there am I with them." Does this mean God does not care if the church is small or large?

In the book of Acts, the growth of the early church is discussed. Acts 1:15 states, "In those days Peter stood up among the believers (a group numbering about a hundred and twenty)," and Acts 2:41 says "those who accepted his message were baptized, and about three thousand were added to their number that day." Acts 4:4 tells of another 5,000 people who believed, and Acts 6:7 describes the "rapid" growth the church experienced. At the end of the Bible, in Revelation 7:9, "a great multitude that no one could count" is revealed.

If God believes a human soul has more value than all the riches in the world, how much worth do a hundred, thousand, million or even a billion souls have? It isn't just about numbers – it is about the salvation of human beings!

These verses teach us that through the power of God, all things are possible. The numbers of Christians started out small, but as the disciples remained faithful to God and each other, more believers were added! It is more than just a number to God. It is about souls for whom Jesus gave His life. We must care! We have to do something about it.

F. Rodríguez

What about you? Are you worried about the large number of people who do not know Jesus?

Anus - Indonesia

Population: 400

The Anus live on a small island in the region of Jayapura. They survive by fishing and farming. Their language, Anus, has some translated biblical stories. Their religion is animistic.

Pray: That the Word of God would reach the Anus and transform their lives.

Here And There

> At daybreak, Jesus went out to a solitary place. The people were looking for him and when they came to where he was, they tried to keep him from leaving them. But he said, 'I must proclaim the good news of the kingdom of God to the other towns also, because that is why I was sent. Luke 4:42-43

In our western world most countries are considered "Christian" and it is relatively easy to preach the Gospel. We face no risk of being arrested or persecuted to the extent of death. However, many people still do not make a decision to follow Jesus. Many people listen to the message of salvation, sometimes hundreds of times, but are unresponsive. Some people know the Gospel message by heart, but they have grown numb to it in such a way that it no longer has an effect on their heart.

The truth is that throughout the world, many people have never heard the Word of God. Some tribes do not know of the existence of the Bible because it has never been translated into their own language. Some people groups are even protected by the government to reduce the influence of other cultures.

Jesus' desire is to take the Gospel "here" in our cities, but His desire is also to take the Gospel "there" where people have yet to hear it. This is the desire of God and it is our responsibility. Do you wonder: how can I reach the unreached people? You can pray for them now! You can play an instrumental role in bringing the Gospel to unreached people.

M. de Rodriguez

Put yourself in the hands of the Lord!

Baiga - India

Population: 526,000
The Baiga are a forest-dwelling tribe whose primary vocation is nomadic agriculture. Their primary religion is Hinduism, and chastity is highly valued in their culture. Their language is Hindi. Only 0.3% of the Baiga have heard the Gospel.

Pray: For doors to be opened so the Gospel may be shared!

MARCH

The Addition

> But seek first the kingdom of God and His righteousness, and all these things will be given to you as well. *Matthew 6:33*

In our lives, we always seek answers. We invest our resources, time, and emotions into fixing the "additions" in our lives. In doing this, we lose sight of the important things. It is easy to lose sight on what is important because we focus on our selfish desires instead of listening to the voice of God.

Have you ever looked up the meaning of "addition"? The dictionary defines it as, "A part that is added to a set of elements." The "additions" we put into our lives are extensions of who we are, what we do, and what we stand for. Anything we add requires effort and time, which creates a struggle between flesh and spirit. Sometimes, we become so focused on meaningless short-term goals that we become distracted from Christ. These distractions often turn into a full-time investment and can lead to burn out, making us lose sight of what we initially desired. Our beloved Father asks us to come to Him for everything and let Him take care of the details. He knows how easily distracted we can become from our relationships with Him when we invest all of our time and energy into the "additions" of life. All He desires is for us to live every day with the goal to please Him. He desires for us to obey Him and seek His heart. Therefore, I invite you to take your hands off of the controls of your life and stop investing your valuable time into "additions" that only distract you from growing in Christ. Instead, surrender all of your burdens at the feet of the Almighty! Let God take care of each of the additions in your life because His plan for your life is perfect. He will grant many blessings in His time and on His terms.

G. Galindo

Do it now!

Baddaga Fertit - Central African Republic

Population: 23,000
Their skin is very dark and they wear white dresses to cover their bodies, except their faces. They are nomadic herders living in tents. Their religion is Islam and they speak Sudanese Arabic. They have the Bible translated into their language.

Pray: For the Word of God to make an impact in their hearts.

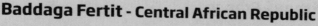

Good Reputation

> *The believers at Lystra and Iconium spoke well of him, so Paul decided to take him along on his journey. Read Acts 16:2-3*

Often, I am asked by university students to write letters of recommendation to help them find new employment. People do everything they can to have a good reputation in the workforce. A good recommendation from a reliable source can be the most important factor in acquiring a job.

Timothy was very young when Paul decided to take him on his missionary trip to be trained. Despite his youth, Timothy had a very good reputation among his fellow believers. He was respected in Lystra, where he lived and in neighboring places such as Iconium. Timothy was recommended to Paul because they believed he would be a good asset for Paul in his journey. Regardless of age, disciples of Jesus should work to be in good standing with the community. In fact, Paul advised Timothy through a letter to be an example for those around him. "Don't let anyone look down on you because you are young, but set an example for the believers in speech, in life, in love, in faith and in purity" (1 Timothy 4:12). If I asked your friends, colleagues, or classmates to write a letter of recommendation for you, what would the letter say? Would it say you were a Christ-like example? Would it speak of you like the believers spoke of Timothy?

W. Bello

Cultivate a good
reputation!

Brittany - France

Population: 229,000
The Brittany are a group from France, scattered along the border with Spain. They speak Breton and French. They call themselves Christians, but their lives do not reflect Christ. Less than 1% live a life obedient to Jesús. They need to live by Biblical truths.

Pray: For a spiritual revival for the Britons, for Jesus to take control of their lives.

Collaborator

> I thank my God every time I remember you. In all my prayers for all of you, I always pray with joy because of your partnership in the gospel from the first day until now... Philippians 1:3-5

Living out the Gospel means partnering with the people of God to complete His mission. We must get involved and cooperate in order to help bring others to Christ. An example of this was Epaphroditus, who risked his life to serve the needs of Paul. He is mentioned as Paul's brother, co-worker, "comrade in arms", and "fellow soldier" (Philippians 2:25-30, 4:18). This illustrates the strong unity of their partnership. During this time in history, Roman soldiers would fight the enemy with a partner. Soldiers would stand back to back throughout the battle so the enemy could not tell where one soldier ended and the other began. They would rejoice together, suffer together, and experience everything together. This is what Paul meant when he called Epaphroditus a "fellow soldier."

We are called to serve one another because of the passion we have for the Gospel. While serving the Lord, we to need have the mindset of 1 Corinthians 12:21-22. We are all part of the same body. No one can say to the other, "I do not need you." The challenge is to work in unity, communion and solidarity.

C. Scott

Am I being a fellow soldier in the mission?

Ava Guarani - Paraguay

Population: 9,450

The Ave Guarani speak Guaraní, which has a translation of the Bible. Many have had an encounter with Jesus, but still need the assistance of missionaries to understand the Scriptures. The challenges of modern life have left many families struggling financially.

Pray: For missionaries to invest their lives within this group, and for the younger Ava Guarani generation.

Love Brings Pain

{ *There a centurion's servant, whom his master valued highly, was sick and about to die. Luke 7:2*

Identifying with people means to share in the feelings of what they are going through, whether it means feelings of joy or despair. We cannot expect to love others if we do not share in what they're feeling. A loving mother always shares the pain of a sick child. Paul writes in 2 Corinthians 11:29, "Who of you is weak, and I do not feel weak?"

A centurion, like the one we read about in Luke 7, was known to be emotionally cold because Roman law required it. A centurion was the commander of a portion of the Roman army. If a servant of a centurion couldn't fulfill the job assigned him, the centurion could simply replace the servant with someone else to do the job. For this reason, a centurion was told not to "love" his servants or grow attached to them.

Someone we love occupies a unique and special place in our hearts. Love can often bring pain because we don't want to lose the people we love, as was the case for the centurion in Luke 7. He had seen past the label of his servant and had begun to value him highly.

Jesus also saw people with compassion. In love, he identified with people and was willingly led to the cross. Because of his love, he suffered great pain. Love prefers to suffer with the object of its affection. Jesus was a perfect example of this. Because he loved ALL of mankind, he died for ALL of mankind! He not only talked about His love for people, he also acted on it. His love was true.

W. Altare

How is our love?

Asilulu - Indonesia

Population: 12,000
They live on the island of Ambon, in the province of Maluku. They share their territory with other ethnic groups that have similar lifestyles, but very different languages. Their religion is Islamic, and they have no Biblical translation.

Pray: For a Bible translation to begin for the Asilulu language.

Faith And Trust Are Synonymous

> Blessed is the one who trusts in the Lord, who does not look to the proud, to those who turn aside to false gods. Psalm 40:4

Confidence comes from God when we place our trust in Him. David experienced this in many different situations in the Psalms. As he grew up and saw the Lord at work in his life, he learned to put his trust in God rather than rely on himself. He wrote, "I am in a desolate hole" and a "well of turmoil." He was expressing his powerlessness in his life.

Each life experience that leads you to put more trust in the Lord brings insurmountable blessing. David himself acknowledges this in Psalm 40:4, which says, "Blessed is the one who trusts in the Lord." As you connect intimately with God by putting your faith and trust in Him, He will reveal more and more of His plan for your life: "I took you from the fold."

We all know God has called us from our life of sin. At the same time, He continues to show compassion each and every day and shows us His will for our lives. What kind of turmoil has He brought you out of to bring you to the point you are at today?

Romans 12:1-2 says, "...in view of God's mercy, to offer your bodies as a living sacrifice, holy and pleasing to God—this is your true and proper worship. Do not conform to the pattern of this world, but be transformed by the renewing of your mind. Then you will be able to test and approve what God's will is—his good, pleasing and perfect will."

D. Duk

Trust in God!

Arbil - Israel

Population: 3,000
The Arbil are one of the most unreached groups in Israel. Their language is Noshan Lishanid, which has no part of the Bible translated. Their religion is ethnic animist. There are only 5 believers among the 3,000. There is a lack of discipleship.

Pray: These Christians can grow in their faith and be a witness to this people group.

The Testimony Of The Incarcerated

> About midnight Paul and Silas were praying and singing hymns to God, and the other prisoners were listening to them. Acts 16:25

Paul and Silas were severely beaten and unjustly imprisoned at Philippi. Paul later recalls this incident in one of his letters to the Corinthians (2 Corinthians 11:23-25). What is incredible is instead of complaining of the injuries, pain, and discomfort at midnight, they sang hymns to God. Instead of cursing those who had wrongly accused and sentenced them, they prayed to God. The public testimony for Christ that led to their injustice ended up placing them in an environment conducive for spreading the Gospel. Since the melody was quite different from what was heard daily in the gloomy prison, Paul and Silas immediately had the attention of the other prisoners.

At one point, an earthquake shook all of the prisoners' chains loose and the prison doors wide open. The jailer woke up and assumed most of the prisoners had escaped. Knowing he would most likely be severely punished, he was about to take his own life in despair. But then, he heard words of hope: "Don't harm yourself! We are all here!" The jailer dropped to his knees and asked Paul and Silas, "What do I have to do to be saved?" So, they gave him the answer that has endured for centuries: "Believe in the Lord Jesus, and you will be saved..." Are you bearing witness to God with your lives in the midst of difficulties, and thus giving hope to the lost?

M. Chiquie

God, use us!

West Coast Bajau - Brunei

Population: 12,000
The Bajau are known as nomads of the sea. They have developed the maritime trade and live on their boats. To be Bajau, you must be a Muslim and observe all the pillars of Islam. Their main dialect is the Sandakan Bajau, which has no Bible translation.

Pray: God places a follower of Jesus within this people group.

The True Focus

> But the Lord said, "You have been concerned about this plant, though you did not tend it or make it grow. It sprang up overnight and died overnight. And should I not have concern for the great city of Nineveh, in which there are more than a hundred and twenty thousand people who cannot tell their right hand from their left–and also many animals?" Jonah 4:10-11

We lose our focus when we get angry, unhappy and worried about little things. How much time do you spend praying for material things and for your personal dreams, while there are millions of people who go to bed each night without ever hearing the Gospel? How many people are going to spend an eternity without Christ because people won't take His love outside the four walls of the church building?

It is, by no means, wrong to pray for personal things. However, the more we seek the heart of God, the more we begin to care about the eternity of the millions of lost souls. What will you do now? Will you look at a few Facebook photos of your unsaved friends and continue on with your normal life? There is an incredible need in every part of the world to reach those who are lost and don't know God's Word. Whenever we open the Bible, we are exposed to the reality of the downfall of people who don't know Christ. There is no hope for those who will not turn from their worldly ways and follow Jesus. How will they ever hear about the love of Jesus if somebody doesn't go share it with them? The Church must put more emphasis on reaching the "120,000 of Nineveh" than "the vine" that sprouted overnight!

A. Gulard

Will you do it?

Bernde - Chad

Population: 6,500 inhabitants
They live in a mountainous and arid region, lacking basic necessities, such as water and electricity. Education is primary, and they live from gardening. Their language, Morom, has no Bible translation. They profess Islam.

Pray: For the Gospel to penetrate into the lives and hearts of the Bernde.

Why Go Right Now?

> *And this gospel of the Kingdom will be preached in the whole world as a testimony to all nations, and then the end will come. Matthew 24:14*

One night in an Indian village, the men were sitting around the fire while a missionary was sharing the Gospel with them. He had done this before, but today was different. He noticed a growing interest among the natives. The power of the Gospel was having its effect, they were starting to understand why Jesus came to this world and the difference He could make in their lives. Suddenly, the chief rose and came close to the missionary.

Pointing to the Bible, he asked, "How much time has gone by since this story was written?"

The missionary, who was somewhat surprised, answered, "Nearly 2,000 years."

The chief responded, "And you still believe the story that you just told us?"

"Since my childhood," answered the missionary.

"And your father believed the story?" asked the native.

"Yes, not only my dad, but also my grandfather and even my grandfather's grandfather," the missionary answered with pride.

"Then, why didn't you come sooner?" asked the chief with pain.

I was told this story as a child and it has stuck with me ever since. Sadly, this story can be a reality today. While you have five or more Bibles in your home, there are still billions of people who have never heard the beautiful Gospel of Jesus Christ. They are waiting for YOU!

M. Eitzen

Change this story!

Baggara - United States

Population: 2,300

The Baggara are an African Arab Group that speaks the Shuwa dialect. They profess Islam and only 0.5% have received the Gospel of Jesus. They are open to the Gospel.

Pray: For Baggara believers to disciple others and bring the Gospel back to their people group in Africa.

Other Sheep

> I have other sheep that are not of this sheep pen. I must bring them also. They too will listen to my voice, and there shall be one flock and one shepherd.
> John 10:16

I once saw a dynamic presentation at a missionary conference I attended. A woman distributed a plate full of cookies to the first row of people. Then a second person came with a bowl of candy and distributed it to the first and second rows of people. Finally, a lady came and distributed sodas, but also only to first two rows. Soon the rest of the crowd reacted in a natural way. Young people in the rest of the rows began to protest, "Hey! When do we get some! We want some too!"

When the preacher came on onstage, his first words were, "It's not fair that some people hear the Gospel many times, when there are millions who have never heard it even one time. It's not fair that we have four or five different versions of the Bible in our language, but there are millions who have never heard the name of Jesus in their own language."

Jesus spoke of the "other sheep" and said, "I must bring them also. They too will listen." For those of you who have dedicated your life to the Lord, think of the other sheep. When you pray, don't just think about your own needs. Think about those who have never heard! Someday, there will be "one flock and one shepherd."

F. Rodríguez

Do it!

Bakumpai - Indonesia

Population: 165,000
They live in the province of Kalimantan, along a river. Their lives revolve around water (fishing, rice cultivation, manufacture of river transport vessels). Their religion is Islam. They have some Biblical audio passages in their language.

Pray: The light of the Gospel would shine among the Bakumpai tribe.

Ask, Search, Call

> Ask and it will be given to you; seek and you will find; knock and the door will be opened to you. For everyone who asks receives; he who seeks finds; and to the one who knocks, the door will be opened. Matthew 7:7-8

What do we need in order to serve the Lord? In this passage, we see Jesus has provided you with all the tools you need. Often, our problem is we don't turn to God to use these tools and instead, we rely on ourselves. The first thing you need to do is ask Him for help. Asking the Father for help only strengthens your relationship with Him. As your relationship with God grows, you will develop a deeper desire to serve Him and use the tools He has given you. So first, present your requests to God and ask Him for guidance in your service for Him.

Second, there are times when you should assess whether the things you asking God for will bring Him glory. Sometimes, people get into the habit of asking God for things out of selfishness. Other times, we don't ask for enough in our prayer requests. Consequently, God will often shut the door on a prayer request and later give you abundantly more than what you asked for. You need to be constantly seeking what the Lord has for your life.

Third, Jesus tells us to knock or call. This means you must be proactive in your ministry and get other people involved. Jesus wants us to work together. Discipleship is not the work of one man by himself. God is pleased when we work together. He enjoys seeing His children meeting the needs of others. When an opportunity arises to serve, pray about it and then be proactive in pursuing it. In other words, if you see a door you think will bring glory to God, pray about it and then go knock on it. If God opens the door, don't be afraid...walk through it.

D. Travis

Do it!

Cashubian - Poland

Population: 100,000

Cashubians live in northern Poland. They have adopted Roman Catholicism as their religion, but most take it very lightly. Small Christian congregations comprise less than 1% of the population. Their language is Kashubian, which has a New Testament translation.

Pray: The testimony of the Gospel grows in this ethnic group.

With Humility

> Each of you should look not only to your own interests, but also to the interests of others. *Philippians 2:4*

The Gospel passionately teaches servants should work in cooperation. In Philippians 2, we find unique descriptions of Jesus, Timothy, and Epaphroditus as servant leaders. Philippians 3 warns about evil works (3:2) and in chapter 4, Paul pleads with Euodia and Syntyche to agree in the Lord (4:2).

The Bible has many references of servants experiencing problems as they work together. In the midst of these problems, we should follow the example of Jesus Christ, who was the ultimate servant. As servant leaders, we should long for Christ's attitude while working with others.

This is the heart of Jesus (Philippians 2:5-11):

- He made himself nothing, taking on the very nature of a servant, being made in human likeness (v. 5-7).
- He became obedient to death - even death on a cross (v. 8)!
- He was exalted (v. 9-11).

Because of His servant's attitude, Jesus was able to cooperate with people around Him. He ended up being exalted to the highest place. The first step to unity and cooperation begins with a capital H: Humility.

C. Scott

Does my life look like this?

Baori - India

Population: 27,200
The Baori are a low-ranking caste in India. They survive by selling used clothing and begging. Normally, they can be seen gathering discarded food from restaurants. Their language is Marwari, which has a translation of the New Testament.

Pray: The humanitarian groups, who minister to them, would be bold in sharing Jesus with them.

Life In Abundance

> The thief comes only to steal and kill and destroy; I have come that they may have life, and have it to the full. John 10:10

One day, as I was sitting at my house in the village of Sooninke, a friend came to visit me. Although he didn't understand it, I had been reading the Bible with him in French for several months. But this time when he came to visit and we began to read, I knew something was different. Suddenly, Saajo said his heart was heavy. I knew it was not a physical illness, but rather a spiritual one weighing him down.

The Bible assures us the thief comes to steal, kill, and destroy, so I assumed Saajo's past rejection of the Word of God was causing the heaviness inside him. Sadly, the prince of this world has many people locked in darkness and oppression. Even though this darkness comes from evil, we are assured Jesus came to give life, and life abundantly. Isn't it amazing that we can partner with God and help people receive the abundant life Jesus offers?

After my friend shared his heart's feelings with me, I prayerfully guided him through a time of recognition of Biblical truths. Later that afternoon, Saajo said with vivid joy, "My heart is renewed and refreshed!" From that day on, reading and studying the Word of God was never the same for Saajo. He had confessed to God his need for Jesus as Savior and Lord of his life. Saajo started living his life abundantly!

Pescador

Are you making this possible for people around you?

Barasana - Colombia

Population: 2,200
They live near the Caño Colorado and Pira- Paraná rivers. Their religion is animistic. Hallucinogens and their flute secrets "Yurupari" play an important part in the festivities and ceremonies of the Barasana.

Pray: God would break down any barriers hindering the salvation of this people group.

Voyage To Blessing

> You intended to harm me, but God intended it for good to accomplish what is now being done, the saving of many lives. Genesis 50:20

Joseph was taken to Egypt against his will. His brothers were jealous of him so they sold him into slavery to get rid of him. But God took this sad story and used it to bless many people. After his forced voyage to Egypt, Joseph ended up becoming governor and Pharaoh's second in command, where he was able to do good not only for the people of Egypt, but also for his family. This fulfilled the promise God made to Abraham: "his descendants would be a blessing to the nations of the earth."

Today, thousands of people are forced out of their home countries and find themselves in foreign places. Some leave for political reasons, others because of financial need, and others to escape catastrophes or persecution. In each case, God can use their situation as a blessing. As God's people, we are called to bring the hope of the Gospel to all nations. In Christ, as seeds of Abraham, we are instruments of God, set apart to be a blessing to the nations. In every situation, we can complain or submit it to God, while seeking to understand His purpose. Let's be missionaries where we are placed and let the light of Christ shine through us.

F. Rodríguez

Are you a missionary in the place where God has you?

Ble Jalkunan - Burkina Faso

Population: 1,500

They are farmers who live in the province west of Banfora Leraba. They adopted Islam, but in practice follow an animistic religion. They have some stories of the Bible in their language, Jalkunan.

Pray: The Bible recordings in their language would be made widely available.

Born Of God

> *...Children born not of natural descent, nor of human decision or a husband's will, but born of God. John 1:13*

Contrary to popular belief, people of God are not called to convert souls. No man can cause this transformation in another person or cause them to have a life-changing experience. The Church must present the Gospel of our Savior to the world. The people who hear must make a decision on their own; they can choose life or death by accepting or rejecting the Gospel. The Church cannot make the decision for these people, or give them the new birth. Our mission today is to present Christ, regardless of the reaction of those who hear (2 Corinthians 2:14-15). Paul, as a servant of God, became frustrated if he saw no fruit for God's kingdom. But whenever this message is preached, it always leads us to victory in Christ Jesus because it is a mark of obedience. As an apostle of Jesus Christ, we should not feel discouraged, for if we preach Christ and His Word, we are fulfilling the purpose God has for us. It is not our responsibility to save or condemn the world through our preaching.

O. Simari

Just preach the Gospel;
God will save them.

Attar - Pakistan

Population: 500

The Attar are 100% Islamic and are very proud of their religion and traditions. Their language is Pashto Nortino. They are mainly livestock farmers who market their own products.

Pray: God would bring down barriers so salvation can reach this group.

Demonstrating Love Of The Lord

> The third time He said to him, "Simon son of John, do you love me?" Peter was hurt because Jesus asked him the third time, "Do you love me?" He said, "Lord, you know all things; you know that I love you." Jesus said, "Feed my sheep."
> John 21:17

Over the years, there have been times when I have felt like abandoning my service to God and going back to my safe, comfortable life. Serving people is not easy; feeling disappointed and let down is natural when you serve people who are ungrateful and slanderous. God has given me the privilege of being used in leading many gifted young people to a life of service. However, because of disobedience, some of the youth I have led have now decided to depart from their calling. This has brought me a lot of pain and I have had to learn to understand I must follow God's calling despite the circumstances.

Peter left everything behind for Christ: the security of a profitable business, the convenience of living in his home, and the peace of doing what he loved to do everyday. Three years after leaving his comfortable life behind, he felt sick. He felt like he had disappointed his Lord and was ready to leave the calling God had placed on his life. He wanted to return to the safety and comfort of his former life as a fisherman. However, one night, the Lord restored him and reminded him of his divine calling. He was called to serve others, to guide them and show God's love to ungrateful, difficult and complicated people. In the same way, you are to show your love for God to others. There's no turning back! If Jesus is your Lord, you have to live a life of service to others! You are to live a life for others just as Jesus lived his life for you. If you love Jesus with all your heart, you are called to show love to others even if you feel like they don't deserve it. Feed His sheep.

G. Vergara

> We are to show Jesus' love to people who are hard to love.

Bawean - Malaysia

Population: 86,000
They live on an island near Java that bears their name. They practice Sunni Islam; they speak the language of Mature, which has a complete Bible translation and the New Testament in audio.

Pray: God's Word will have an effect on their hearts.

Reflections Of God

{ *And God created mankind in his own image, in the image of God he created them; male and female he created them. Genesis 1:27*

God created man in his image, which is PERFECT. However, that image was distorted because of man's sin. When we return to communion with God, we become adopted as His children. As His adopted children, we reflect His character. But when we sin, we reflect His character inaccurately and portray a God with attributes not in line with who He is. What kind of God do you reflect when it comes to your attitude about your work or your behavior toward the unlovable people in your life? If you choose to be whiny and resentful, you are unconsciously portraying God as whiny and resentful. In the same way, if you struggle to forgive or love others, why would people think the God you serve can forgive and love?

The choice is up to us to decide what kind of God we want to reflect. Some Christians reflect a God who is only in the church building: well dressed, discriminatory, and unwelcoming, both to outsiders and Jesus himself. When our behavior runs low on love, how can we say we believe or trust in a loving God? After all, the second commandment is, "Love your neighbor as yourself" (Leviticus 19:18). When the world sees churches that do not live out the mission of God, they see a God who is elitist, selfish, and only ensures the salvation of a few select people. But this is not the true reflection of God; we must seek Him to become like Him.

F. Chinatti

Reflect the true GOD!

Cabecar - Costa Rica

Population: 11,000
They live in the region of Turrialba. They mainly grow bananas to survive. Their religion is indigenous polytheistic. Some now know Jesus, but there is much confusion among these believers. Their language has the New Testament translation.

Pray: The Gospel reaches their hearts, removing any confusion.

Is There A Biblical Basis For Missions?

> He said to them, "Go into all the world and preach the gospel to all creation."
> Mark 16:15

When we speak of global evangelism, we are speaking about the Great Commission God entrusted to us in the Bible. This is our main purpose as Christians.

Only four chapters in the entire Bible do not speak of the great mission of reaching the lost and establishing the kingdom of our Creator. In Genesis 1 and 2, we see man and woman in full relationship with God. Before their fall and spiritual death, Adam and Eve were in perfect communion and full obedience to the will of their Creator. In Revelation 21 and 22, we see a description of the new heaven and the new earth. Imagine, in this time, there will be no need to save, restore, seek or recover lost people!

Of the 1,189 chapters of the Bible, 1,185 highlight the need for salvation and restoration. That's 99.7% of all Scripture! We don't have to wonder if God's will is truly focused on missions. His mission is based on the history found in 1,185 chapters of the Bible.

H. Ziefle

Will you do it?

Baliaga - Indonesia

Population: 56,000 Populations

They are the original inhabitants of the island of Bali. They store the dead in bamboo cages under a sacred tree. When there are 100 or more bodies, they are burned in a religious ceremony. They practice animism. Their language is Bali, which has a complete translation of the Bible.

Pray: For missionaries to continue to explain the Word of God to this people group.

Obedience In The Small Things

> Now Jesse said to his son David, "Take this ephah of roasted grain and these ten loaves of bread for your brothers and hurry to their camp" ... David complied with the instructions of Jesse. Read 1 Samuel 17:17-20

Imagine the scene: Samuel anointing David with oil as he kneels before his feet. When David gets up, there is no sound of trumpets, no one bowing before him, and no horse waiting to take him to his castle. I wonder if David thought, "This is my day of glory." But nothing happened. Instead of experiencing the glory as the new king of Israel, David returned to tending sheep and living his usual life. I picture David sitting bored in the field and thinking, "When will it really be my day of glory? When will it be my time to jump on the public stage?"

When his time finally came, it happened in such a unique and interesting way that it makes me laugh. Jesse, David's father, sent him to war. This was the moment David had been waiting for! He was ready to become a man and fight for his people. Unfortunately, David's father was only sending him to take food to his brothers. But he was told to go, so he obeyed.

I'm sure David thought, "What a shame! I'm going to war, where the soldiers are all tough and manly, and they are all going to see me skipping over the hill with a picnic basket in my hand. This is going to be humiliating."

If David ever dreamed of doing an extraordinary act, I'm sure he did not imagine it would come from his obedience in carrying a lunch basket, but it did! He reached the battleground and was filled with zeal for God. We all know the story from there. David took a leap of faith and killed a giant twice his size. From that point on, his life was not the same. His name became famous and the rest is history. So the next time you are asked to be obedient in what seems to be something small, do it! If you ride the wave and go with the flow, you might end up killing a giant of your own!

W. Núñez

> Everything can start with a small job.

Catalan - Spain

Population: 6,648,000
The Catalan are a people group originally from Spain. They live in Catalonia and Valencia. They retain their language, Catalan, but also speak Castilian. They have many Biblical resources available. They profess Roman Catholicism.

Pray: For a spiritual revival in the Christian churches.

Personal Value

{ *You are justified freely by his grace through the redemption that came by Christ Jesus. Read Romans 3:21-26*

From childhood, many of us are taught to find our value through what others say about us. Every time our parents or other adults celebrate our abilities or congratulate our achievements, we learn self-worth depends on our achievements or abilities. However, neither the recognition from the world for our achievements, nor applause for our abilities is able to fill our hearts with true joy and peace.

The inner dissatisfaction every person experiences is caused by sin. When we live with our backs to God, we do not live reflecting the glory of God. But God, in His great love for humanity, has given a way to be free from sin and its eternal consequences. This freedom comes through the death of God's Son on the cross, as a sacrifice for our sins. Through Jesus' resurrection, God forgives and reconciles us to himself.

Through Christ's sacrifice, you are now found worthy in the sight of God. However, this is not because of your achievements, what you have said, or what you think about yourself. Instead, your acceptance is dependent on believing in what God has done. God sees you and accepts you through the righteousness of His Son's death on a cross. He has accepted you through the Lamb of God who took away the punishment of sin for the world.

A. Betancur

Take this message to everyone!

Bilala - Chad

Population: 177,500
The Bilala men grow and trade cotton, sorghum, millet and cassava. Women grow food in gardens and raise small animals. They profess Islam. Their language is Naba, which has some audio Bible stories.

Pray: For God to be revealed, to the Bilala, through Jesus!

The Only Way

> *I want to know Christ—yes, to know the power of his resurrection and participation in his sufferings, becoming like him in his death... Philippians 3:10*

The Gospel is the Lord's desire for everyone to know Him. Within life's busyness, we cannot neglect having a passion for people to know Jesus. We are constantly being tempted to lack passion for both Jesus and His people. Often, the excitement of different church programs or activities can overshadow our passion for Jesus. Our first priority must be to know Him. In Philippians 3, the apostle Paul's desire was to know Christ. His passion led to the desire of working together with a body believers and sharing Jesus' love throughout the world. When you meet Jesus in a profound way, He will change your life, give you passion, and direct your steps. Although it requires much effort and sacrifice, it is worth it to grow closer to the heart of God. Your top priority should be to worship God and let Him use you to be a messenger to other people about His love!

C. Scott

Do you remember your
salvation every day?

Ayore - Paraguay

Population: 2,015
The Ayore live in the eastern region, in Alto Paraguay and Boqueron. They have the New Testament in their language. Their beliefs are a mixture of Christian and animism. They are in a literacy program organized by missionaries.

Pray: For the new generation, who will have a better education and access to the Word of God.

Bible in a year: Matthew 19:1-15 / Numbers 9-10 / Ecclesiastes 7

He Has Always Been There....

> So do not fear, for I am with you; be not be dismayed, for I am your God. I will strengthen you and help you; I will uphold you with my righteous right hand.
> Isaiah 41:10

Although we know the love of God, we often fear change in the future. If we would simply remember how God brought us through our past, we would realize He has always been with us, sustained us, and given us victory. You may think what you are going through is extremely difficult, but you need to realize God is still with you. He is strengthening you, providing for you and will never let you fail.

Unfortunately, we are constantly tempted to doubt Him. We might think, "He helped me then, but maybe this time is different. Maybe now I don't deserve it." It is in this mindset the problem lays. All of the blessings, all that we are and all that we have are by the mercy and grace of God. Nothing we do will change the circumstances unless God allows it.

Therefore, cling to His promises and stand firm! God created us and He knows the full story of our lives, from beginning to end. Everything happening in your life is by His sovereign will. Nothing is accidental; everything is in His plan. Do you fully trust God and always put Him first in your life? If that is the desire of your heart, I invite you to believe in and enjoy a constant relationship with your heavenly Father. Join Him every day in prayer and praise!

M. Inciarte

Fear not!

Bayad - Mongolia

Population: 57,000
The Bayad are a Mongolian tribe living in the west of the country. Although the people are very friendly, they live in a remote area and are difficult to access. They have had a complete Bible translation in their language since the year 2000. However, it is estimated only 0.1% are Christians.

Pray: The believers of other Mongol tribes would minister to the Bayad with the Gospel.

In Jesus

> *Fixing our eyes on Jesus, the pioneer and perfecter of faith. For the joy set before him he endured the cross, scorning its shame, and sat down at the right hand of the throne of God. Hebrews 12:2*

Recently, I have been learning a lot about how to have joy despite my circumstances. During a Bible study I was leading, a verse spoke to my heart and revealed shocking truth. Hebrews 12:2 says, "Let us fix our eyes on Jesus, the author and perfecter of our faith, who for the joy set before him endured the cross, scorning its shame, and sat down at the right hand of the throne of God."

This is incredible! The verse says I should fix my eyes on Jesus, not on the circumstances around me. When I go through trials, there are times when all I can think about are my problems and how to fix them. I find it difficult to think about having joy in the Lord during these challenges. Jesus became the greatest example of having joy in difficult circumstances when he experienced a cruel and shameful death on the cross. So, with joy, I now accept the challenges and trials my Lord and Savior has for me.

Every day in my ministry, I face decisions that affect the course of my life. It is not always easy to make decisions of obedience when walking into unfamiliar territory. But when I walk into unfamiliar territory, I fix my eyes on God, who is always faithful and trustworthy. I release any worry I might have and walk forward knowing my heavenly Father is taking care of me! You can rest in the fact God is always with you, guiding every step you take. Be filled with joy!

MyT. Goddard

Fix your eyes on Christ!

Bozo-Tie - Mali

Population: 236,000

Bozo means "straw house". There are three ethnic groups classified as Bozo. They live in the Mopti region, surviving from fishing and some crop cultivation. They speak Bozo Tieyaxo, which has some portions of the Bible translated. They profess Islam.

Pray: Each member of this ethnic group can hear the message of salvation.

Interrupting Their Routine

> If you knew the gift of God and who it is that asks you for a drink, you would have asked him and he would have given you living water.
> Read John 4:1-26

As we meet new people and build relationships, we begin to notice they are either fully satisfied with life (which can only come from a relationship with Christ) or they are dissatisfied with their life (which is usually the case). Those who are not happy with their lives are usually easy to recognize: bad attitudes, no motivation, and no purpose.

Many of these people are probably stuck in a Christ-less, monotonous routine like the Samaritan woman. Because of her social status in the community, she always went to the well at a certain time in order to avoid other women. The day she met Jesus, she was doing the same thing she always did. However, Jesus interrupted her routine and unexpectedly spoke to her. He turned an ordinary conversation about water into a conversation about eternal life. We should also interrupt people's routines and challenge them to think about spiritual truths, using terms they will recognize. Instead of expecting people to come to us, we need to go to them. Jesus did not despise the Samaritan woman, but spoke in a way she could understand. In doing this, she realized her life was not hidden from God's sight. Jesus did not judge her, but instead, loved her and showed His desire for her to be in a relationship with God. Do you talk to nonbelievers in such that attracts them to Christ? Do your conversations with them have a loving balance between revealing their need for a Savior and inviting them into a relationship with God?

N. Rivas

Get people out of their routine!

Bajelani - Iraq

Population: 57,000
The Bajelani are traders and professional soldiers. They strictly follow Islam. Women dress in all black, covering their entire body and face. They speak Bajelani, which has portions of the Bible translated.

Pray: The Bajelani have the opportunity to hear about Jesus.

Give Your Best

> "When you bring blind animals for sacrifice, is that not wrong? When you sacrifice crippled or diseased animals, is that not wrong? Try offering them to your governor! Would he be pleased with you? Would he accept you?" says the LORD Almighty. Malachi 1:8

In this passage, God rebukes His people for their lack of love and respect when giving their offerings. They were giving less than what the law of the Old Testament required. They thought God could not see the flaws in the offerings they gave. Today, it is also common to offer defective sacrifices. However, it no longer comes in the form of lame animals. It comes in the form of a song sung halfheartedly, a message delivered without preparation, or a prayer prayed without much thought. When we offer something to the needy, it is usually something we have extra of or can no longer use. Sadly, it is often useless to the person we give it to. Unfortunately, we can trick ourselves into believing these are acceptable sacrifices, when in reality, they are no sacrifice at all.

Jesus rebuked the Israelites because they thought their sacrifices were pleasing to Him, when in fact they were disappointing. Everything we offer as a service to our neighbor should be given as though it were being given to Jesus. What are you offering to God? Do you give your unwanted leftovers to the blind, the lame, or the sick? Do you think God is happy with that? If this is not the case with you, praise God! But, there is always room for improvement!

F. Rodríguez

Always give your best!

Bhojpuri - Fiji

Population: 26,000

They are immigrants from India, and have preserved their language, Bhojpuri. They practice the Hindu religion. They are devoted to rice and sugarcane, which serves the entire region. They have the New Testament in print and audio, as well as the Jesus film, but few have responded to the Gospel.

Pray: For a greater impact of the Word of God in their lives.

Useful Servant

> "Return home and tell how much God has done for you." So the man went away and told all over town how much Jesus had done for him.
> Read Luke 8:26-39

This passage has always intrigued me. Within the verses, we see some of the people were more concerned about the pigs drowning than the man who had just been healed. Instead of glorifying God for the act of salvation, they became afraid and drove Jesus out of the country. What catches my attention is the Gerasene man wanted to follow Jesus, but instead Jesus told him to return home. He wanted to go where Jesus went, but Jesus asked him to stay and serve Him by being a living witness to the wonders God had done in his life. Jesus sent the man to the people who did not recognize the powerful miracle that had just taken place. The Gerasene accepted the mission immediately, without questioning Jesus' orders. He was obedient and did not become discouraged about the plans Jesus had for him.

The Gerasene man not only went back home as he was told, but he did so much more. He proclaimed to all the people the saving work of Jesus Christ. He was an effective servant who did what he was told to do. What a great example we can take from this character! We should also surrender our will and service in gratitude to God for our salvation. Be a testimony to the wonders of God, even if people reject you and God's miracles!

M. de Rodríguez

Imitate his example!

Betoyes - Colombia

Population: 800
The economy of the Betoyes is based solely on agriculture and the trade of bananas. They have lost their native language and now speak Spanish. Numerous Bible resources were distributed into their villages, but only about 1% have responded to the Gospel.

Pray: The Betoyes would find life in Jesus.

Unconditional Love

> { *A new command I give you: Love one another. As I have loved you, so you must love one another.* John 13:34

My wife and I serve as missionaries with the Mastanawa people of the Purus River. They live on the border of Peru and Brazil. In this region, there are eight people groups. Most people have the New Testament in their native language. This is not true for the Mastanawa people because they don't have a written language to call their own. While other ethnic groups are advancing in their knowledge of God, the Mastanawas cannot.

One day, I came across several drunk Mastanawas. When I saw them, I immediately became upset and said things I cannot repeat in this devotion. I thought about the life and salary I had left behind to come serve these people. Although I never said it, I secretly expected a sign of gratitude from the Mastanawa for my service and sacrifice. However, they showed no gratitude and treated us as if we were obligated to give.

Through similar events, God taught us He wants us to love these people with a love that is unconditional and expects nothing in return. This kind of love is freely given out of obedience to Christ. Christians are expected to show this kind of love, but we should not expect to receive it from the world. Only those who recognize Jesus as Lord of their lives are capable of giving the amazing unconditional love God displays. Out of obedience and gratitude toward God, I will continue to love the Mastanawas and others who lack this kind of love in their lives.

G. Rivas

You have to give to understand!

Bisu - Thailand

Population: 700
The Bisu are a group with Chinese origin who have moved numerous times, but are still not accepted by other ethnic groups. They are marginalized, persecuted and considered of a lesser rank. They have the Bible translated into their language, Bisu.

Pray: That their intense search for identity and belonging leads them to Christ.

Bible in a year: Matthew 22:1-22 / Numbers 21 / Song of Songs 1:1-2:7

God Will Provide

> He told them: "Take nothing for the journey—no staff, no bag, no bread, no money, no extra shirt. Whatever house you enter, stay there until you leave that town." Luke 9:3-4

Jesus gave these instructions to His disciples before sending them to preach the Gospel. He told them not to worry about material things or about basic things they needed to stay alive. Jesus instructed His disciples to remain in one place and not go from house to house looking for better accommodations.

We are tempted to use the excuse: "I need specific material things before I can go out and preach the Gospel." Naturally, every person has basic needs, but God is capable of providing for these needs. He provides in ways we least expect by using people we least expect. Jesus encourages us to go without fear because we can trust He will go before us and prepare the way. We can be assured He will provide for our needs so we are able to testify to His provision. God provides in His time. Our responsibility is to preach His Word and have faith in Him. When we have faith in God, there is no need to be dependent on man. However, God uses people to provide basic needs. Are you willing to welcome missionaries into your home? Are you being sensitive to the needs of others? God wants to use you! Will you allow Him to bless others through you?

F. Rodríguez

Do not let love for material things hinder you!

Czech - Czech Republic

Population: 9,870,000
The majority of these Slavic people are Atheist and are not interested in religion. The country has a strong Russian influence. Only 26% claim to be Roman Catholic and less than 1% Protestant Christian. They have many Biblical resources in their language, Czech.

Pray: For the chains of atheism to be broken and hearts readied for the Gospel.

Bible in a year: Matthew 22:23-46 / Numbers 22:1-40 / Song of Songs 2:8-3:5

Christ Above All

> This is to my Father's glory, that you bear much fruit, showing yourselves to be my disciples. John 15:8

A true disciple of Jesus Christ is willing to put God above all other life aspirations. A devoted disciple recognizes Jesus Christ as Lord. Jesus spoke to the Jews who believed in him and said, "If you hold to my teaching, you are truly my disciples." It's extremely important to remain faithful to Jesus and his teachings! But, how can this become a daily discipline?

In the book of John, Jesus tells us how we can recognize his disciples. "By this all will know that you are my disciples, if you love one another" (John 13:35). In another section of Scripture, Jesus challenges his disciples by telling them if they did not give up everything, they couldn't be his disciples. Jesus wanted to express the most important thing in their lives was to put Him first in their lives. It is ok to be successful and have material possessions, but these things should not control your life. Today, remember the Father will be glorified in your life if you are obedient to His Word and recognize His lordship over all things.

D. Duk

Are you being
a good disciple?

Chakali - Ghana

Population: 7,600

The Chakali are farmers who live east of Wa. Their religion is based on the belief in wandering spirits, which makes them afraid to walk at night. Their language, Chakali, has some audio Bible stories. The Christian church is 3% and growing!

Pray: Chakali believers would give a powerful testimony of their faith in Jesus.

Let's Go!

{ *Do not make us cross the Jordan. Numbers 32:5*

The story in chapter 32 of Numbers describes two tribes who began to think only of themselves and put aside any concern for the rest of God's people. For these tribes to remain in God's will (Exodus 3:7-8), they needed to trust and follow Him wholeheartedly. It wasn't easy for them to leave Egypt and go to the Promised Land. After 400 years of being slaves, they were challenged to have a new mindset, lifestyle and spiritual attitude. Just as the tribes of Reuben and Gad were about to realize their dream of entering the Promised Land, they decided they wanted to stay where they were, rather than accepting the high risk, high reward command God had given them. They said to Moses, "Do not make us cross the Jordan."

Here we see two different views and attitudes contrasted: greed versus generosity, cooperation versus individualism, disobedience versus obedience, rebellion versus compliance, ethnocentrism versus local and global outreach. We, like these tribes of Israel, need to experience a transformation of character. We are called to be like Jesus, remaining in His will and living as a light to the nations (Isaiah 49:6). But we often refuse to cross the Jordan. We refuse to leave our comfort zones and deal with problems that might lie ahead. We don't always want to invest in others, but we must obey God in order to reach the Promised Land!

C. Scott

Are you going to cross the Jordan?

Cayuga - Canada

Population: 3,500

The Cayuga live in the province of Ontario. Their main language is Cayuga, but they have received the Gospel in English. About 10% believe in the Gospel, but the rest follow a nominal Catholicism.

Pray: The witness of Christ will reach the entire ethnic group.

Identity

> Yet to all who did receive him, to those who believed in his name, he gave the right to become children of God. John 1:12

We all know the human race is far from perfect. We have a number of weaknesses and limitations. We are also faced with floods of problems on a daily basis. But none of this should keep us from being who God wants us to be. We are His children; our destination is eternal life in heaven with Him. When life gets complicated and seems as if there is no way out, focus on God and His eternal purpose. Frame every so-called "disaster" with this question: Does this problem matter in the scope of eternity? Being His child not only gives you access to His blessings and protection, but also gives you courage to influence others with enthusiastic, God-focused leadership.

Each person only has one life to live on earth, so as children of God, we need to let His light shine through us by loving others and being generous with a constant attitude of service (Matthew 5:16). A child of God should never evoke fear or doubt, but rather confidence. Since Christ died for ALL mankind, a follower of Christ should not be exclusive, but include everyone in generosity. You can be a bright light in the lives of your unsaved friends because you can bring peace in conflict, harmony in debate, and acceptance in the midst of rejection. You are a child of God. Live it!

W. Altare

> You can be a light to the world.

Bit - Laos

Population: 2,800

There are a variety of beliefs in their villages, but animism and ancestor worship are the strongest among the Bit religions. Linguistically, it is a very complex tribe, as most can speak the languages Lao, Lu, Khmu and Hmong. There are currently no Christians among them.

Pray: For the tribe to hear the message of salvation in a language they know.

Walking Together

> Then the man and his wife heard the sound of the Lord God as he was walking in the garden in the cool of the day, and they hid from the Lord God among the trees of the garden. Genesis 3:8

I remember the first walk I took with my wife like it was yesterday. I wanted our walk to last forever; simply being next to her was enough to satisfy me. Now, I am presented with so many demands for my time: work, ministry, children, and the tasks of everyday life. Sadly, I cannot take time to enjoy hand in hand walks with my wife as often as I would like.

Today's passage gives us the impression God walked in the Garden of Eden regularly. On this specific day in the Garden, like many others, He was going to walk with the man and woman He created. Can you imagine what it would be like to walk next to God? Sadly, Adam and Eve's sin separated them from His presence. From that day on, they never walked with God or enjoyed His presence the way they once had.

Fortunately for us, God didn't cross His arms and say, "You sinned against me, so we're through." Instead, He put together a plan to rescue man from his sinful nature. The sole purpose of God's plan is to bring Himself more glory through the restoration of the broken relationship caused by sin. God wants to walk with you just as He did with Adam and Eve in the Garden of Eden. As a Christian, you are responsible for showing the world how much they need a restored relationship with their Creator.

H. Bascur

What are showing with your life?

Biami - Papua New Guinea

Population: 200
The Biami survive by fishing and gathering wild fruits. They live in small villages near rivers. They have not heard the Gospel in their language because no part of the Bible has been translated into their language, Piame. Their religion is animistic.

Pray: For Bible translators to bring the good news of salvation to this group.

APRIL

Do Not Be Discouraged!

> Moses said to the Gadites and Reubenites, "Should your fellow Israelites go to war while you sit here? Why do you discourage the Israelites from crossing over into the land the LORD has given them?" Numbers 32:6-7

Moses had to address a serious moral problem within the Israelites. The tribes should have been united and cooperative with one another, but instead two tribes were thinking only about themselves. Moses reminded the tribes what had happened to the spies sent to survey the land at Kadesh Barnea. The spies discouraged the people (32:9) and brought down their morale. The consequence was waiting many years to enter the Promised Land (32:11). This led to the death of all of Israelites except Caleb and Joshua, whom the word of God says, "... followed me with all their heart" (32:12).

To follow God with your whole heart means to daily renew your mind with His Word and Holy Spirit. Following God means to believe no task is impossible in His hands. A vibrant faith is the opposite of fatalism, resignation and selfishness. Faith leads to perseverance, dedication and generosity. When we follow God wholeheartedly, He has promised blessings greater than we can imagine. Do not focus on your own desires, but instead think of God's global mission. Do not be discouraged because you will receive the blessing of God's promises.

C. Scott

Are you going to be left behind?

Barias - Pakistan

Population: 3,200
Some are Muslims, but the majority follow Hinduism. Their language is Sindhi, which has a translation of the Bible. No known Christians live among them. Many Barias are illiterate, so it is important the Word of God is spread with audio.

Pray: They hear the Good News in their native language.

His Will

> Therefore go and make disciples of all nations, baptizing them in the name of the Father and of the Son and of the Holy Spirit.
> Matthew 28:19

Many people wonder what God's purpose is for their life. It's a valid question. We want to do His will. We pray for His guidance and cry out for God to use us in His Kingdom. However, His will often remains a mystery.

Knowing God's will is discovered through a process of walking with Him daily. There are some things you should never forget. First, God loves you and cares deeply for your heart. No work or ministry can bring you closer to God. Only a daily relationship with Him can create intimacy. How wonderful!

Second, God entrusts "much" to the ones who have been faithful with "little." Do not expect to jump into big things if you're not willing to work faithfully with the little things. There is a process everyone must experience, but it takes place at God's pace. He will allow you to go through different situations (some tougher than others) so you grow, learn, and mature.

Third, His will is found in His Word. If you study it each day, you will find God's Word will never ask you to do something that goes against His will. In the Bible, we are given clarity on what the Lord expects of us. Start to understand His will by reading Matthew 28:18-19, John 17:18 and Isaiah 61.

L. Ashmore

Have you opened your Bible?

Chenoua - Algeria

Population: 82,000

Their main language is Chenoua, but it has four dialects that are very different from each other. They live in scattered villages in the interior of Algeria. Their history is marked by poverty and poor education. They profess Islam and do not accept other religions. They have the Bible in their language.

Pray: The Gospel would find a way into their lives.

Proclaimed In All The Earth

> *But I have raised you up for this very purpose, that I might show you my power and that my name might be proclaimed in all the earth. Exodus 9:16*

Today's verse is part of the message Moses delivered Pharaoh as he announced the coming of the hail plague. It's during this message God used Moses to indicate the purpose of His displays of power throughout the plagues. I invite you to read the context of the verse (Exodus 9:13-19).

God tells Pharaoh there is no one like Him in all the earth and God alone has the power to take everything away (including his life). Yet, God left Pharaoh alive so His name might be proclaimed throughout the world. God always intended the world to know His purpose. The 10 plagues on Egypt were not just to deliver Israel from bondage and to show God's power, but they were also for the nations of the world to recognize the wonders of God for the years following Israel's deliverance. In fact, forty years later, Rahab testifies that they had "heard how the Lord dried up the waters of the Red Sea." Today, you can find countless resources re-telling the story of Moses delivering God's people out of Egypt. The plagues were given all for God's glory! God has not changed. Today, He is not satisfied that some people are unaware of His wonders. He wants all nations, ethnicities, and people to know the one true God. Are you aware of this reality? Do you want to know the wonders of God for you and your church?

F. Rodríguez

> Do you want the whole world to know about His truth?

Brao - Vietnam

Population: 400

The Brao live on the border of Cambodia and Laos. They are hunters and gather wild fruits. Their language is Wash, which is in urgent need of a Bible translation. They have heard of Jesus through other languages. A small church is among them.

Pray: Bible translators and teachers of the Word would disciple the church.

Different, But Not Alienated

{ *...by setting aside in his flesh the law with its commands and regulations. His purpose was to create in himself one new humanity out of the two, thus making peace. Ephesians 2:15*

When God gave the law to Israel, it was not intended to distance them from the other nations, but to bring them closer. Israel should have become a model for the people of God, worthy of imitation by all nations. But Israel failed to properly obey this divine missionary call to be a light to the nations. Instead their possession of the law made them proud. They increasingly grew apart from the other nations because they were trying to keep clean according to the law. They made matters worse by adding human commandments, which is what Paul was referring to when he mentioned "the law with its commands and regulations." A religious faith always produces a religious culture and a religious culture is formed by human interpretation. Israel believed that their religious culture was the sole expression of the will of God. Unfortunately, this caused hostility and distance from other nations.

The same thing that happened to Israel can also happen in our churches today. By rejecting Biblical truth and adding traditions we call "Christian", many churches repel themselves from the lost people of the world. As followers of Christ, we need to be drawing ourselves to the lost people. This allows us to share the love of Jesus with them. Does the truth you believe repel you from the people of the world? How can you be an instrument of salvation if you avoid people?

A. Neufeld

Stay close!

Cabiyaris - Colombia

Population: 280
They live along the Apaporis River in Colombia. They follow their indigenous religion and their rituals often focus on anacondas. It is estiamted 6% have given their lives to Jesus. Portions of the Bible have been translated into their language.

Pray: For Cabiyaris believers to share a strong testimony.

Beyond Material Needs

> When Jesus landed and saw a large crowd, he had compassion on them, because they were like sheep without a shepherd. So he began teaching them many things. Mark 6:34

The compassion of Jesus is shown in the well-known miracle of feeding the 5,000 people with a few loaves of bread and fish. You can also notice, by reading the story, feeding these people was more of a concern of the disciples than Jesus Himself.

Jesus was concerned more about the eternal circumstances of the crowd than their temporary circumstances of hunger. After multiplying the food, so everybody had enough, Jesus began to teach them because they were like "sheep without a shepherd."

Sometimes we, as disciples, tend to be more moved by the material needs of people, than their spitual needs. We tend to spend much of our time relieving them of their physical ailments (which is very good and necessary), while overlooking their need to be spiritually filled. People need a Savior, more specifically, they need a relationship with God through His son, Jesus Christ! Jesus knows people cannot live on bread alone, which is why He desires to give them eternal life. Jesus wants to deliver them not only from their hunger, but from death.

The Lord will take care of all the needs of His people, but everything in its proper priority. May the Lord enable you to feel what He felt when He saw the crowds.

M. Chiquie

> The spiritual need is first priority.

Ani - China

Population: 104,000

The Anis are a group of Tibetan origin. They live in the province of Yunnan. Although the majority of Anis ignore Him, they believe in a creator. They follow an ethnic religion. They worship ancestors and believe in disease causing spirits. Their primary language is Axi, which has some translated portions of the Bible.

Pray: The Anis would receive the Gospel of salvation in their own language.

Trust In Him

> We do not want you to be uninformed, brothers and sisters, about the troubles we experienced in the province of Asia. We were under great pressure, far beyond our ability to endure, so that we despaired of life itself. Indeed, we felt we had received the sentence of death. But this happened that we might not rely on ourselves but on God, who raises the dead. 2 Corinthians 1:8-9

In this letter to his Christian brothers in Corinth, Paul was trying to explain the severity of his troubles in Asia. In the midst of his trials, he also gave thanks to God for the incredible hope he received. Paul hit the nail right on the head when he explained God's purpose for the trials he experienced. "That we might not rely on ourselves but on God."

How often do trials make you feel hopeless and abandoned? As believers, we often assume we're free from the problems and sufferings of this sinful world. But that couldn't be further from the truth! God uses trials in our lives to teach us to trust in Him during everything we do. Are you presently going through difficulties, opposition, economic hardship, diseases, or other problems that you can't handle on your own? God is letting you go through these things for a reason! The more trials you go through, the more God has the opportunity to show His protection, His provision, His love, and His care. A practical way to start trusting God through your trials is to simply talk with Him in prayer. God is waiting for you to ask for help in your trials!

F. Rodríguez

Are you praying?

Cagayan Negrito - Philippines

Population: 1,300
They live in the northern region of Cagayan. Most follow an ancient animistic religion, but some have heard the Gospel. It is estimated 5% are Christians. Their language is Atta-Pamplona, which has a translation of the New Testament.

Pray: Cagayan believers' faith is strengthened and multiplied.

The Priority Of The Kingdom

> But seek first his kingdom and his righteousness, and all these things will be given to you as well. Matthew 6:33

What is the first priority in your life? It's clear from His Word that God wants us to share in His kingdom, to have an eternal mindset, and to desire what He desires. Recent studies have shown the three main desires of students around the world are: 1) success in school/job 2) more money 3) a boyfriend/girlfriend.

Most people believe if they can have these three things, they are on their way to a good life. They believe these three things automatically lead to: a good family, a good house, a good steady income and "security." The problem with this "security" mindset is all these "things" are temporary, just like the world we live in. Having these "things" doesn't equal living "happily ever after" or living "the dream". Life on this earth is just a tiny sliver in the scope of eternity!

Would you spend the majority of your time decorating a room on a ship that's sinking? Jesus reminds us not to worry about anything other than seeking His Kingdom. If we do this, He promises to fill in the details of our life in accordance to His plan and timing. With this promise, there is simply no use in worrying about the things the world desires. Let your King be your top priority! It's the least we can do when He takes care of everything else!

D. Travis

Have an eternal mindset!

Cao Lan - Vietnam

Population: 170,000

Like most of the ethnic groups in Vietnam, their religion is based on spirit, earth, water, fire, and animals. Their quality of life is very precarious and their villages lack basic services. Their language, Caolan, has portions of the Bible translated.

Pray: For God to become real to the Cao Lan. Pray God brings life, salvation, and new opportunities for growth.

Passion – Compassion

> He prayed to the Lord, "Isn't this what I said, Lord, when I was still at home? That is what I tried to forestall by fleeing to Tarshish. I knew that you are a gracious and compassionate God, slow to anger and abounding in love, a God who relents from sending calamity." Jonah 4:2

Jonah knew the loving attributes of God because he was educated in the Scriptures. Although Jonah knew about God's loving attributes, he did not desire for the attributes to be shared as God intended. Jonah knew God was forgiving, compassionate, and merciful, but he did not want God to manifest the characteristics over the Ninevites.

God is glorified when people repent because it allows Him to forgive and heal. Jonah didn't share God's gracious mindset. He wished God would judge the Ninevites harshly because of their sin against God. It is difficult to understand why someone would be so harsh, but we often act the same way. It is easy to become proud of being Biblically educated or to spend time debating theological issues. Meanwhile, millions live their lives without ever hearing the name, "Jesus".

Do not take my point the wrong way. We need to be studying the Bible fervently and fighting to understand sound Biblical doctrine. One of the biggest problems in the church today is a lack of Biblical knowledge. But knowledge itself doesn't guarantee a heart after God's heart. The more we study the Bible, the more we should fall in love with God and the Bible. Our studies should lead us to acquiring the same loving attributes as God. Is your heart beating for the same things God's heart beats for? Do not be like Jonah!

A. Gulard

Let's have more passion for God and more compassion for people!

Western Cham - United States

Population: 3,200

The Western Cham are immigrants from Cambodia. Most are young people who have gone to study in universities. Almost all claim to be followers of the Islamic faith. Although they have had contact with the Gospel, they do not wish to accept the Savior.

Pray: For the few believers who have dared to leave Islam.

One Body

{ *Now Moses was a very humble man, more humble than anyone else on the face of the earth. Numbers 12:3*

Throughout the life of Moses, we see God allowing him to face extremely tough challenges with the Israelites. How did Moses handle the problems he had with the people of God?

1. He confronted them about their sin. The call for unity, communion, and mutual support is a challenge for the global church.

2. He demanded compromise. Having a Christ-like attitude means adjusting our vision to the vision of God. Instead of taking situations into our own hands, we must learn to do what God asks of us.

3. He gave a warning: "If you refuse, you will be sinning against the Lord. And you can be sure that you will not escape the consequences of your sin." The great challenge of the church is to think as "one body". What the entire "church body" can achieve together will always be greater than what an individual can achieve. Unity begins to develop when everyone willing admits their need for a healthy interdependence.

Are you unified, humble and encouraging others? Do you cooperate and have fellowship as one body of believers?

C. Scott

You are part of the Body!

Bozo-Tiema Ciewe - Mali

Population: 5,900
Bozo means "straw house". The Bozos are made up of three distinct groups. Each group is extremely unique and has little in common with the others. Bozos are more educated and culturally advanced than their neighbors. They control the water transport in their area. The majority are Muslims. Only a few Biblical stories are translated into their language.

Pray: The Word of God would make an impact in their lives.

The Faith Of A Child

> *Truly I tell you, anyone who will not receive the kingdom of God like a little child will never enter it. Luke 18:17*

A few days ago, I stood before more than a hundred children from ages four to ten and told them the story of Jesus calming the storm. At the end of the story, most of them sat with crossed arms anxiously hoping I would say something else. It seemed as though there wasn't an ounce of doubt about the ability of Jesus to calm the storm! These kind of instances help me to better understand what Jesus is talking about in Luke 18:17. When we become adults, we sadly lose the innocent, yet bold faith of a child. It is no surprise the Lord asks us to have the "faith of a child", a blind faith that believes God can do anything!

When I was nine years old, my dad asked me to pray for a girl who had been born premature and had many physical disabilities. Even after three years of life, she still couldn't walk. The doctors said they had done everything they could and there was no hope for her to walk. That night, my younger brothers and I prayed just like we had done so many times before....with faith. After a few hours, my parents were shocked to find that the little girl found a balance in her stance that she hadn't had before! But my brothers and I were not surprised! After all, we knew it was what we prayed for and knew God simply heard us! Today is a day to pray with confidence, simplicity, humility, and the faith of a child!

W. Altare

Is your faith like a child?

Bathari - Oman

Population: 200
The Bathari are indigenous, Muslim Indians. They live in Dhofar. They have no Christians or churches among them. They do not know the Bible. Their language is Bathari.

Pray: They would have the opportunity to hear the Gospel.

To Do Missions?

> *For God so loved the world that he gave his one and only Son, that whoever believes in him shall not perish but have eternal life. John 3:16*

The word "mission" comes from the Latin word "missio" which means to "to send." We know "missions" was on the heart of God from the beginning of life because He decided to send His only Son into the world to be a missionary (John 3:16). This verse clearly describes the love of God in action. It describes God's intent to rescue men and women within all tribes, peoples, races, languages, nations, and generations.

Why do we do missions? We do missions because it is a command from the Word of God to go! We also do missions to bring glory to God and salvation to lost souls. God wants all Christians to take part in His "call to missions". We must spread the message of salvation to the ends of the earth while constantly reflecting on the character of Christ in our lives. GOING, GIVING, and PRAYING should be part of your daily routine.

L. Díaz

Let's do missions!

Chak - Myanmar

Population: 4,000

Due to the wealth of their territory, Chaks enjoy a high social status. They are fervent Buddhists, with some animistic beliefs. They have heard the Gospel from Portuguese Catholics, but have shown no interest in changing their religion. Their language is Chak.

Pray: The Chaks would receive the Gospel in their own language.

The True Taste of Vegetables

> { *You will seek me and find me when you seek me with all your heart.*
> *Jeremiah 29:13*

As a child, I absolutely hated vegetables. When I grew up, I kept the memories of their horrible taste and I also remembered how every meal was a battle for my mom to prepare and a night-mare for me to eat. But recently, I met a woman to whom God gave the gift to cook vegetables in a way that made their taste captivating!

I think this is how many of us have experienced God. In some cases, you may have been intro-duced to a punishing and distant God, who you only feared and respected. On the flip side, you may have been introduced to a "human" God, who wants you to meet Him in ways you do not understand.

Jeremiah 29:13 shows the true God who desires to be close to your heart in every circumstance. Sometimes we hear of believers who have lived under difficult circumstances. An example is family members or close friends who turn away from God because they have had a "bad taste" experience. The "bad taste" controls their minds, just like my experience with eating vegetables controlled me.

Today discover God in a new way! Allow your mind to forget any memories of a "bad tasting" God. I pray you discover the closeness of God as your Heavenly Father and friend for all eternity.
G. Galindo

Experience God in a different way!

Chamacocos - Paraguay

Population: 1,450
Chamacocos are also known as the Ishir. Their beliefs are Christian and Animis-tic. They live in four communities in the north of Paraguay. It is estimated only 100 faithful Christians live among them. They have the New Testament in their language and the Old Testament is in the process of being translated.

Pray: For the spiritual maturity of believers and for a desire to reach their communities with the Gospel.

The Tongue

> Let your conversation be always full of grace, seasoned with salt, so that you may know how to answer everyone. *Colossians 4:6*

The tongue, even though it is a small part of our bodies, has incredible power to do good or evil. For this reason, it's imperative that we, as Christians, learn to continuously monitor what we say. It's amazing how only a few words can affect the lives of people for eternity. The simple words "I love you" have great power. When the words are said, strong relationships can be built. When the words are not said, relationships can be destroyed.

In James, we read that a man must learn to tame his tongue. James compares the tongue to a "wild beast" that continuously refuses to be tamed. Solomon wrote about the tongue long before the book of James was written. He wrote:

"The words of the reckless pierce like swords, but the tongue of the wise brings healing" (Proverbs 12:18).

"Anxiety weighs down the heart, but a kind word cheers it up" (Proverbs 12:25).

"Those who guard their mouths and their tongues keep themselves from calamity" (Proverbs 21:23).

"Those who guard their lips preserve their lives, but those who speak rashly will come to ruin" (Proverbs 13:3).

Peter also experienced several difficult situations because of the way he used words. In 1 Peter 3:10 he wisely advices, "Whoever would love life and see good days must keep their tongue from evil and their lips from deceitful speech." Numerous Biblical characters struggled with the same struggles Christians have today! Use your speech to build others up! Love and encourage with your words!

D. Duk

Are you taming your tongue?

Danish - Denmark

Population: 4,996,000
They are a Scandinavian group whose language is Danish. They call themselves Christians, but they are very nominal. It is estimated only 4% adhere to the Biblical doctrines. Recently cults have began to gain in popularity.

Pray: For Christ to reign supreme in the hearts of the Danish.

Not In Vain

> Therefore, my dear brothers and sisters, stand firm. Let nothing move you. Always give yourselves fully to the work of the Lord, because you know that your labor in the Lord is not in vain. *1 Corinthians 15:53-58*

One day my friend Buubu and I were visiting the house of our brother and friend, Hamidu. We were visiting because he had recently died and was being prepared for burial. While we were there, people were discussing if he should be buried in the Muslim cemetery. As we were discussing one of the leaders said, "His father was a Muslim, wouldn't he want to be buried in the same cemetery as his father?"

Hamidu died trusting in the redemptive work of Jesus. We were sad because he was no longer with us, but we were excited to know God had given him eternal life. Our hearts were at peace because we knew we would see Hamidu again!

Sadly many Muslims die without hope, but this was not the case with Hamidu. He had access to the Word of God and it led him into a relationship with Jesus. Death had no victory over Hamidu because he was resurrected through Christ!

I'm not sure if you have seen death face to face, but I do know all people will one day face death. Be assured Jesus has overcome death! Nothing can separate you from His love.

Pescador

Keep preaching the Gospel!

Chenapian - Papua New Guinea

Population: 400

They live west of the Sepik River. They gather wild fruits, hunt small game, and fish. They have no translation of the Bible in their language, but they have heard Biblical stories from Catholic missionaries! They urgently need to know Jesus.

Pray: For Bible translators and missionaries to work among them.

The Divine GPS

> *Whether you turn to the right or to the left, your ears will hear a voice behind you, saying, "This is the way; walk in it." Isaiah 30:21*

In the world today it is incredibly important to recognize the voice of God. If you don't know God's voice, the voices filling the world will quickly confuse you and lead you astray. A GPS always shows you the correct path to your desired destination. If you happen to take a wrong turn, the GPS never gets angry, but instead corrects your path.

I imagine a GPS is similar to God. He knows exactly the steps you should take to get to your desired destination, but He never forces you to follow His instruction. Often we get off track in our lives, but then we hear His voice of compassion redirecting our path. To be redirected onto the path, two things are extremely important. First, you have to let God be the ultimate guide in your life. Even if the instructions He gives seem wrong, you need to trust that His route is best. Second, for a GPS to be able to guide you, you need to have a desired destination or goal. If you are living your life without goals, how can God guide you? Talk to God and ask Him to give you a goal in life. Once you have your goal, you can enter it into the "divine GPS" and let God guide you with His gentle and loving voice.

J. Segnitz

Be guided by God!

Chali - Bhutan

Population: 1,600

The Chali language is different from all other Eastern Tibetan varieties spoken in Bhutan. They are devout Buddhists. They do not have the Bible in their language and no known Christians live among them.

Pray: For Christians of India to reach out to them.

Provision Of Resources

> *...Taking the five loaves and the two fish and looking up to heaven, he gave thanks and broke them. Then he gave them to the disciples to distribute to the people. They all ate and were satisfied, and the disciples picked up twelve basketfuls of broken pieces that were left over. Luke 9:16-17*

This well-known passage from the life of Jesus teaches a great lesson that should be remembered when doing ministry. We see in the story 5,000 hungry men gathered to hear from Jesus, but this doesn't include women or children. We can imagine there might have been around 15,000 total people gathered, all of who were starting to grow restless from hunger. Having compassion for them, Jesus took what little food was available (5 pieces of bread and 2 fish), blessed it, and handed it to the disciples to distribute to the people. After all of the people had eaten, the leftover food was gathered. The leftovers amounted to more food than what they started with! It's important to see that the food had multiplied in the hands of the disciples after they had given it to Jesus to be blessed.

Often material needs limit us in being able to bless others. Jesus calls us to trust in His provision and power and not our material possessions. He invites us to put what we have in His hands and let Him work with it. Multiplication of resources cannot happen without taking the first step of faith and placing it in the Lord's hands. Sometimes, we find ourselves trying to do things our own way. We try to justify it by calling it "working hard for the Lord," but that's not having faith in the power and provision of God.

God challenges us to stretch our faith and to trust His provision for all of our needs. Jesus expects us to be good stewards of the things He provides us with, even if His provision is just "pieces" in our eyes. The first step in being a good steward is putting it back in His hands so that it can be multiplied! M. de Rodríguez

Be a good steward of what God gives!

Cherokee - United States

Population: 292,000

They live in northern Oklahoma, mostly on indigenous reservations. They have the New Testament in their language and it is estimated 5% are believers. Most struggle with their culture, which has strong roots in Animism.

Pray: God would strengthen the church among the Cherokees.

God The First Missionary

> Then the man and his wife heard the sound of the Lord God as he was walking in the garden in the cool of the day, and they hid from the LORD God among the trees of the garden. But the LORD God called to the man, "Where are you?" Genesis 3:8-9

It's alarming the great amount of apathy among many Christian churches today regarding world missions. Many churches claim evangelism within their neighborhoods is enough and world missions is the job for missions organizations. However, what we need to realize is God's call to world missions was a call to the church! Followers of Christ, who decide to go to other cultures to spread the love of Jesus, need to be sent and supported by their home churches!

Missions have been at the heart of God since the fall of man! When Adam and Eve sinned, God immediately came to meet them. Even when they hid in fear and knew they had disobeyed, God in his infinite love sought them out. The Bible is a perfect missionary book, and from cover to cover, it breathes a single focus: to proclaim the saving plan of God for every human being. God wants all to be saved; so much that He designed the plan to rescue mankind from eternal separation from Him! What other king do you know who would come off his throne and be sacrificed for those who don't deserve it? We serve an incredible God!

If your heart is after God, there is no longer a choice between being called and not being called to global missions. Whether you are going or sending, world missions is for every believer. You should love every single lost person in the world, whether it is your neighbor or a stranger on the other side of the world.

G. Vergara

Is world missions in your heart?

Cineni - Nigeria

Population: 4,900

They live in the state of Borno. The men are farmers and the women make baskets and other crafts. Their language is Cineni, which doesn't have a translation of the Bible. They practice an animistic religion, led by the village leader.

Pray: The Gospel comes to their villages and frees them from darkness.

Easter Week

> When they came to the place called the Skull, they crucified him there, along with the criminals–one on his right, the other on his left.
> Luke 23:33

This passage takes place during Easter. During this Easter season, take time to meditate on Jesus' words as He was being crucified. During Jesus' crucifixion, He said, "Father, forgive them, for they do not know what they are doing." Within this passage, we see the patience Jesus had with His oppressors. In Jesus' situation, He had the right to demand justice, but instead he lovingly interceded for His persecutors.

Regardless of what you are experiencing, Jesus reminds us our hope is beyond or present circumstances. In Luke 23:43, Jesus speaks to the man being crucified next to Him. He says to the man, "today you will be with me in the paradise." Jesus fixed His eyes beyond His present pain and suffering. He focused on the Kingdom that was to come! What are you focusing on? Are you focusing on the Kingdom of God or your present circumstances? One day you will be with Him in paradise!

S. Langemeier

Have refreshing time with God today!

Cornish - United Kingdom

Population: 517,000
The Cornish come from the United Kingdom. Their first language is Cornish, which has a translation of the New Testament. Eight percent of the population are members of the Anglican Church. It is estimated 35 percent are atheists.

Pray: For believers to give testimony of God's grace among the Cornish.

In Unity

> The Gadites and Reubenites answered, "Your servants will do what the Lord has said." Numbers 32:31

The Kingdom of God requires us to be brave and accept the call into action when needed. Our natural tendency is to revert back to what we know and what is comfortable for us. This particular chapter of the Bible challenges us to be different than the rest of the world and to embody the values of the Kingdom of God, such as unity, integrity, and truth.

In this story the tribes of Reuben and Gad tried to separate themselves from the rest of Israel, by living a comfortable life. Moses strongly responded to them and the two tribes humbly accepted his criticism. They said, "we will not return to our homes until every Israelite has received his inheritance." (v18)

The tribes of Reuben and Gad then became servants who did not seek their own good but instead, the will of God. When this happens, God is glorified because His ways triumphs over our own. God is even more glorified when a community unites in Christ and decides to answer His call to love one another. Each local church is a small "community" within the Kingdom of God. Therefore, we should practice unity, cooperation, communion, and fellowship with the other communities within the global church!

C. Scott

Look for the common good!

Bedouin - United Arab Emirates

Population: 765,000
The Bedouins are Muslim, but they have some animistic beliefs. They believe in Sufism, which is a belief that some have acquired a special inner knowledge direct from Allah. They reject the Gospel, but do have some portions of the Bible in their native language.

Pray: God will break the barriers so they can be evangelized.

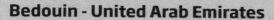

The Double Mission

> This day I call the heavens and the earth as witnesses against you that I have set before you life and death, blessings and curses. Now choose life, so that you and your children may live.
> Read Deuteronomy 30:15-19.

It is not Biblically accurate to believe the sole ministry of Christians is to evangelize the unsaved people of the world. With this belief, defeat is often experienced when results are not clearly seen. The ministry of a follower of Christ should also include helping other followers strengthen their relationships with Christ and warn them about possible sin in their lives. In this passage, Jeremiah's ministry was to condemn the sin of people who didn't repent.

Although we get confidence from seeing the results of the number of people who have been saved, our ministry should not be dependent on numbers. Our goal should be dependent on bringing glory to God. Even when the world rejects Christ, God's Word does not return void. His Word always accomplishes that for which it was sent. When we faithfully preach the Word, we do not need to worry about "results" because the Word accomplishes its mission on its own. Our task is to invite souls to make decisions for Christ. We do not have to compete with the Holy Spirit in its job of moving within the hearts of people. Let the Spirit and the Word of God serve its purpose to accomplish its dual mission.

O. Simari

Spread the gospel!

Churu - Vietnam

Population: 17,000

Churu is a town isolated in the mountains of northern Vietnam. They are spiritual slaves under the power of local shamans and witch doctors. They received the Gospel through foreign "tourists" and some have put their faith in Jesus.

Pray: For the faith of the Churus to strengthen and grow.

Rahab

> But Joshua spared Rahab the prostitute, with her family and all who belonged to her, because she hid the men Joshua had sent as spies to Jericho—and she lives among the Israelites to this day.
> Joshua 6:25

When you hear the name "Rahab", what comes to your mind? Before I did a deep study on her story, I only knew she was a prostitute from Jericho who helped two Israelite spies. But last year, I looked deeper into her story and was amazed at what I found.

What stuck out to me, as I was studying, was the fact that after Jericho was taken by the Israelites, Rahab and her family were allowed to live among the Israelites as foreigners. This was incredible because it had never been allowed before (Joshua 6:23). At times, she must have felt rejected and out of place in her new home. It is interesting to know before joining the Israelites, Rahab had to learn all the new customs and laws of the Israelites. Understanding all of the laws God gave the Isrealites had to be extremely overwhelming for Rahab as she integrated into the new culture. Yet through this tough time, God used Rahab to show the Israelites His character! After my study, I don't identify the name "Rahab" with a prostitute who was a simple assistant to the Israelites. Rather, "Rahab" now means: a woman who experienced salvation, redemption, forgiveness, and transformation by the power of God. God blessed her by not only by making her a part of the genealogy of the Messiah (Matthew 1:5), but he blessed her by referring to her as a "woman of faith" in Hebrews 11. Rahab was a foreign woman who God used for His glory!
MyT. Goddard

Be used by God!

Dampelas - Indonesia

Population: 12,000
The Dampelas are farmers who live in the mountains northwest of the Sulawesi Peninsula. They are proud of their culture and Muslim religion. They use amulets to ward off spirits. Their language, Dampela, has no translation of the Bible.

Pray: For the message of salvation to come to them in their language.

Martha And Mary

> "Martha, Martha," the Lord answered, "you are worried and upset about many things, but few things are needed—or indeed only one. Mary has chosen what is better, and it will not be taken away from her." Luke 10:41-42

What would you do if the doctor told you that you had one year to live? Some would travel the world. Some would make sure all their relationships were in the right place. Others would contemplate suicide to escape the anticipation of death. But let's say you're part of a mission team with the task of translating the Scriptures into an indigenous language. What would you do with the short time you had left?

Recently, my wife and I answered this question for ourselves. Our response: We need to prioritize our lives in such a way that leads us to fulfilling the task we have been called to do.

The reality is most people spend the majority of their time on things that will be "here today and gone tomorrow." The motto our world now lives by is, "Satisfy your desires." The tragedy of this mindset is it is directly opposite to the life that imitates Christ.

In today's Scripture, we see Mary chose a life desiring Jesus, while Martha lived occupied with preparations. Martha's activities weren't bad, but Jesus made it clear that He preferred Mary's attention rather than Martha's service. We need to make sure we aren't getting so busy with life's activities that we forget to give Jesus attention and hear from Him! Your daily life is your reflection of your relationship with God! We need to be living each day with one purpose: to glorify God in everything we do.

G. Rivas

What did you do today?

Chiapanecos - Mexico

Population: 40

Their ethnicity is endangered because most Chiapanecos are elderly. 15% have clung to indigenous beliefs and the rest have adopted Catholicism. Only one known person is believed to have received Christ.

Pray: For the one believer to shine the light of Jesus among the other 40.

Bible in a year: Acts 9:1-25 / Joshua 3:1-5:1 / Job 22

Mission Tasks

> Do everything you can to help Zenas the lawyer and Apollos on their way and see that they have everything they need. Our people must learn to devote themselves to doing what is good, in order to provide for urgent needs and not live unproductive lives. Titus 3:13-14

How would you define a "missionary" in the world today? In 1 Peter 2:9, we see that being a missionary is not an option; it is a command for Christians to obey. We are all missionaries because every Christian is called to participate in fulfilling the Great Commission. But be encouraged! Jesus Christ has given us (the church) gifts and strengths from the Holy Spirit to complete this mission. This means we are called to be Christ's "transformation agents" as we seek to bring the Gospel to the ends of the earth. However, we must remember this mission is not limited to our local churches, nor is it limited to foreign countries. God calls us to link our local churches with world missions and to serve with the intent of crossing barriers with Christ's love in both "word and deed", for the glory of His Kingdom!

With Christ's love we need to serve all, even the most forgotten people of the world. Each person needs to hear the Good News and see the love of God. In this devotional book, we highlight the work of the faithful, courageous missionaries working within the animist, Hindu, Buddhist, Muslim, atheist and postmodern world.

Let us serve these missionaries in such way that we become part of the work! Supporting missionaries financially or prayerfully is an awesome way to get involved in the mission! It's either that or....GO!

C. Scott

What part will you take in the mission?

Dabarre - Somalia

Population: 37,000

They are farmers who raise bananas and sugar cane. They are regarded as Muslims, but their understanding of their faith is minimal. They believe Christians are inferior and thus discriminate them. Their language, Dabarre, does not have evangelistic resources.

Pray: For God to start a project translating a Dabarre Bible.

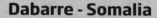

Who Are You Walking Alongside?

> *And I will ask the Father, and he will give you another advocate to help you and be with you forever. John 14:16*

In John 14:16 Jesus talked about the Counselor, the Comforter who would come, the parakletos, the lawyer, and the one who motivates. In various occasions Paul uses the same Greek root word, parakletos, to talk about the comfort and encouragement from God, the Holy Spirit, Scripture, and from other believers.

A former mentor of mine once spoke wise words that continue to inspire and challenge me, "You can become a great evangelist and preach to large audiences, or you can be a great teacher to a large crowd. But your biggest impact will result from the investment in the lives of a few people who long to be faithful disciples of Christ."

Over and over again I am encouraged by this quote. It motivates me to invest my life by serving, listening, encouraging, defending, and comforting others.

Do you have a dream to serve the Lord in another culture? Do you long to change the world as an evangelist or a teacher? What do you want to do with your life? This world desperately needs more people to invest in the lives of a few disciples and to encourage them to be faithful to Christ. Do as a "parakletos" would and accompany a few people in their walks with Christ! God has many blessings in store for those who help others in their relationships with Him!

T. Sandvig

Doing this will impact your life!

Koreans - North Korea

Population: 24,052,000

The beliefs of the North Koreans are a mixture of Confucian thought, Buddhism and Shamanism. The worship of ancestors is very important. They have the complete Bible in their language, but Christians are not allowed into the country

Pray: For an opening in North Korea for Christian missionaries to enter.

April 25

A World Feat

> And this gospel of the kingdom will be preached in the whole world as a testimony to all nations, and then the end will come.
> Matthew 24:14

Having been with Jesus for a while, the disciples started to wonder what the world would be like during the end times. Jesus described how it would be a terrible time, with persecution against Christians, and religious confusion. This troubled the disciples because they couldn't fully grasp what Jesus was talking about.

Jesus then said something that brought encouragement to the small group of disciples. Even amidst the darkness, the Good News of the Kingdom would be carried to the very ends of the earth. The disciples, who were few in number and insignificant in the eyes of others, would be the start of the greatest feat in history. The Way, the Truth, and the Life, the crucified and resurrected Messiah, would one day be announced to all corners of the planet and reach every living soul on earth. Is there anything else in the world that can compare to this feat?

Just like the disciples, you and I are called to be part of this amazing task. What a privilege it is to be a participant in the work of bringing His Word to the ends of the earth! God's plan in completing this work is perfect and He's calling YOU to be a part of it!

A. Betancur

What will you do?

Chilcotin - Canada

Population: 3,500
The Chilcotin are an indigenous group native to North America. Chilcotin consist of seven different communities. They have heard the Gospel in English and it is estimated 20% have responded. The majority of Christians are young people. They have some portions of the Bible in their native language.

Pray: The native church would reach out to their people for Christ.

The Reality Of Sin

> *The kings of the earth rise up and the rulers band together against the Lord and against his anointed, saying, "Let us break their chain and throw off their shackles." Psalm 2:2-3*

Sin originated when Satan wanted to be like God. He didn't want to submit to his Creator and declared himself dependent on God. In reality, this is exactly what sin is: "a declaration of independence from God."

Adam and Eve knew eating from the tree of knowledge of good and evil was wrong because God had said it was. But Satan, in his cleverness, offered them the ability to know what right and wrong was. He offered them the power to be like God and to declare themselves independent from Him. Sadly, his temptation worked.

Today millions of people throughout the world declare themselves independent from God and deny His existence. Others make God conform to their own plans and hearts' desires. Unfortunately, evil ran rampant when Israel had no king because everyone did what seemed right in his or her own eyes. We can be thankful that we have God's Word to show us what is right and to help us remain dependent on Him. We are all ambassadors of the Great King and are called to submit to His lordship and be reconciled with Him through Jesus Christ!

F. Rodríguez

Do you understand the great value of our mission?

Dangaleat - Chad

Population: 77,000
The Dangaleat live in rocky land, but they still produce millet. The majority are farmers, but some have moved to the cities as government or construction workers. Their religion is Islam. Their language, Dangaleat, has some Biblical audios.

Pray: For God to open doors for the preaching of His Word within this people group.

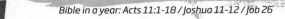

The Initiative

{ *But the LORD God called to the man, "Where are you?"*
Read Genesis 3:6-10

After the disobedience of Adam and Eve in the Garden, the Bible gives us God's reaction to their fall. In the story, we see Adam and Eve deliberately disobey God. In shame and fear we see them hide from God in the Garden. But what does God say and do?

Genesis 3:10 says, "But the LORD God called to the man and said, 'Where are you?'" After the fall, who took the initiative? Who sought out whom? Who blamed whom? Who cared for whom? Who was the one who forgave and restored? God initiates the search, He initiates communication, and He initiates the restoration of His creatures.

Today, God is initiating a conversation with you. He is calling you to repentance so that your relationship with Him can grow stronger through forgiveness! When you draw closer to His heart, you will begin to better understand the importance of the Great Commission. Like God did with Adam and Eve, we need to be initiators with other people and help them towards restoration. We need to be praying and caring for the lost, fearful, and ashamed. Who knows, they could end up being bold proclaimers of the truth or courageous missionaries to distant lands where the name "Jesus" has never been heard!

H. Ziefle

Do you take the initiative?

Estonians - Estonia

Population: 899,000
They are a Baltic community. Most are not religious, but approximately 40% are members of the Orthodox or Lutheran church. The main language is Estonian, but many speak the "Tallinn" dialect.

Pray: For the Gospel to speak into their lives.

You Are An Extension

> When Jesus spoke again to the people, he said, "I am the light of the world. Whoever follows me will never walk in darkness, but will have the light of life. John 8:12

Last Christmas, I decided to decorate the balcony of my house for the holidays. I bought beautiful lights, strung them up over the railing, and fastened them with tape. Satisfied with my work and ready to see the lights in full-glow, I went to plug them in. To my horror, the cord did not reach the wall outlet! I knew the lights were not going to work if they couldn't be connected to electricity. So I found an extension cord, plugged one side into the outlet and the other side into the lights. Instantly, the balcony illuminated with the soft beauty of hundreds of lights. I then sat satisfied in a chair and started to think.

A great illustration can be drawn from this Christmas lights story. There is a world full of people who have the potential to shine for Christ, but they aren't connected to the power source. Many are sitting in the dark, not aware Christ is waiting to illuminate them. He, in His grace and mercy, wants to use you for the world to receive His power. Just as the lights cannot shine without power from the outlet, you and I can do nothing without Christ.

When God turns on the lights, you become "plugged" into the Lord and you receive His power to reach a world standing in the dark. Reach others with the power our Savior has given you!

L. Ashmore

Stay connected to Christ!

Western Cham - Saudi Arabia

Population: 100

The Western Chams are immigrants from Cambodia who came to Saudi Arabia in search of a better life. They continue to speak their native language, but have adopted Islam as their religion. There are no known Christians among them and they have no translation of the Bible in their language.

Pray: The Gospel would advance among this people group of Saudi Arabia.

Act Of Grace

> After he drove the man out, he placed on the east side of the Garden of Eden cherubim and a flaming sword flashing back and forth to guard the way to the tree of life. *Genesis 3:24*

In Randy Frazee's book, *The Heart of the Story*, he wrote about Genesis 3:24 and said, "Driving them out of the Garden of Eden was actually an 'act of grace.'" How can shortening the life of people be an act of grace on the part of God? Through our eyes, it is difficult to understand because we interpret life as a blessing and death as a curse. But from the perspective of God, the world we live in is ruled by sin, hatred, selfishness, and injustice. God knows our lives in this kind of world cannot be eternal and thus, need an expiration date.

Although there are many movies and myths about achieving immortality, can you really imagine living in this sinful world for all eternity? Thank the Lord for not allowing us to live forever in these circumstances!

It's understandable that we hold onto our life on earth because it's all we know. But Jesus, through His sacrifice, has opened a door to eternity into a new world with Him. We just need the faith to believe Him.

Our years here on earth are just a sliver of time in the scope eternity, thank God! What will you do with your time? As a continuing act of gratitude for His grace, you should serve Him until the day He calls you home.

H. Bascur

Will you serve?

Chakma - Myanmar

Population: 26,000
They are a Buddhist group with a reputation for honesty, diligence, and reliability. Their language is Bengali, which has a translation of the New Testament and a few audios. No known Christians live among them.

Pray: For the distribution of the Word of God.

With The Guidance Of The Holy Spirit

> *The two of them, sent on their way by the Holy Spirit, went down to Seleucia and sailed from there to Cyprus. Acts 13:4*

It's important to allow the Holy Spirit to guide you when making important decisions. But in what ways do you allow Him to guide you? The Bible clearly teaches our lives need to be filled with the Word of God, fellowship with believers, prayer, worship, and evidence of the fruit of the Spirit. Doing these things helps us to clearly discern the doors God is opening or closing. Some people do not take initiative, but rather wait for opportunities to come. Others have no patience and attempt to force doors open. A life led under the influence of the Holy Spirit seeks to walk through the doors being opened and stops at the doors being closed (2 Corinthians 2:12). When God closes a door, be patient. His will can sometimes be difficult to decipher, but you can be at peace knowing you are being led by the Holy Spirit (Revelation 3:8). Being daily in the Word is key to remembering what God expects.

"He has shown you, O mortal, what is good. And what does the Lord require of you? To act justly and to love mercy and to walk humbly with your God" (Micah 6:8).

What doors are open before you?

C. Scott

Let God guide you.

Chimilas - Colombia

Population: 480
They live in the Magdalena region of Colombia. They maintain their native religion and culture, especially funeral traditions (ex. Placing the deceased in a certain position and prohibiting repeating his/her name). They have a few scriptures available in their language. It is estimated four percent of the population are believers.
Pray: For an effective response to the Gospel among the Chimilas.

MAY

Persevere

> I, John, your brother and companion in the suffering and kingdom and patient endurance that are ours in Jesus, was on the island of Patmos because of the word of God and the testimony of Jesus.
> Revelation 1:9

When John wrote these words of the book of Revelation, he was nearly 100 years old. It had been about 60 years since Jesus had ascended into heaven, and He had not yet returned. By this time, all of the other apostles had died as martyrs. Although John was still alive, it didn't mean his life was free from suffering! He was often tortured for the sake of Christ and had even witnessed the death of many of his Christian brothers. John was banished to an island called Patmos for almost 20 years. The only inhabitants on the island were a few convicts who had also lost everything.

Despite his difficult circumstances, John remained faithful and continued to worship God. Day after day, John had to constantly fight off illness caused by poor living conditions and frequent cold, wet nights. During this time, I'm sure even dry clothes would have done John's heart well. If you lost everything today, would you still praise God for who He is? What was it that prevented John from becoming discouraged and giving up his faith? Perseverance!

Are you willing to leave your comfortable life to serve the Lord? Are you willing to sacrifice your dreams for the dreams of God? If God called you to live a life of sacrifice, would you accept it for the sake of His name?

Missions is not about going on a luxurious vacation to a distant land, experiencing a new culture for a few days, or sightseeing with family. Just like God did with John, God can call you out of your comfort-zone and ask you to follow him. Missions means stepping out of a world of comfort and proclaiming, "God is worth more than any possession or position!"

A. Gulard

Follow Jesus with perseverance!

Daya - Indonesia

Population: 82,000

The Daya are located south of the island of Sumatra. The Daya speak a dialect of Lampung Api. They are devoted to farming rice, a product that they trade with their neighbors. Although the New Testament and the Jesus film are available in their language, Islam is still the predominant religion.

Pray: God touches the hearts of the Daya and they start to have interest in knowing Jesus Christ as their personal Savior!

Divine Direction

> *A man's heart plans his way, but his steps are directed by the Lord.*
> *Proverbs 16:9*

In Acts 16:6-10, we read of how the Holy Spirit didn't allow Paul and his team to go into the province of Asia and preach the Word of God. Later, they went to Mysia, but when they tried to enter Bithynia, the Spirit of God did not allow them to enter. It wasn't until they went to Troas that Paul had a vision indicating their mission should begin in Europe. After Paul had his vision, he was convinced God had called them to preach the Gospel throughout Europe.

Prayer, God's Word, fellowship with believers, and divine events all play a key role in directing you towards God's will for your life. However, it is not enough to know only what the will of God is, you must also be obedient in doing His will. This includes brining His message of salvation to the nations!

Missionary work involves the Spirit of God moving in the hearts of people by showing them where to preach salvation. If you are an active member of God's church and are dedicated to being a doer of the will of God, He will show you what step to take!

C. Scott

Be alert!

Dulia - Bangladesh

Population: 6,800
The Dulia live in the provinces of Dhaka and Khulna. They speak Bengali. Their primary religion is Hinduism. The Bible and the Jesus Film are available in their language, but they have still not accepted the Gospel.

Pray: God would open their hearts and help them see beyond Hinduism.

A Mystery Revealed By Jesus

> In reading this, then, you will be able to understand my insight into the mystery of Christ, which was not made known to people in other generations as it has now been revealed by the Spirit to God's holy apostles and prophets. This mystery is that through the gospel the Gentiles are heirs together with Israel, members together of one body, and sharers together in the promise in Christ Jesus. Ephesians 3: 4-6

God's missionary purpose, in the Old Testament, was not understood by the scholars of the Torah 2,000 years ago. Although the Old Testament had numerous passages of prophecy, regarding the future blessing and salvation of other nations, Jesus still had to reveal to Israel God's true intention for the Messiah. In the Old Testament, God's covenant with Israel at Mount Sinai was to bless "all the nations on the earth." The lives of Isaiah and Jonah are two examples of how Israel was to be a light and blessing to the nations. However, the majority of Jews believed God was to be only the God of Israel. Their selfishness was so strong, some Jewish rabbis even wanted to remove the book of Jonah from the Hebrew Bible because they didn't want their people to focus on the conversion of the despised Gentiles in Nineveh.

The Old Testament missionary concept was radical. Nations were to be "co-heirs" with Israel, nations were to be "of the same body" as Israel, and the nations were to be "partakers of the divine promise" given to Israel. Today, God has extended these benefits to all nations so all people can share in their joy. If you know this is true, is it fair for you to keep God's salvation only for yourself instead of sharing it with other nations?

A. Neufeld

Share the Gospel!

Daza - Niger

Population: 13,000
Daza live in a hot and dry climate. They consider themselves tough murderers and thieves. They speak Dazaga, which only has a few translated portions of the Bible. They are Muslims and practice of polygamy.

Pray: The Word of God would cause radical changes in their lives.

Bible in one year: Acts 15:22-41 / Judges 1 / Job 33

Thanks Man!

> Dear brother, you are faithful in what you are doing for the brothers, even though they are strangers. In front of the church they have testified to your love. You will do well to send them on their way in a manner worthy of God. Read 3 John 1:5-8

In these verses, we see the example of a man who offered his faithful service to God:

1. Gaius was a faithful disciple of Jesus, "you are faithful."

Jesus instructed His disciples before the first missionary journey: "Whatever town or village you enter, search there for some worthy person and stay at their house until you leave. As you enter the home, give it your greeting. If the home is deserving, let your peace rest on it; if it is not, let your peace return to you" (Matthew 10:11-13). Gaius, a faithful disciple, knew Jesus' teachings. He knew because he was faithful, the Spirit of God came upon his house.

2. Gaius was an example of love, "have testified to your love."

The love known as "agape" is manifested through works. Jesus said, "Do not take along any gold or silver or copper in your belts, no bag for your journey, or extra tunic, or sandals, or walking stick" (Matthew 10:9-10). Inevitably, Jesus wanted His disciples to be helped and loved by other people.

3. Gaius was a contributor to missionary work, "You will do well to send them on their journey." Missionary work is a task for the entire church. Each member must participate in the mission. Gaius' supported missionaries by allowing them to stay in his house.

F. Rodríguez

Follow this example!

Chocholtecas - Mexico

Population: 900
The Chocholtecas live in mountainous areas on the Pacific coast. They speak both Chocholtec and Spanish. They are goat herders and they market their products. Some of the young people have started to migrate to big cities.

Pray: Those who are now living in the city would come to know Christ and would return home and share it with their people.

The Perfect Miracle

> I will not venture to speak of anything except what Christ has accomplished through me in leading the Gentiles to obey God by what I have said and done— by the power of signs and wonders, through the power of the Spirit of God. Read Romans 5: 18-21

Hawa was the wife of a believer in the village of Sooninke. Already having one baby die, she now found herself unable to get pregnant. She had heard of Jesus and his miracles. So one day, she opened her heart and simply said to us, "I want to have a son!"

What would you have thought in this situation? Would your mind have been filled with doubt? Or would you have had the faith to believe God could give this barren woman a son? That day, we prayed for Hawa. We prayed God would give her a baby boy, just as she had asked. We invited her to trust God that night, but it wasn't until later when God really moved in Hawa's heart. During the following months, we showed several videos about Old Testament prophets. Thankfully, the videos were in the village's native language, Sooninke. To our surprise, the most receptive person to the videos was....Hawa! Slowly, her heart started to open to the idea of putting her trust in Jesus. But what happened next was a complete miracle. God honored our faith-filled prayers and we received the news she was pregnant! As the baby grew inside her tummy, she had no doubt that her child would be a boy, just like we had prayed. When the healthy baby boy was born, she was overcome with thankfulness and decided to accept Jesus as the Lord of her life. God can do miracles in any life where faith is present! However, the greatest miracle is the ability for Jesus to give salvation to the lost!

Pescador

Keep preaching
the Gospel!

Diuwe - Indonesia

Population: 100

They live east of the Catalina River, near Papua New Guinea. They fervently follow Islam. They do not have a translated portion of the Bible in their language, Diuwe. They are fisherman and some cultivate gardens.

Pray: Each Diuwe would have the opportunity to know Jesus.

Bible in one year: Acts 16:16-40 / Judges 4-5 / Job 35

The Works Of The Holy Spirit

{ *Since we live by the Spirit, let us keep in step with the Spirit. Let us not become conceited, provoking and envying each other. Galatians 5:25-26*

In the past when I was under a lot of pressure, I always struggled to be patient with others. For example, if someone asked me a question when I felt impatient, my response would reflect the pressure I felt. Often, that meant I would respond in a rude and unfriendly manner. Even though I knew this was wrong, I didn't know how to fix it.

One Saturday afternoon, I attended a workshop at my church. During the workshop, one passage of scripture changed my perspective. The speaker quoted Galatians 5:22-23, "The fruit of the Spirit is love, joy, peace, patience, kindness, goodness, faithfulness, gentleness and self-control. There is no law against such things."

I had heard this a thousand times, but that day, I finally understood: the Spirit of Christ lives in me. I finally realized if I let God lead me and entrust Him with every aspect of my life, the fruits talked about in Galatians would manifest themselves, even when I feel impatient. After coming to this realization, I apologized to God. Since that day, I have continued to come back to this passage. When I feel under pressure or impatient, I simply give my worry to God in order for the fruits of the Spirit to be revealed in my life.

D. Duk

I invite you to do this as well!

Extremadura - Spain

Population: 1,272,000
They are native to the region of Extremadura. Although Roman Catholicism is their main religion, it is estimated only 0.8% have actually put their faith in Jesus. Most can read the Gospel in Spanish.

Pray: The Word of God reaches the Extremadura.

Address Unknown

> *If any of you lacks wisdom, you should ask God, who gives generously to all without finding fault, and it will be given to you.* James 1:5

How can we have confidence God is leading us through His Holy Spirit? First, there is internal evidence (what God is telling me). We see this manifested in Paul (Acts 9:15, 13:47, 22:21, 26:14-18, Galatians 1:15-16). Secondly, there is external evidence. You should surround yourself with mature Christian brothers who are spiritually discerning (Proverbs 11:14, Acts 13:1-3, Galatians 2:7-9). Finally, there are events or circumstances guiding your next steps and opportunities (Acts 16:6-10, 2 Corinthians 2:12, Acts 14:27, Colossians 4:2-4). There are numerous instances in the Bible reminding you God is the only one who holds the power to create and take away opportunities. According to His will, He opens and closes doors in your life. When all the evidence points to an open door and it is in line with God's Word, you can be assured He is confirming the path for you to take.

Is God guiding you toward a specific path? Are you seeing doors open? Or is it still not clear in your mind?

C. Scott

Ask God for wisdom!

Cochin - Israel

Population: 14,000
Although the Cochin have the entire Bible translated into their language, Malayalam, only 2% call themselves Christians. The majority practice animistic religions. They live a very secular life.

Pray: In the midst of a prosperous life, they will feel a spiritual vacuum, which will lead them to know Jesus.

Only Sinners

> *For all have sinned and fall short of the glory of God, and all are justified freely by his grace through the redemption that came by Christ Jesus. Romans 3:23-24*

If we preached only about God's justice, it would make the sinner's situation even more desperate, terrible, and tragic. On the flip side, if we only emphasized the love of God in our preaching, it would awaken more sentimental admiration for Jesus Christ, but it would also fail to give conviction of sin and the need for repentance, which is necessary for salvation.

Often, we present the Gospel improperly. We forget the cross of Christ not only speaks of love and mercy, but also of justice and law. God doesn't save by withholding His justice but instead He is "just and the justifier of the one who has faith in Jesus" (Romans 3:26). The justification of a sinner is made possible through Jesus' forgiveness and mercy. Through Jesus' brutal death on the cross, we see the penalty of sin being paid. Therefore, the law and the cross, justice and mercy, should be part of the Gospel!

O. Simari

> Preach not only the love of God, but also the consequences of rejecting his love. Always!

Eka - China

Population: 3,000
The Eka live in a mountainous area. They are dedicated to the cultivation of corn and rice, as well as raising poultry. They are polytheistic, worshiping many gods and deities. They speak Lahu, which now has a translation of the Bible. It is believed only 25 Christians live in this people group of 3,000.

Pray: The Eka believers testify to their faith with boldness.

Easier Said Than Done

> For by him were all things created ... all things were created through him and for him. Colossians 1:16

This title refers to a saying we use in Costa Rica: "del dicho al hecho, hay mucho trecho", which means, "easier said than done." When I attempt to grasp all what God has created, this saying immediately comes to my mind.

In this verse, Paul tells us absolutely everything was created by God. As Christians, we are certain of this truth and so we shouldn't spend time justifying it. The verse also says: "... and for him." In theory, we know all things have been created for Him. We find it in Christian song lyrics, poems, on bumper stickers, and on T-shirts. However, the way we behave and the way we pray makes it seem like we forget all things were created for Him. We say, "God, give this to me, save me, bless me, take things away, give me prosperity, help me." Sometimes, it seems we have reduced God to a genie who is waiting for us to rub His magic lamp and ask for wishes we want Him to grant.

If you've been limiting God in this way, now would be a good time to speak with Him personally, ask for forgiveness, and adore Him for who He is. What decision or action could you take to show God you were created to glorify Him?

W. Núñez

Lord, I want to glorify You!

Chortís - Guatemala

Population: 41,000

They are indigenous people of Mayan origin who are very interested in Roman Catholicism. There is a strong New Testament audio broadcast available to them. Only 6% of the Chortís are Christians, but they have little knowledge of God.

Pray: Discipleship programs would become available for the Chortís believers.

The Nations By Heritage

> Ask me, and I will make the nations your inheritance, the ends of the earth your possession. *Psalm 2:8*

In Psalm 2, one of the Messianic Psalms, God promises His Anointed to the nations as an inheritance. Whenever the Bible speaks of the Messiah's reign, it talks about it being an everlasting kingdom over all the nations and the earth. The Kingdom of God is within us and began when Jesus Christ came to earth. Now, the kingdom continues to spread to the ends of the earth through faithful missionaries.

The church, as the body of Christ and Embassy of the Kingdom of Heaven, is called to bring the message of salvation to every nation on earth. "Ask me and I will give the nations." This is a promise from the Father to His son, Jesus. This is also a promise we, as ambassadors, can take to the world. In the world, there are millions of people who do not yet belong to Jesus Christ. They are people we can ask God for, but then we must go to them and share the Good News of Jesus Christ. God is not content with just your neighborhood or even your country becoming "Christianized." Think beyond where you call home and start praying for the nations. Ask God for a particular nation, pray for it, and look for opportunities to GO!

F. Rodríguez

Forward!

Duaish - Mauritania

Population: 7,100

The Duaish live on the southern Atlantic shores of Africa. Most of their activities revolve around the sea. They have the Jesus film and some audio Bible stories available in their language, Hassaniya. They are Muslims, and there are no known Christians among them.

Pray: The Gospel will penetrate their hearts and transform their lives.

Where Is My Attention?

> But whoever looks intently into the perfect law that gives freedom, and continues in it—not forgetting what they have heard, but doing it—they will be blessed in what they do. James 1:25

In this day in age, many things are competing for our attention. Studies show people are finding it increasingly more difficult to concentrate on basic daily tasks and relationships. The television, Internet, and mobile phones are all demanding our attention. Without realizing it, we are constantly bouncing from one technology device to another. However, the apostle James calls us to pay attention to the law of God and persevere in it. How is this accomplished?

1. Set aside time in your day to read the Word of God without interruption. If necessary, turn off the computer and phone.

2. Try to memorize a Scripture passage from the Bible every day. Memorizing Scripture will help you pay more attention to God in your daily life.

3. Persevere in what you read. Put it into practice. Reading and listening is not enough. There must be a change in your life when you read and hear the Word of God.

This particular passage, in the book of James, also gives us a promise: "But whoever looks intently into the perfect law that gives freedom, and continues in it—not forgetting what they have heard, but doing it—they will be blessed in what they do" (James 1:25).

This promise given to us in James, is the same promise given to Joshua by God many years earlier: "Keep this Book of the Law always on your lips; meditate on it day and night, so that you may be careful to do everything written in it. Then you will be prosperous and successful" (Joshua 1:8).

W. Bello

Is your attention on the Word of God?

Fortsenal - Vanuatu

Population: 600
They are located in the South Pacific, off the coast of Australia. Their religion is animistic and it governs all aspects of their daily lives. Their native language has no Bible translation. They have only heard the name of Jesus from Catholic priests.

Pray: For the Gospel to be provided in their language, so they may know Jesus.

Spiritual Direction

> Behold, I have left before you an open door that no one can shut.
> Revelation 3:8

God is the one who opens and closes doors. One of the keys to knowing God's will is to realize every opportunity from Him will be aligned within the values and principles of His Word. If God opens a door for you, it will not contradict His values and principles. God has given His Word so we may become more and more like Christ every day, discerning each decision with truth.

With knowledge of God's Word, we have wisdom to discern and distinguish when God does not allow advancement through a door, or if we are undergoing an attack from Satan (For an example, look at what happened to the team of apostles in 1 Thessalonians 2:17-18). We are called to be mature believers and to have the capacity to distinguish between right and wrong, while exercising the power of spiritual perception (Hebrews 4:12, 5:11-14).

You should ask the Lord to give you spiritual understanding to know which doors are open and to have faith to walk through them. How can you develop a greater spiritual understanding and obtain wisdom to be discerning?

C. Scott

Stay in Prayer!

Halang - Laos

Population: 5,600
They live on the border with Vietnam. All of the male names start with the letter "A" and the female names start with the letter "Y." Although the Halang living in Laos have not heard the Gospel, there are missionaries who have planted churches among them in Vietnam.

Pray: The missionaries among this people group would boldly proclaim the love of Jesus.

Helplessness

> Simon answered, "Master, we've worked hard all night and haven't caught anything. But because you say so, I will let down the nets."
> Read Luke 5:1-11

During this day along the lakeshore, the perfect combination came together for a miracle: frustrated fishermen, an eager crowd, and a willing Master.

When Jesus saw the crowds were eager to listen, He asked Simon to take him away from the shore so he could teach the crowd as they listened attentively alongside the bank. After ending his talk, he challenged Peter to row out into the deep and cast his net. He did this as if he didn't know what it meant to be frustrated after an entire night's work of catching no fish.

Peter looked at Jesus and said, "We have caught nothing, but because you say so, we will let down the nets." After a few short minutes, their helplessness and discouragement was replaced with euphoria and amazement because fish filled their nets to the brink of being torn.

Generally we give our best effort, but fall short of achieving what we want. At times, we have unpleasant feelings of helplessness, feeling worn out and ready to give up. But it's then, in the breaking point, when our impossible situation becomes possible through the power of God. Human inability is the door to divine action from God. You need to come to the point in your life where you surrender everything to God and realize that without Him, you can do nothing. I encourage you to cry out like Paul ... "I can do everything through Christ who strengthens me" (Philippians 4:13).

F. Chinatti

Do you dare?

Bozo-Sorogama - Mali

Population: 285,000

Bozo means "straw house." There are three ethnic groups that are classified as Bozo. Because they live near a river, they have fish in their diet. They also grow rice and millet. They are Muslims. They have some Bible stories translated into their language, Corogama Bozo.

Pray: God would touch their hearts so they would be open to hear His Word.

FAITH: Question Of Science Fiction?

> Now faith is the assurance of things hoped for, the assurance of things not seen. Hebrews 11:1

Today, as I was walking through the aisles of the movie store, glancing at the movie titles, I spotted a movie I had never seen before: "Faith Like Potatoes". The movie is based on a true story about God showing a man the greatness of His glory in exchange for the man's faith.

Two rows down, I found the movie: "Facing the Giants". I was thrilled to find another movie about our Heavenly Father. This movie is about the power God gives us to overcome our fears, circumstances, and obstacles.

I decided to rent both movies and as I grabbed them off the shelf, I noticed both of the movies were in the Science Fiction section. I couldn't help but think they were not classified correctly! However, this thought made me realize there are millions of people in this would who do not understand faith. They have not experienced a real faith with our Heavenly Father and only consider Him to be imaginary and intangible.

Every day as a Christian, it is a challenge to have faith: "certainty in what we hope for and certainty of what we do not see" (Hebrews 11:1). Yet, our faith grows when we spend time each day communicating with God, reading the Word, and putting it into practice!

We cannot afford or permit the word "faith" to be classified as Science Fiction. It is by faith we are saved. If your faith is in the fiction section of your life, ask yourself this question: Am I living every day by walking step by step in faith?

G. Galindo

Examine your faith!

Coconucos - Colombia

Population: 6,140
They live in the central area of Cauca. They are dedicated to the cultivation of potatoes and corn. They are animists who live in fear of spirits embodied in pigs and volcanoes.

Pray: God would free them from their fears and give them freedom in Christ!

Persecution: What If It's My Turn?

> *Blessed are you when people insult you, persecute you and falsely say all kinds of evil against you because of me. Rejoice and be glad, because great is your reward in heaven, for in the same way they persecuted the prophets who were before you. Matthew 5:11-12*

Through the media, we are used to hearing about "rights": rights for women, men, children, and minority groups (whether racial or social). With all the influences about rights, it's crazy how we develop false images of what our "rights" as evangelical Christians should be.

Many Christians act as though they have the right to lives of comfort and respect. But does this "right" line up with the Word of God and the life of Jesus? Paul, Peter, and the other disciples were persecuted and even martyred for their faith in Jesus. Did they claim their alleged "right" to a comfortable life?

This very second, millions of our Christian brothers are remaining faithful to Christ while suffering oppression, injustice, persecution, and even martyrdom. Even in their human weaknesses, they continue to allow the Word of God and the love of Christ to transform their lives despite persecution. For this reason they are able to say, as Paul did, "I have lost everything in order to know Christ and the power of his resurrection, and I am sharing in his sufferings and in order to become like him in his death" (Philippians 3:10).

Would this be the conviction of you heart if God were to take you to a place where you would suffer persecution?

T. Sandvig

Are you ready?

Halwai - Nepal

Population: 60,100
The Halwai are known as bakers and traders of chocolates and sweets. 99% are Hindu and 1% are Muslim. They have the entire Bible available in their language, Nepali. Nevertheless, there is no knowledge of a single Christian among them.

Pray: For a keen interest to develop within the Halwai to learn about Jesus.

Missions Start With Your Relationships

> *Andrew first found his own brother Simon and said to him: "We have found the Messiah"... Philip found Nathanael and said to him: "We have found Jesus of Nazareth" ... of whom the prophets wrote. John 1:41, 45*

When you hear the word "church", what comes to your mind? Do you immediately think of a building with a pulpit and stained glass windows? Or do you think about a group of people? The Bible teaches the Church is not a building, nor is it the meeting that takes place inside of the building. God's blood-bought children are the Church! The Church is a living body, not an inert element. As we gather each week to celebrate the presence of the Lord, we should also be working together, in Him, to become "one body". This body of believers should function together to glorify God and build His Kingdom on earth. When the Church does this, it is fulfilling the purpose God intended!

Most believers of Christ have put their faith in God because of the influence or invitation from another believer who is close to them. If we know this to be true, why are we holding back? In the book of John, both Andrew and Philip were so excited to know Jesus, they couldn't help but share their faith with their loved ones. God equips each of us with the tools we need to be able to fulfill the mission He has called us to. As a Christian, you are called to be a light for Jesus wherever you are, whether in your hometown or in a foreign country, your mission is to always spread the love of Jesus. You might be the only reflection of Christ that some people will ever see. Some people may feel intimidated by going to church services and listening to preachers, but everyone listens to their friends. You don't always need to talk. If your life is filled with passion for Jesus, it will speak for itself. Other times, words are necessary. If the Lord has touched your heart, He will undoubtedly move in the heart of those around you.

W. Altare

No Doubt!

Dzhidi - Israel

Population: 98,000
The Dzhidi are of Jewish-Persian heritage. Their religion is animist with some features of Judaism. They don't have any Scripture translated into their language, Dzhidi. Only a few have had contact with the Gospel and have accepted Christ.

Pray: The few who know Jesus will be light to other Dzhidi.

Bible in one year: Acts 23:23-24:9 / Judges 20 / Psalm 45

A Wise Decision

> Now all has been heard; here is the conclusion of the matter: Fear God and keep his commandments, for this is the duty of all mankind.
> Ecclesiastes 12:13

Today more than ever, people are recognizing our world is in a state of moral decay. For example, if you pick up any newspaper, what do you see? You'll find atrocities and disasters all over the world. Add those with the human degradation happening through the recent advancements in technology, and what do we have? It seems as though we have lost a moral standard that once shaped our key principles and values. We have lost respect for others, and even ourselves. All these things are just a culmination of leaving God out of the picture, pushing Him aside, and living each day without a healthy fear of Him.

Look at the life of King Solomon, a man of incredible wisdom, we see even as a child, he had a healthy fear of God. Sadly, he later turned away from God and set his eyes on the worldly desires of his heart instead of the desires of the Lord. This proved disastrous for him, his family, and his kingdom. At the end of his life, he wrote the book of Ecclesiastes and explained everything in this life is meaningless if not lived out of respect and worshipful obedience to the Lord and Creator.

Although having a healthy fear of the Lord is the wisest decision you can make in your life, it is not a decision you make just once. Rather, it is a daily decision to follow, respect, worship, and obey God. It's not easy! In my daily life, God challenges me to give up things I believe are valuable. However, I understand these "valuable things" become distractions from my relationship with Him. Every day, we struggle against our worldly flesh, against the temptations of the world and the army of Satan. However, living in awe of our Lord is the best thing you can do in this world. This way, you will be able to avoid the disastrous consequences in your life. Just ask Solomon. G. Vergara

What decisions do you need to take today to live in fear of God?

Faroese - Denmark

Population: 2,800

The Faroese are originally from the Faroe Islands, an archipelago of 18 islands near Norway. They speak Faroe and British English. They are dedicated to the trades of the sea. 80% belong to the Lutheran church, but many have left the truth of the Bible for modern theological trends.

Pray: Sound Biblical doctrine returns to the hearts of the Faroese.

Bible in one year: Acts 24:10-27 / Judges 21 / Psalm 46

Spiritual Surgeon

> For the word of God is alive and active. Sharper than any double-edged sword, it penetrates even to dividing soul and spirit, joints and marrow; it judges the thoughts and attitudes of the heart.
> Hebrews 4:12

The word "discern" in the New Testament is used in reference to cutting. It is generally what a surgeon does: separate the "sick" from the "healthy", while using precision when cutting. Discernment is a gift and spiritual skill you can develop. Discernment is the ability to decide between what is true and what is false. It is having good judgment and being able to look clearly and deeply. Just for clarification, we do not have to judge one another (Romans 14:10-14). If a sharp object is not used properly, it can cause much damage.

Hebrews 4:12 says we are not the ones who discern; rather, it is the Word of God that discerns. You need to have good judgment as you are studying, understanding, and applying the Word of God in your life. You gain your wisdom and discernment from studying the Word of God, along with asking the Holy Spirit to help you understand and practice what you learn.

You need to delicately and accurately discern the relevant topics in our local and global society. You need to extend yourself to the forgotten people of your city, the nation, and the world. With all the controversial topics in our society, you need to develop discernment and be a light of truth to the world.

C. Scott

Prepare your hands to do the work!

Futunanes - Wallis and Futuna

Population: 4,000
They speak Malay and French. All they know about the Bible is what Catholic missionaries have taught them. Their lives are simple, yet modern. They are avid fishermen because their island has no suitable land for agriculture. It is estimated only 1% of the Futunanes have put their faith in Jesus.

Pray: For those who have a Bible to develop a greater interest for studying and growing from it.

When The Lights Go Out

> By day the Lord went ahead of them in a pillar of cloud to guide them on their way and by night in a pillar of fire to give them light, so that they could travel by day or night. Neither the pillar of cloud by day nor the pillar of fire by night left its place in front of the people.
> Exodus 13:21-22

When I was a kid, I don't ever recall being afraid to turn out the light when it was time to go to bed. However, I do remember sleeping with my parents for almost 5 years. When the lights went out, it wasn't a trigger of fear, but rather the sign for me to hop in my parents' bed and settle down between them. I found security from their presence around me!

Looking back, I realize things don't always turn out the way I would like. Often, I find myself trying to make things go my way. When I do this, I fall into the harsh reality that not everything is under my control. When this happens, a flood of fear and doubts start racing through my mind. I realize now I wasn't all that brave as a child because my security came from the presence of my parents. The dark shadows aren't so scary when you are in a familiar place with familiar people.

The arms of your Heavenly Father are around you. When you think you may be lost, remember His love is a pillar of fire to warm you up, guide you, and shine bright in the darkness.

A. Corrales

If you turn off your light, seek God. His presence will be your light.

Cocopa - Mexico

Population: 200

The Cocopa live in the northern part of Mexico. It is a group of low class people, with few educational and job opportunities. Almost 50% have put their trust in Jesus, but they lack quality discipleship and an understanding of the Gospel.

Pray: For the church to grow not only in numbers, but also in the knowledge of God.

Blameless

{ *... the one whose walk is blameless will minister to me. Psalm 101:6*
(See also Romans 5:20)

Before becoming a missionary, my job with the Aviation Police in Lima occupied the majority of my time. Working in a military institution can be extremely difficult for Christians because of the surrounding temptations. Each day, before going to work, I would tell myself, "I'm entering my mission field." I did my best to be a man above reproach. Sometimes I emerged triumphantly, but other days, I would leave ashamed. I wondered: How can I be a missionary if I don't live a blameless life? I assume many other Christians who want to be missionaries struggle with the same question. The enemy often tries to skew our view of our incredible God. When you sin against God, you can be sure consequences will follow. However, you can also be certain about the promise of Jesus' victory on the cross. God forgives your sin through the death and resurrection of Christ. For where sin abounds, grace abounds more. Should you stop striving to be blameless then? Of course not! Every Christian is called to live above reproach. However, being blameless does not mean you have to be perfect and never sin. Blameless means: "there is no accusation against you." It means if you sin, you must recognize it and confess it to God and the people who were affected by that sin. As God forgives each and every sin you confess, there is nothing to accuse you of! You are blameless when you recognize and repent of your sin. By the grace of God, you are blameless!
G. Rivas

Is this a reality in your life?

Koreans - South Korea

Population: 47,087,000
The South Koreans are known for their high status in life. They enjoy affordable comfort and are at the forefront of technology and communication. 30% are Christian, but most declare themselves non-religious.

Pray: The modern lifestyles do not take over their hearts and replace Jesus.

Nothing Is Impossible

> Who is this King of glory? The LORD strong and mighty, the LORD mighty in battle. Psalm 24:8
>
> For with God nothing is impossible. Luke 1:37

If you are involved in any kind of Christian ministry, you will constantly battle spiritual warfare. There will be times when it seems impossible to continue. These are the moments you can remind yourself of people in the Bible who also went through tough spiritual battles. For example, David went through numerous hardships and came out of each one with a newfound strength. Psalm 24:8 says, "Who is the King of glory? The LORD strong and mighty, the LORD mighty in battle."

He is your strength! Your God is the King of glory. I'll say it again... He is the KING! This means no matter what happens in ministry, everything is under His control and sovereign hand. His plan is perfect and and He is by your side!

When you find yourself without the strength or courage to continue, turn to the truths of the Bible. In the midst of spiritual warfare, you can get everything you need to persevere from the Word of God. Luke 1:37 says, "For with God nothing is impossible." Nothing is impossible for your God or His children who are doing His work.

MyT. Goddard

Keep going!

Duwinna - Tunisia

Population: 4,600
They live on Jerba, a Mediterranean island. They live off of fishing and the cultivation of fruits and vegetables. Their community is 100% Muslim. Their language, Nafusi, does not have a translation of the Bible.

Pray: : God would remove any barrier preventing them from hearing the Gospel, so that they would come to know Christ.

The Joy Of Giving

> God loves a cheerful giver. 2 Corinthians 9:7
> (See also Mark 12:41-44)

One day, Jesus sat near the altar to watch people give their money offerings. Many rich people approached the altar with a great display of pageantry and threw large amounts of money in the box. Then, a widow appeared from the crowd, a very poor woman who depended on the charity of others to survive. The woman gave two small coins, barely worth anything.

Amidst the pageantry, almost no one noticed the presence of this poor widow... except Jesus. Knowing her heart, Jesus said, "This poor widow has given more than all the others." The others gave out of their abundance, but she gave all she had. Jesus teaches us the value of our offering does not depend on the quantity but rather, the attitude of the heart.

The widow's might teaches us the only real motivation to give should be love. God loves a cheerful giver. Because He has forgiven us and filled us with promises for all eternity, God expects us to love Him and to give everything we have in response to the undeserved love He has given us. God does not look at how much or how little you have, or how important you are in the eyes of others. Rather, God expects you to give your whole life to His service and glory because of your love for Him.

A. Betancur

Are you giving with joy?

Cree - Western Canada

Population: 74,000
The Cree are a people group native to North America. They live in Alberta and Saskatchewan. 10% of the people are Christian.

Pray: Their identity would be found in Christ and not their economic achievements.

Follow The Goal!

> Brothers and sisters, I do not consider myself yet to have taken hold of it. But one thing I do: Forgetting what is behind and straining toward what is ahead, I press on toward the goal to win the prize for which God has called me heavenward in Christ Jesus. Philippians 3:13-14

Throughout our lives, we encounter numerous tests of our faith, which give us a chance to persevere toward what lies ahead in Jesus. Argentine Pastor John Masalyka gives three ways to help us:

1. Hear God (Genesis 22:1). You must be sensitive to the Spirit and listen to where God is leading you. There are none as deaf as those who choose not to hear God. "If you hear His voice, harden not your heart."

2. Believe God. The circumstances God allowed in Abraham's life were very difficult. These circumstances tested his faith, yet he still believed (Hebrews 11:17, Genesis 22:18).

3. Work with God. This involves prayer and hard work. Remember, His plan is perfect. If there is no work being done, there is no progress.

Being united as a body of believers for the mission of God involves hearing, believing and working in accordance to His will. Forget the successes and failures of the past and strain toward what is ahead. Our responsibility is to live in love, be generous, and stay committed to serving. Looking back on what "could have been" will only cause you to stumble and become discouraged. Press on towards the goal to win the prize!

C. Scott

Eyes on the prize!

Fala - Spain

Population: 12,000

This people group originated in Spain and they speak Fala. They live in Extremadura, near the border with Portugal. They profess Roman Catholicism. Only 8% embrace faith in Jesus Christ, but there is no emphasis put on evangelism.

Pray: God would strengthen the Fala church. Pray the Fala people would find reason to share the love of Christ.

No Fear

> Get yourself ready! Stand up and say to them whatever I command you. Do not be terrified by them, or I will terrify you before them.
> Jeremiah 1:17

In the 1950's, a man by the name of Adrian House was serving as an Officer in the United States Marine Corp. On the weekends, he worked as a bouncer of a bar. Standing at 6"4" tall and weighing 240lbs, Adrian rarely faced someone who challenged his authority. In fact, he struck fear in the hearts of most men, due to his commanding presence.

One Friday night at the bar, a man who was about 5'0" walked up to Adrian and said to him, "I have come to tell you about Jesus and you're going to listen." The man went on to explain he was a chaplain for the Marines and God told him Adrian would one day be a mighty warrior in God's Kingdom. That night, because of the fearlessness of one man, Adrian accepted Jesus Christ as his Lord and Savior.

Over the next 30 years, Adrian House went to pastor and plant many churches in the United States, lead hundreds of people to decisions for Christ, and shared about the incredible love of Jesus to thousands of people through radio ministry. Today, I have the signature of my grandpa, Adrian House, tattooed on my wrist to "remember the leader who first taught me the Word of God" (Hebrews 13:7). However, every time I look at my wrist and remember the faithful life of my grandpa, I also remember the fearlessness of the man who shared Christ with him and started an amazing "chain of grace"!

Today, I encourage you to share your faith in Christ with someone. You never know, God might use you to start a "chain of grace" and be a messenger of His love to the next world changer! "Get ready!...Do not be terrified by them..." Go share!

G. House

No fear!

Huay - Thailand

Population: 600

The Huay are a group who have lived in northern Thailand for centuries. They are very friendly and helpful. They preserve a culture totally different from their neighbors. The women carry loads on their heads. 100% of the population is Buddhist and they do not accept other beliefs.

Pray: Their eyes would be opened to the Gospel and they would fall in love with Jesus.

Where Is Your Delight?

> Delight yourself in the Lord, and He shall give you the desires of your heart. Psalm 37:4

Whenever we eat a good meal, we take delight in enjoying and savoring each flavorful bite. Another advantage of eating a good meal is the fact it nourishes us and meets a physical need that our bodies require to function. In the same way, spiritual food is needed for our spiritual bodies to function. The more spiritual food we take in, the more we will find joy in doing the will of God. Do you feed your spiritual body by walking in fellowship with God? After you read and meditate on His Word, do you apply it to your life? If you do, you will find the desires of your heart are in harmony with God's plan for your life.

As you seek His presence in your quiet time, He makes His will known for your life. The Bible teaches as a child of God, you can ask for anything according to His will. It is these requests, which are in-line with the will of God, that give a lasting peace and joy in your life. Make it a priority to seek Him with all of your heart. Experience the peace, joy, and hope that comes from seeking God! Delight yourself in the Lord because he promises your heart's desires will be fulfilled. I pray you believe it is a priority to read the Word every day, so your spirit may be fed. God will speak if you learn to listen. When you follow Him, He will always give you the desires of your heart.

M. Inciarte

Delight in God and His Word!

Galeshi - Iran

Population: 2,500

The Galeshi live in a mountain town difficult to access. Currently, they have only the Jesus film available in their language, Gilaki. They are faithful to Islam and no recorded Christians live among them.

Pray: God would transform their hearts and they would become obedient to Jesus.

Bible in one year: Romans 1:1-15 / 1 Samuel 8 / Psalm 54

Blessing Of God

{
May God be gracious to us and bless us and make his face shine on us—so that your ways may be known on earth, your salvation among all nations. Read Psalm 67:1-7

In this passage, we see a man from the Old Testament with a global vision, but the man has never heard of Jesus or the Great Commission. This man had his "ear tuned" to the Word of God and was close to God's heart. Therefore, he knew God's desire was for every nation to hear about His plan for salvation.

Within these seven verses, the psalmist speaks about "missions" ELEVEN times.

But what is more interesting is in the first and last verse, the psalmist asks blessings for others. When you ask God for blessings, what kind of blessings do you ask for? Do you ask for health, materials, benefits, and physical protection?

Normally we pray and ask for the needs in our lives or for the needs in the lives of our family. However, the psalmist focuses on God's desire for all nations to know Him and to be saved. In your prayers, are you focusing more on your desires or on Gods desires? The Lord says, "But seek first the kingdom of God and His righteousness, and all these things shall be added?" Matthew 6:33

Evaluate the "how" and "why" of your prayer life. Make sure your prayers put heavy emphasis on the unreached people of the world. Pray for those in your neighborhood, in your city, in your country, and those at the ends of the earth.

H. Ziefle

Are your prayers going in the right direction?

Earn - Indonesia

Population: 4,700
They live north of the Maluku and Halmahera Islands. They are fishermen and farmers and are 100% Islamic. The Gospel has not yet been introduced to them. Therefore, they have no testimony of the Word of God.

Pray: For the introduction of the Gospel to this people group. Pray the Bible would be translated into their language, Win.

My Need For Christ Comes First

{ *What must we do to do the works God requires? Read John 6:25-40*

One recent survey showed 40% of missionaries, who enter the mission field, decrease their average quiet time with God. While it is very possible a missionary won't be as spiritually filled when living in a foreign country, due to lack of churches or leaders, it is extremely important they do not become part of that 40%. The desire of my heart is for my life to reflect my alone time with God.

Jesus said, "I am the bread of life." Bread, or food, is necessary in order for growth to occur. By saying, "I am the bread of life," Jesus is indicating time with Him is essential for growth to occur in our spiritual lives. The average amount of time missionaries spend with Jesus is gradually declining and is being replaced with "ministry plans". Because they are to busy with their ministry, many missionaries don't believe they can take a half an hour for quite time with God. However, we can be certain of one thing: God owns time. If we are nourished by His word every day, we will accomplish and have enough time for ministry things, such as learning a language, evangelism, discipleship, church planting, or translating the Bible.

When you are spiritually malnourished and not utilizing spiritual strength from God, you will notice your "flesh" quickly shows itself in different life circumstances. Giving your whole life and service to God starts with your daily alone time with Him. Today, pray for all the missionaries who struggle to make time to spend alone with God.

N. Rivas

Do not leave Him!

Chiricoa - Colombia

Population: 200
The Chiricoa are farmers of cassava and live under the rule of a Shaman, a sorcerer. The Shaman officiates their native ceremonies and funerals. They speak Cuiba, which has had a New Testament translation since 1998. It is believed there are less than a handful of Christians among them.

Pray: God would break the chains of sorcery within the Chiricoas.

Are You A Fragrant Offering?

> *Epaphroditus, my brother, fellow worker and fellow soldier...are a fragrant offering, a sacrifice acceptable and pleasing to God.*
> *Philippians 2:25 and 4:18*

When we decide, as a body of believers, to work together in God's mission, it is a sign that Satan is being defeated. It is evidence of God's church working in unity and love to bring the message of Jesus to the world! This is exactly what happened with the apostle Paul and the church at Philippi.

We must ask ourselves: Why is there still 27% of the world's population who have little or no access to the Gospel? Our world now has seven billion people living in 234 countries with more than 16,000 races. Of these different ethnic groups, more than 6,600 remain unreached. I present this information not to discourage you, but to encourage you because we know the goal will be reached!

"We live with the challenge of working in unity and fellowship, although we have differences in culture, wealth, and background. We need the help of the Holy Spirit and a willingness to lay aside our differences for the sake of our mission!"

C. Scott

What could I do for the unreached?

North Fali - Cameroon

Population: 1,800
They were divided into northern and southern regions because of their religious differences. The South adopted Christianity and the North continued to practice Islam. They have audio Bibles for evangelism in their language, Fali.

Pray: For a burning desire to know Jesus and a willingness to give up their community for Christ.

The Conquest Of God

> So great is your power that your enemies cringe before you. All the earth bows down to you, and sing psalms, sing praises to your name. *Psalm 66:3-4*

History tells us of rulers, kings, and emperors who conquered other nations by subduing and enslaving them with force. According to Psalm 66, the expansion of the Kingdom of God is being built by other means and has different purposes than the great kingdoms of the past. God's dedication, care, protection, and forgiveness are "weapons of love" that have been used throughout time to draw people to Himself.

Unlike vicious rulers of the past, God does not desire destruction or enslavement of His enemies. He simply wants His enemies to repent of their rebellion, join His Kingdom, and experience the same blessings and privileges the people in the Kingdom are already experiencing. God wants His current enemies to sing praises to His name! Let all people praise God so it may be heard!

The expansion of the Kingdom of God is not like the Crusades of the Middle Ages. It is made with a revolution of love, for the benefit of every inhabitant of the earth, not to enslave, but to liberate. God is now in the process of sending ambassadors to bring His love to everyone. Are you one of them?

F. Rodríguez

Will you join the revolution of love?

Illanon - Malaysia

Population: 17,000
They live on the south coast of the province of Sabah. Although they are nominal Muslims, they are not accepting of a change in religion. A neighboring ethnic group has tried sharing the Gospel with them, but so far, it hasn't made a significant impact. The Bible has not yet been translated into their language, Iranun.

Pray: The Gospel would be presented to them in their own language and their hearts would be open to change.

The Purpose Of The Law

> *Therefore no one will be declared righteous in God's sight by the works of the law; rather, through the law we become conscious of our sin. Romans 3:20*

When preaching or evangelizing, most prefer not to speak about the law, sin, or damnation. We don't want anyone falling into the bondage of law and the error of legalism. However, while these topics bring an uncomfortable environment, they often help sinners recognize their spiritual hopelessness without Christ! We forget people cannot believe in the living, real, and saving Jesus until they realize their own conviction of their sin against Him. According to Paul, the law is the knowledge of sin.

When we, as Christians, don't care for the law of God, non-Christians will despise the law and end up despising His amazing grace as well. We need to reach out to souls who are full of despair – people who know they cannot save themselves. We need to reach out to those who are ready to cry out to God with all their might. When we do this, sinners can understand the Gospel is not for those who think they're righteous, but rather for those who know they are not! At this point, the soul receives the ability to understand the Gospel and believe it with saving faith. We must preach both: the law and the amazing grace God gives sinners.

O. Simari

Does your preaching reveal the reality of sin?

Cubeo - Brazil

Population: 7,800
Their religion is animistic and revolves around the work of a medium. They are hunters and fishermen. They speak Cubeo. Since 1989, they have had the translation of the New Testament.

Pray: God sends missionaries who will live with them and teach them about Jesus.

The Insanity Of The Gospel

> *For the message of the cross is foolishness to those who are perishing, but to us who are saved it is the power of God. 1 Corinthians 1:18*

Two women have just witnessed a triple execution at the foot of Golgotha. Two of the men executed were accused of being thieves, and the other, a blasphemer. The women knew the "blasphemer". In fact, there was hardly a person in the region who had not heard of the famous Jesus, the Nazarene. After He was crucified, they started to talk to each other about him. One person questioned the innocence of Jesus and proposed He "must have done something" to deserve that kind of death. One other woman spoke more positively about Him and said He died for love and His ideals. She said He was a very good man, guilty only of being honest and wanting to change the society of His time.

What were these women missing? Sometimes, it is very easy to lose the real focus (Jesus) and the purpose of the cross. Jesus was more than a good teacher, and His death meant much more than just martyrdom for good ideals. On the cross, He was playing the main character in the cruelest and yet, most wonderful scene in the history of mankind. Jesus carried the sins of all humanity to the cross with Him, so that we might receive forgiveness!

What does the cross mean to you? Is it power? Is it madness? There are millions of people in the world who have never heard of the purpose of the cross. Who will tell them? There will be many people who will think you're crazy for wanting to invest your life in telling people about Jesus Christ. But don't worry! They don't understand the power of the message!

A. Gulard

> Let the world call me "crazy," I know whom I serve!

Finnish - Finland

Population: 4,879,000

The Finns belong to the Lutheran church. They live out their faith through baptisms, funerals, and religious festivals. Most believe in God as a vital spiritual force and nothing more. They need to be re-evangelized.

Pray: For a revival in Finland and for mighty leaders of God to step up.

JUNE

Our Influence On Others

> *Therefore this is what the Lord says: "If you repent, I will restore you that you may serve me; - if you utter worthy, not worthless, words, you will be my spokesman. -Let this people turn to you, but you must not turn to them..." Read Jeremiah 15:19-21*

It's as if God were saying, "separate the precious from the disgusting in your life; then you will be my spokesman." In order to be a spokesman of God and be able to publicize truth about Him, we need to make sure there is no sin in our lives that has not been dealt with.

We may "talk the talk" of a Christian life, but often, our attitudes don't match our talk. Too often we let gossiping and unkind people influence our daily behavior. In Genesis 13, we read Lot "lifted up his eyes and chose for himself the plain of Jordan." Lot knew the land of Jordan was inhabited by negative influences, but he chose it anyways. Spending the majority of your time with negative influences can and will hinder your relationship with Christ! In Genesis 19:14, we read Lot, after living in a land of negative influences, tried to save his family from destruction but they wouldn't listen to him. Often, our testimonies become weak and useless for encouraging others to seek God because of our bad choices. This is exactly what happened to Lot.

As the saying goes: "Your actions speak louder than words." Today, examine your attitude and the influence non-Christians have on your life. In this way, you will be able to keep your testimony strong and speak truth into the lives of other people.

D. Duk

Guard your testimony!

Fezara - Sudan

Population: 280,000

The Fezara live in the western region of Sudan. They make their living by raising goats and sheep. Most households also have a garden for food. They profess Islam and it is common for a man to have two wives in separate houses. Their language is Sudanese Arabic, which has a New Testament translation.

Pray: Their hearts would be open to the Gospel.

Religion Versus Redemption

> *For it is by grace you have been saved, through faith—and this is not from yourselves, it is the gift of God—not by works, so that no one can boast. Ephesians 2:8-9*

Ever since the Tower of Babel was built and destroyed, man has continually sought ways to create a path to God. Even though Ephesians 2:8-9 specifically states the only way to God is through faith, thousands of alternative systems, philosophies, and idols have been created to "get to God". People today are no different than the people who build the Tower of Babel, thousands of years ago. People still fall into the same religious trap.

1. GOD WILL LOVE ME IF I AM OBEDIENT.

This religious trap gives you a list of things you can and cannot do for love and acceptance. But God loves us with an UNCONDITIONAL love, which means he loves the same, regardless of our actions.

2. IN THE WORLD THERE ARE GOOD PEOPLE AND THERE ARE BAD PEOPLE.

This religious trap separates people based on what they do. If you do good, God will give you favor. If you do wrong, the punishment is imminent. But God says, "not by works, so that no one can boast" (Ephesians 2:8).

3. APPEARANCE IS VERY IMPORTANT.

This religious trap looks at the surface level of a person. Were you blessed to be born in a Christian family? Did you go to a Christian school? How long have you been going to church? Do you dress "properly"? None of that matters. God looks at the heart.

Are you religious or do you have a personal relationship with Christ? When you understand God's grace and salvation, you will have the desire for others to enjoy it also.

L. Ashmore

What are you doing for others to enjoy it?

Gaius - Indonesia

Population: 365,700
The Gaius live north of Sumatra. They came to the area after the devastating tsunami of 2004. The majority are fishermen and farmers. It is an Islamic state, but most follow animism practices. They speak Gayo, which has no Bible translation.

Pray: The light of the Gospel would reach this group.

167

Provision Of Resources

> Taking the five loaves and the two fish and looking up to heaven, he gave thanks and broke them. Then he gave them to the disciples to distribute to the people. They all ate and were satisfied, and the disciples picked up twelve basketfuls of broken pieces that were left over. Luke 9:16-17

This is a well-known passage from the life of Jesus and it gives us a great lesson. With women and children included, the people in need was estimated to be around 15,000. Jesus took what little food was in possession of one of the followers, blessed it, and broke it to give to His disciples. If we read through the passage, we see the miraculous multiplication did not actually happen in the hands of Jesus, but in the hands of His disciples. The disciples had given everything they had to Jesus for Him to use. Jesus simply gave it back with the power for it to be multiplied! When the 15,000 people had eaten until they were full, the leftover food was collected and stored in baskets...12 of them.

Often, the desire for material possessions and our tendency to hold them with "closed hands" limits our ability to bless others. Jesus has called us to trust in His power and provision, and not in the material possessions we have. He has invited us to give everything we have up to Him and let him work miracles with it. Also from the passage, we see there is no multiplication of resources without distribution. Sometimes, we expect resources to multiply first before we distribute them. That is not faith in the power and provision of God.

Our faith requires trusting God will provide for our needs as we freely and joyfully give to others. We have experienced God's provision time and time again. Within this provision, you must learn to be a good steward of what is placed in your hands, not wasting anything, even if they are just "pieces." Everything can be used to serve Him and fill the needs of the lost.

M. de Rodríguez

Be a good steward of what God gives!

Garwis - Afghanistan

Population: 1,700
The Garwis are Muslims in Afghanistan who speak Kalami. They practice endogamy, marrying only within their clan. No Christians live among them and there is no Bible translation in their language.

Pray: For this group to be reached with the Gospel.

The Purpose Of The Law

> *I have fought the good fight, I have finished the race, I have kept the faith. 2 Timothy 4:7*

Many people find themselves fighting a war by themselves, struggling with not knowing whom they are fighting, or realizing they are fighting for lost causes. In this passage, Paul speaks about the important aspects of "fighting the good fight". What Paul is talking about is not just finishing the race, but keeping the faith during the race.

Fighting the good fight requires three things:

1. Know when a battle is ok to fight and who you're fighting against (2 Corinthians 2:11, 2 Timothy 2:5).

2. Know what you need to go into battle (Ephesians 6 - Armor of God).

3. Know the battle is God's, not yours (Exodus 14:14, Revelation 17:14).

With these three things in mind, how can we finish the race before us, while keeping the faith?

-When, at the end of each day/season of life, we can say we decided to glorify God in all we did!

In 2 Timothy, Paul gives us three very important suggestions:

1) Kindle the fire within you (1:6).

2) Retain the beautiful teaching entrusted to you (1:13).

3) Be strong in the grace that is in Christ Jesus (2:1).

M. Chiquie

Are you fighting the good fight?

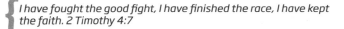

Fur - Egypt

Population: 3,300

The Fur live in the very dangerous Darfur area. They are farmers who profess Islam 100 %. No known Christians live among them. They speak Fur, which has the Jesus film and some audio Bible stories. There is strong resistance to the Gospel.

Pray: For God to bring down all barriers hindering the evangelization of these people.

God's Provision

{ *Before he had finished praying, Rebekah came out with a jar on her shoulder. Genesis 24:15*

Eliezer, the oldest servant of Abraham, was given a mission one day to find a wife for Isaac, Abraham's son and his future boss. You can imagine how daunting of task this could be. Most people find it quite difficult to find their own spouse. How much more difficult must it have been for Eliezer to find the appropriate partner for someone else!

In Genesis 24, we read he took ten camels, supplies, and gifts as he traveled to the old home-town of Abraham. Upon reaching the city, where would Eliezer start looking?

There was no social media like Facebook, and he didn't know any girls in town. So he did the only thing he knew was right: he knelt and prayed to God - and asked for a sign. The sign he asked for: the woman, who voluntarily offered to water his camels, would be the future wife for Isaac. It was a far-fetched sign. A camel can drink up to 120 liters of water, Eliezer had 10 camels, and the pitchers women used to draw water from a well did not exceed 10 liters. He knew any woman willing to lift 1,200 liters of water for his camels was a woman worthy to be Isaac's wife. As you prepare for missions and think about who will be alongside you on this adventure, do the right thing: ask God.

M. Eitzen

And wait for His provision!

Dominicans - Dominican Republic

Population: 8,523,000
The natives of the island are mostly black, speak Spanish, and have lost their indigenous language. They are Catholics. Among the youth there is much sexual immorality, drug addictions and alcohol abuse. The church is very weak.

Pray: God frees the youth of the Dominican Republic from sin.

To Be Or Not To Be

> *For we are God's masterpiece. He has created us anew in Christ Jesus, so we can do the good things he planned for us long ago.*
> *Ephesians 2:10*

Jenny: Do you ever dream, Forrest, about who you're gonna be?
Forrest Gump: Aren't I gonna be me?

Forrest, played by Tom Hanks in this well-known 1994 movie, didn't exactly understand the question asked of him. I can't help but pull a real "truth" from his answer. It seems very natural for children and adults to dream of who or what they want to be in the future. When I was a little kid, I remember wanting to be a professional baseball player, even though I had never played baseball in my life! I ended up never playing, unless you want to count the church softball league. Then, I wanted to be the President of the United States....that is, until I figured out how much everyone hated the president.

Dreams of who I'm going to be have come and gone in my 26 years of life and while I think having dreams is great, I can't help but wonder what the body of Christ would look like if all His followers focused each day on being the people God created them to be. These people would not conform to the world (Rom. 12:2), would rejoice in sufferings (Rom. 5:3), and would experience a freedom incomparable to the world (John 8:32). They would know how to love, (1 Cor. 13) but be hated by most (Mark 13:3). They would be faithful in the little things (Matt. 25:23) and forgive no matter what (Col. 3:13). If all followers of Christ lived to be who they were created to be, a masterpiece to glorify the Creator, I truly believe the Great Commission (Matt. 28:19-20) would look less like the "Great Suggestion."

G. House

Today, Are you being who God created you to be?

Jarai - Cambodia

Population: 21,000
They live on the border with Vietnam. They eat rice, cassava , fish and berries. Although the majority of the people are animists, a small Christian church has been planted. They have a New Testament translation in their language.

Pray: The Jarai church in Cambodia continues to grow and would be strengthened in the Word of God.

Normal? No!

> *"This is amazing," Moses said to himself. "Why isn't that bush burning up? I must go see it." Exodus 3:3*

It was a normal day for Moses, doing a regular job in the middle of a regular spot, where a normal bush was burning, which was common due to the dryness and heat. Everything was normal, that is until God suddenly appeared on the scene and transformed it into something so amazing, so spectacular that Moses decided to have a closer look. The bush was burning, but not burning up. Little did Moses know, his life was about to drastically change.

If anything catches my attention the most in this scene, it's the method God used to initiate the conversation with Moses. He used something so simple and graceless, if it weren't for that "amazing touch" of God, it would have gone unnoticed.

I don't know why we often think that to be used by God in missionary work, we need to drastically change our location. The truth is the only requirement of those who serve God is simply God Himself acting and working in their lives. I'm sure you can look back now and see how God has used the simplest things and transformed them into something "incredible" or "amazing" just to get your attention. Once God got your attention, He revealed Himself in a special way and entrusted you with a task or service. I invite you to deny yourself today! Deliver yourself into the hands of God, asking Him to give you the opportunity to be a "divine distraction" in the life of someone else.

W. Núñez

Put yourself in the hands of God!

Gorontalo - Indonesia

Population: 1,042,000
They are originally from the island of Sulawesi. They are farmers and fishermen, but also sell clothing throughout their region. They have a good economic status. They are Islamic by tradition, but in practice, animistic. They have the New Testament in audio. Only 1.8 % has responded to the Gospel.

Pray: For a spiritual awakening among the Gorontalo.

Promises Of The Father

> Jesus reached out his hand and touched the man. "I am willing," he said. "Be clean!" Immediately he was cleansed of his leprosy.
> Matthew 8:3

The phrase, "I will" is used approximately 4,000 times in the Bible and most of the time, it's said by God. In the New Testament, Jesus contently says, "I will."

Christ came to fulfill the "I will" of the Father. Therefore, His will is supreme. When Jesus said, "I am willing" to the leper, He showed what kind of will He had. His will is good, gracious and positive. The Bible declares that His will is perfect.

We know God by what He does. Unlike other gods, who do absolutely nothing, He is an active God. Having faith in God means having faith in a God who acts. When God says, "I will," He makes a covenant, a promise to be fulfilled. We know God is faithful, he keeps His promises, and His word is reliable. Examine the promises God has made in your life, remember the times He has said, "I will", and walk with conviction that He will keep His word. Be aware of the covenants that will be fulfilled in you!

D. Duk

Trust in His promises!

Friesian - Netherlands

Population: 496,000
The Friesian are originally from the northern lands in Friesland. 50% declare themselves nonreligious. Secularism and materialism are the foundation of their lives. Some follow Roman Catholicism, while only 3% live an authentic Christian life. They speak Frisian, which does not have a Bible translation.

Pray: A revival would start within the Friesian people.

Everyone

> For all have sinned, and fall short of the glory of God.
> Read Romans 3:21-23

Have you ever heard of Jeffrey Dahmer? "The Butcher of Milwaukee " killed and dismembered 17 victims between 1978 and 1991. Some he even ate! Creepy isn't? At his trial, he was very collected and did not show regret or apologize for his actions. He was sentenced to fifteen life sentences with no hope of parole. His story doesn't end there. In prison, he heard the Good News and accepted Jesus Christ as his Savior. He was changed by the power of God. In 1994, he was killed by another convict.

How much should a person pay for taking seventeen lives? Should a man like this be forgiven? We find it hard to understand someone like Jeffrey was free from eternal damnation. We think, if Jeffrey is measured against us, then we're fine. However, that's not how God sees it.

Even though different sins have different earthly consequences, is one sin worse than the other when it comes to judgment before God? Do we have the right to say one deserves more eternal punishment? No. As Romans 3 plainly declares: ALL have sinned; all means ALL.

Christ died for ALL. There is no sin so terrible that it cannot be forgiven. Anyone who comes to God will not be cast out by Christ (John 6:37). Have you judged others with the thought your sin is less severe than theirs? It is a good idea to stop looking at the sin of others and instead, thank God for your own salvation.

L. Ashmore

Already on your knees?

Giziga - Cameroon

Population: 1,800

The Giziga are farmers who grow corn, mill, and some fruits. They live in clans, with each clan having their own healer. The healer organizes all the religious services and festivals, and treats all the diseases. Their religion is animism, but they have the entire Bible in in their native language.

Pray: For a spiritual awakening that will make them see the light of Christ.

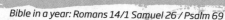

The Grace Of God

> *"Why are you so angry?" the Lord asked Cain. "Why do you look so dejected? You will be accepted if you do what is right. But if you refuse to do what is right, then watch out! Sin is crouching at the door, eager to control you. But you must subdue it and be its master."*
> *Genesis 4:6-7*

Cain was furious. His offering was not seen with pleasure, jealousy consumed him, and he schemed on how to best release his anger with God and his brother. When we remember the story of Cain, we immediately evaluate him negatively, judge him, and use him as an example of what not to do when angry. It's fairly obvious why no one ever thinks to name one of their kids, "Cain." In the midst of our evaluation, we see the Lord give an awesome display of love and mercy in today's passage. God comes to meet Cain with the sole purpose of rescue.

It is encouraging to understand no matter how difficult it may seem, it is possible to show love and mercy to those who choose evil over good. How great is the grace of the Lord!

We are called to show love and compassion for every human being, especially for those who our society believes are not worthy of it. Your responsibility is to show everyone hope, without exception.

H. Bascur

Do you?

Enlhet - Paraguay

Population: 14,200
The Enlhet live in Alto Paraná, Boqueron, and Presidente Hayes. They will soon have the complete Bible in their language, Enlhet. Animism is still very strong among them, but some have responded to faith in Jesus.

Pray: For missionaries who are working among them and the existing church.

What I Have I Give You

> Then Peter said, "Silver or gold I do not have, but what I do have I give you. In the name of Jesus Christ of Nazareth, walk." Acts 3:6

Sadly, many Christians make excuses for not obeying the Biblical command to evangelize. Sometimes it is the fear of being rejected or losing a friendship. Many believe they need more Biblical knowledge to better defend their faith. Some may believe if their churches had more entertaining preachers or better worship music, it would attract more people to the feet of Christ. However, every single one of these excuses, based on the inner fear of rejection, should be thrown out when we take a look at this particular story of Peter. He had, just a few days earlier, denied his Lord three times, but still he had the courage to share Jesus with a cripple who, for years, sat at the church door begging. Peter was completely clear in explanation to the beggar: he had absolutely nothing to give him except to share his salvation in Christ. What he knew, he shared; from there, the saving power of Christ took over.

Often times, we pray for God to take away the fear of sharing Christ with others so that we can be effective messengers (like Peter) of the saving power of Jesus. Just like the crippled man sitting at the church door, the world is desperate to experience the love of God. We have opportunities every day to share this incredible love; we just need to take them!

G. Vergara

Are you making excuses to share the saving power of Jesus?

Jeh - Laos

Population: 11,000

They live in the southern part of the country. Women share their marital status in the style of their hair: over the shoulders if they are single and long braided when they are married. They speak Jeh, which has some translated portions of the Bible. About 3% of these people are Christian.

Pray: For the native church to have a powerful testimony among the people.

What For?

{ *So that your ways be known on earth, your salvation among all nations. Read Psalm 67:1-7*

Through Psalms 67, we see the Psalmist asking for God's blessing because he knows the blessing will serve a purpose in two different ways:

1. For God's ways to be known throughout the Earth (Remembering now that Jesus is THE WAY).

2. For God's salvation to be known throughout the nations (Remembering that salvation is through Jesus and ONLY Jesus)

These may seem like two simple things, but if we want to let God use us as effective tools for all to achieve salvation we must ask ourselves: Do we pray for all the people of the earth, from all languages and ethnic groups, to receive blessing from our Lord?

The Psalmist, who was a man with a global mission, gives us an example of how to pray for the world:

Psalm 67:1: "May God be gracious to us and bless us and make his face shine on us."

Psalm 67:2: "so that your ways may be known on earth, your salvation among all nations."

I can't help but wonder what it would be like if every one started praying more for heavenly blessings, like this Psalmist prayed. I wonder what our world would be like if people prayed more for missionary and spiritual prosperity than personal prosperity and economic material.

H. Ziefle

How will you pray now?

Domari Gypsy - Israel

Population: 11,000

The Domari gypsies are a group that moves between the borders of Lebanon and Israel. Their religion is Islam. They don't have frequent contact with foreigners, which has made it made it difficult to reach them with the Gospel. They have no Scripture in their native language.

Pray: They will hear about Jesus and choose to follow Him.

Also Around

> Then the eleven disciples went to Galilee, to the mountain where Jesus had told them to go. Matthew 28:16

The disciples knew Jesus was making a statement about how far he wanted them to go when he told them to go to Galilee. It was a rich land filled with poverty because of the exploitation of landowners (large expanses of land were owned by just a few people). Usually, marginalized people lived there with shame and contempt. Galilee meant "poverty" to everyone while Jerusalem referred to the center of power with political and religious privileges. It was clear Galilee was an overpopulated area in relation to the possibilities and privileges. Abandoned orphans, widows, homeless and unemployed were all common characteristics of Galilee.

But, it was in Galilee where Jesus began His ministry and chose His first disciples. Jesus certainly had an abundance of options from Jerusalem, but He chose to fulfill His ministry among the masses neglected by political and religious leaders. The "outer edges" of Galilee represented an uncompromising and urgent commitment to the mission of Jesus, which included all Jews, Samaritans and Gentiles.

Jesus is constantly sending people to bring the good news of the Kingdom of God to all generations and nations. It's a message that has to do with the transformation of the entire human existence.

C. Scott

> Are you extending your boundaries? Are you responding to the call of God?

Hanno - Philippines

Population: 17,000

The Hanno people live in the forests on an island near Luzon. They live in houses made of straw and bamboo. They are animists and each village has a witch who controls the spirits. Their language, Hanno, has a New Testament translation.

Pray: They would be freed from the power of darkness and receive the Word of God.

Not By Works But Yes To Artworks

> For we are God's workmanship, created in Christ Jesus for good works, which God prepared beforehand so that we practice.
> Ephesians 2:10

God has a purpose to save. He shows this by showing His mercy, love and grace are unconditional and selfless. Ephesians 2:7 explains God wants to prove now and in the coming ages "the incomparable riches of his grace, expressed in kindness to us in Christ Jesus." This means, our salvation is meant to be a public showcase of the incredible qualities of God. In a way, it seems as though God is building an undeniable "lawsuit" against Satan, by demonstrating his saving power of grace through the resurrection of Christ.

Verse 10 explains we are created to do good works that have been prepared in advance for us to do. An absolute priority in our lives is to recognize we are made for good works (for God). We aren't just to contemplate doing them, but actually live every day doing them. All of this indicates salvation is so much more than just a status. Rather, it is a way of life centered around the good works God designed for us to do.

The fact salvation is by grace, not by works, does not mean works are not linked to salvation. Good works are the evidence of a new birth and a transformed life that seeks to serve God through love. Does your life show this evidence? Are you walking in the good works God prepared for you to do?

A. Neufeld

If not, start now!

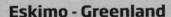

Eskimo - Greenland

Population: 45,000

The life of an Eskimo is dedicated to fishing and marine hunting. Their language is Inuktitut Greenlandic, which has an entire Bible translation. Most are Catholics, but 3.5% are evangelical Christians.

Pray: The witness of the Eskimo church draws others to Christ.

The Order To Witness Is For Everyone

{ *Go therefore and make disciples of all nations. Read Matthew 28:18-20*

The "Great Commission" is the term used to describe the missionary task of the Church: "preach the Gospel to every creature" (Mark 16:15). It is important to remember the responsibility of reaching the world with the Gospel was not just given to the apostles, but to all Christians. This makes the Great Commission a HUGE responsibility because the mission of Jesus is now our mission (2 Cor. 5:18).

While carrying out the Great Commission, it is important to remember a few characteristics of our "call" from the King: power, purpose, provision and presence! The Bible is the source of authority for the Gospel. We represent God when we use the Bible to testify to others (2 Cor. 5:20). What a privilege! First, we are saved by the grace of God; then we are sent, under His authority, to become partners in building His eternal kingdom (2 Cor. 6:1)!

The command in the Great Commission is to "make disciples." First, Jesus calls us to come to Him and then, He enables us to "go" and continue the mission that He began. As a disciple maker, Biblical evangelism and discipleship should be the focal point of our lifestyle. Our "mission" should be carried out at all times and in all places, to the people who surround us.

However, you must understand after a person receives salvation, your "mission" doesn't stop. Discipleship is a key to the "spiritual transformation" of a new disciple of Jesus! When you teach, you learn! What you learn, you should share!

L. Diaz

Let's obey the command!

Kanarese - Malaysia

Population: 55,000

The Kanarese are an immigrant group of farmers from India with very poor wages. They are discriminated against because of their religion, Hinduism. A few of the Kanarese now embrace Islam. They have an entire Bible translation in their language, Kannada.

Pray: For them to be released from the idolatry of Hinduism and seek Jesus.

Stop Worrying

> So do not worry, saying, "What shall we eat?" or "What shall we drink?" or "What we wear?"   Read Matthew 6:25-34

Has your worry ever accomplished anything? Except for making things worse? People now, more than ever, care about the clothes they wear. For most, these clothes aren't "needs" but instead "wants". It's the same with food. Jesus said these things are what the Gentiles worry about. I have seen some of the most heated arguments stem from people who can't agree on which restaurant to go to.

More and more, the hearts of Christians are influenced to confirm the mindset of the world. Christians are becoming less willing to be sanctified and consecrated in holiness for the purposes of God.

Do you know someone with a shopping addiction? Millions of people all over the world are addicted to shopping. Unfortunately, like all addictions, it only brings emptiness. On the flip side, if you seek God, satisfaction will overwhelm your heart, regardless of what you wear or what you eat! Let's start thirsting for righteousness and be full of the Living Water that leaves no one thirsty. When you continually seek to serve with this confidence, at some point, you will have the thought, "There is nothing for me to worry about anymore!"

D. Travis

He takes care of you!

Friulano - Croatia

Population: 11,000
This Croatian group emigrated from Italy in the nineteenth century. They are faithful to Roman Catholicism and have the New Testament in their native language, Friulian. The Protestant congregations have very little strength.

Pray: God would strengthen the witness of Friulano believers.

Strength In The Lord

{ *Finally, be strong in the Lord and in his mighty power. Ephesians 6:10*

As believers, we can only move forward when we are rooted in the Lord. If we fail to abide in Him, the influences of this world are so strong, our own human strength will not be enough to stand firm against it and we will fail.

It's encouraging to know we can endure all the hardships of life because God gives us strength when we remain in Him. Often, the opposition, temptations, and negative influences trying to distort our character seem too strong for us to handle. Only in the strength of the Lord will we have the power to live as children of God. That same power not only transforms the way we live, but also makes us "more than conquerors through Him who loved us." With His power, there is redemption from sin!

Think about this: what things have you been doing to receive this redemptive power from the Lord? Have you been devoting the time necessary to read His Word and draw strength from it? Today, decide to surrender to the Father, so you can be transformed into His image and draw His strength for your life. This way, you can live a life not only pleasing to Him, but also a life with a powerful testimony to the people around you.

Pescador

Go ahead, but go with Him!

Hamer Banna - Ethiopia

Population: 88,000

The Hamer Banna are known for dyeing their hair and body like the red color of earth. They are shepherds of sheep and goats. The women and children sleep in the house, but the men and older children sleep among their flocks to protect them. They are animists, speak Hamer Banna, and have just a few portions of the Bible translated into their language.

Pray: For each Hamer Banna to have the opportunity to hear the Gospel.

Run To Win

> *Do you not know that in a race all the runners run, but only one gets the prize? Run in such a way as to get the prize. 1 Corinthians 9:24*

Jesus came not only to save, but also to give a goal for our lives—one that's worthy of achieving. Many Christians begin their relationships with Christ with enthusiasm and dedication, but stumble along the way and lose sight of the goal. Paul encourages us to run the race of life in a sportsmanlike manner. He desires we run with as much enthusiasm, determination and incorruptible effort as possible.

A race has several stages. The beginning of the race is always filled with excitement and fierce determination. The main goal is running as hard as possible towards the finish line. However, when you find a rhythm, it is easy to begin to slow down. Suddenly you will realize you aren't running at the same pace you once were. Although you may face setbacks, the race never stops! While you are running, the race can begin to feel routine. You may even start to question why you are running and ask, "Why do I do what I do?" or "Where is the driving passion I once had?" These questions can distract your mind and cause you to slowly lose sight of the finish line.

Many Christians stop at this stage. However, the Bible clearly says, those who continue to run will make it to the final and most exciting stage! In the final stage you can begin to hear the sounds of the stadium. The applause and music encourage you to push through the last strides of the race. New energy rushes over you, giving your body strength and the desire to finish the race marked out before you!

J. Segnitz

Remember, our goal is JESUS.

French Canadians - Canada

Population: 7,435,000
They live mainly in Quebec. Their culture has a mixture of American and European influence. Most are nominal Catholics and have lost confidence in the church.

Pray: For them understand the difference between a relationship with Christ and a religion.

Blessing Of Purpose

> May God be gracious to us and bless us and make His face shine upon us; so that your ways may be known on earth, your salvation among all nations. Psalm 67:1-2

It is common in many churches, on special occasions, to use the Priestly Blessing found in Numbers 6:24-26: "The Lord bless you and keep you: the Lord make his face shine upon you and be gracious unto thee: the Lord turn his face, and give you peace."

Did you ever think this blessing had a purpose? In Psalm 67, God reveals the exact purpose of this particular blessing! ..."so that your ways may be known on earth, your salvation among all nations." God told Abraham not only would he personally be blessed, but he would also be a channel of blessing to all the nations of the earth (Genesis 12). God blessed Abraham greatly and also used him to bless others! This is the ultimate purpose of the Priestly Blessing.

Jesus, the promised seed, is the source of blessing to the nations. Therefore, God sends us to make disciples (passionate followers of Jesus) to the ends of the earth. The more blessing God gives, the more responsibility we have to share these blessings with others. You're not the final deposit of the blessing of God, but instead, you are simply a distribution channel that should reach out to every nation on earth. Are you aware of that?

F. Rodríguez

Are you using your blessings for world missions?

Kalmyk-Oirat - Russia

Population: 172,000

The Kalmyk-Oirat are of Mongolian decent. In Stalin's time, they were deported to Siberia, where very few survived. The Kalmyk - Oirat language has a Bible translation and some audios. No known Christians live among them, 70% are Buddhist and 30 % atheists.

Pray: For the Word of God to transform those who can read and listen.

Reach Out!

{ *Enlarge the place of your tent, ...do not hold back... Isaiah 54:2*

A missionary awakening usually arises out of bold decision-making. This is exactly what happened in the history of missions because of the decisions of William Carey. He was born into a lower-middle class family in England. He learned the shoemaking trade while also pastoring a church. His motto was: "Expect great things from God, risking great things for God." His opposition had objections to world evangelization: Why should we go there if so many people here still haven't been saved? Carey would explain: just because there is unsaved people in your town doesn't mean you abandon the call to world evangelism. He understood world evangelism is a task for every generation, for every age and should involve the WHOLE church. So he went...

He left for India in 1793 and lived as a missionary for 40 years. He understood the mission and the mandate of obedience. In his first few years, he planted a church and trained local pastors to lead it. By the time of his death, he had translated the Bible, or portions of it, into at least 35 languages and dialects of India. A missionary awakening emerges from within the "silent land" by the bold decisions of Godly individuals.

Are you the next bold individual God will use to start a missionary revival?

C. Scott

Begin praying for them!

Java Banten - Indonesia

Population: 288,000

They live in communities on the islands of Sumatra, Sulawesi, and Maluku. They grow rice, coffee, cloves, beans, and bananas. The dominant religion is Islam, but about 3,000 Christians live among them. They have the complete Bible and the Jesus film in Javanese.

Pray: For a spiritual impact on the lives of the Java Banten.

Towards The Future

{ *There is a way that appears to be right, but the end it leads to death.*
Proverbs 14:12

All decisions have consequences. The consequences may be positive or negative, large or small, but any decision will be subject to the law of action and reaction. For this reason, we must seek God and be guided by the Holy Spirit in our decision-making! The decisions you make today will be what determine your future. If you want to understand why you act they way you do, simply look back at your past choices and their consequences. If you want to know how you will act in the future, simply observe the choices you are making today!

Today is the first step down the aisle to your new job, your new studies, a revived relationship with your children, or deciding your future ministry. The way you choose to travel today will determine your final destination. Your daily walk is marked by the day-to-day decisions you're making.

Are you letting God guide the decisions you're making? Don't jump to conclusions or fast decisions based on human reasoning, but instead look for His guidance in everything. Most people make decisions while seeking comfort, economic stability, and social acceptance, but those are patterns of the world. Instead, follow Christ, invest your life in Him, serve others, reach the lost, and make wise God-centered decisions with the Word as your guide.

A. Gulard

Follow Christ, not the ideals of this world!

Herki - Iran

Population: 20,000
The Herki speak northern Kurdish, which has a New Testament translation, the Jesus Film, and audio resources. Only 4 known believers live among the 20,000. All 4 suffer great persecution. The Herki strictly follow Islam.

Pray: God would protect these brave believers, and give them a powerful testimony.

Jesus Washing the Feet Of His Disciples

> *A dispute also arose among them as to which of them was considered to be greatest. Jesus said to them, "The kings of the Gentiles lord it over them; and those who exercise authority over them call themselves Benefactors. But you are not to be like that. Instead, the greatest among you should be like the youngest, and the one who rules like the one who serves. For who is greater, the one who is at the table or the one who serves? Is it not the one who is at the table? But I am among you as one who serves." Luke 22:24-27*

> *"so he got up from the meal, took off his outer clothing, and wrapped a towel around his waist. After that, he poured water into a basin and began to wash his disciples' feet, drying them with the towel that was wrapped around him." John 13:4-5*

Why does is it so difficult to play the role of a servant, not caring if we are acknowledged for it or not? To what end are you ambitious? Do you like being in control and managing others? The ambition to do good deeds, the pursuit of excellence, and leadership can be good things … but only if they are well monitored and your underlying motives are pure. Do you have the maturity to objectively evaluate your own motives in service and leadership? Do you have someone who can correct you with love and strength when your pride seeks control, recognition, and praise? Do not let the term "servant" have a negative meaning when it comes to sacrificially and cheerfully serving, whether that be in your local church, on a missions team, or somewhere across the world. Study and imitate the attitude and example of Jesus washing the feet of his disciples.

T. Sandvig

Be a servant!

Guaná - Paraguay

Population: 242
The Guaná live in Alto Paraguay and Concepción. They are one of the most culturally integrated and detribalized people in Paraguay. They have lost their traditional techniques of hunting, fishing, and even their way of farming. They have been greatly influenced by the Mennonites.

Pray: For Bible translators; they do not have the Scriptures in their native language.

187

Bible in a year: Mark 6:1-29 / 2 Samuel 15 / Daniel 9

Passion For Missions

> How, then, can they call on the one they have not believed in? And how can they believe in the one of whom they have not heard? And how can they hear without someone preaching to them? And how can anyone preach unless they are sent? As it is written: "How beautiful are the feet of those who bring good news!" Romans 10:14-15

Do you have a passion for missions? When I was seven years old, I had the opportunity to experience missions because my parents decided to quit their jobs and abandon their comfortable lives to serve the Lord as missionaries. During my childhood, I made a decision that no matter the cost, I would be a missionary and be part of the great team of people working to bring the Word of God to unreached people groups in their language.

The call that was growing in me was firmly based on Romans 10:14-15. Throughout my adolescence, those verses continued to encourage me and at the age of 15, they motivated me to raise money for my first short-term missions trip to Bolivia. Actually going, however, was a huge eye opener! On the trip, God worked in my life in many ways. The following two summers, I went to Papua New Guinea and Mongolia on missions trips. The purpose of each trip was to learn, serve, and live out missions. Today, I am a full-time missionary with my husband and children in a country where I never imagined living. Through God's grace, I am serving the people He has given me a deep love for.

MyT. Goddard

How strong can your passion for missions be?

Haratines - Morocco

Population: 51,000
The Haratines live in the north of the Atlas Mountains. They are farmers and speak Moroccan Arabic. They have the New Testament in their language, as well as several films and audios. No known believers live among them; they are 100 % Islamic.

Pray: The light of the Gospel reaches the Haratines.

Drinking Lady

> Jesus answered her, "If you knew the gift of God and who it is that asks you for a drink, you would have asked him and he would have given you living water." John 4:10

Since no one can live without water, I imagine the Samaritan woman in this story had been coming and going from this well for years. Having water is to have life.

She might have had her ups and downs in different situations, but she was probably unconsciously faithful to always fetching water.

I see this woman as any other normal person. I'm sure she had burdens, frustrations, achievements, sorrows, joys, and often contemplated the fabric of her existence.

And then one day (a perfectly normal one, so she thought), four words are unexpectedly said to her that would forever put color into her black and white world: "Give me some water." Over the course of the conversation, she came to understand she wasn't faced with ordinary company, but someone who could give her a life she never knew.

Will you be willing to give water to those in need? Are you letting God use you to be a well that can give living water to the people who need their thirst for eternal life quenched? Remember: you have been promised flowing rivers of living water, "Whoever drinks the water I give will never be thirsty again" (John 4:14). Are you responding to the eternal need of those around you?

D. Duk

> Keep your well available for others to take living water from.

Giay - France

Population: 100

The Giay are Chinese immigrants who are devoted to tourism and gastronomy in France. They continue to retain their ancestral beliefs, with a strong belief to animism and Buddhism. Their language is Bouyei, which has no Biblical resources for evangelism.

Pray: The Giay would soon have the Gospel in their native language.

My Car Has A Little Fish

{ *He said to them, "Go into all the world and preach the gospel to all creation." Mark 16:15*

On several occasions, friends of mine have told me, "I saw your car parked the other day" or they tell me "You passed me and didn't see me." I usually reply, "Are you sure it was me?" or "Are you sure it was my car?" To which, the answer is always the same: "YES, I SAW THE LITTLE FISH ON THE BACK OF YOUR CAR!"

The last time I thought about this, my initial feeling was joy because I knew the decision to buy the little fish carrying the name of "Jesus" had successfully distinguished me from the rest of the cars. The next feeling I had was doubt. I wondered if people could see the "fish of Jesus" in my life; I wondered if they could distinguish me from the rest of the world. I wondered if my life was a powerful testimony each day, which caused others to know I was different. It's not enough to simply say you believe in Jesus; you have to actually live FOR Him, in order for the world to distinguish you from the crowd.

There is a saying in Spanish "es mejor ser que parecer," which means, "it's better to BE than to SEEM." I think this should our daily prayer, rather than just a simple saying. BE a child of God, a person who stands out. BE the "little fish" swimming against the current. To do this, you need to be constantly seeking to grow in your relationship with God, one day at a time. You need to be obedient to what the Father asks of you, read His Word daily, and talk with Him through prayer. Are you living each day with the presence of a "little fish" or are you swimming with the current of the world? Aim to distinguish yourself from the crowd by being a true child of God.
G. Galindo

Aim to be different! That way, the Good News will be brought to all creation.

Kedayan - Brunei

Population: 181,000
The Kedayan are also known as the Malay Bruneians. They differ from other Malays in their culture and language. They practice Islam. It's estimated that Brunei has more mosques per square kilometer than any other country in the world. Their language, Brunei, has a few portions of the Bible translated.

Pray: God would raise up bold Christians who are willing to share Jesus within this Islamic community.

Obedience Through Doubt

{ *When they saw him, they worshiped him; but some doubted.*
Matthew 28:17

Two things in particular characterize the meeting between the disciples and Jesus in this story: worship and doubt. The word "worship" means reverence, which often involves falling prostrate and lacking hesitation.

Even though the disciples react with both worship AND doubt, Jesus doesn't reject them, but receives them. There might be times when doubt creeps into our lives, but we shouldn't let this doubt keep us from obedience in giving God the glory He deserves by fulfilling the Great Commission.

Jesus said all authority has been given to Him in heaven and on earth, which obviously gives unlimited authority to Jesus. This reminds us to fight through the doubt because He gives us a promise: "And surely I am with you always, until the end of the world." This promise of the Lord should be our greatest motivation for obedience. His presence, provision, and comfort are attached to the task that has been given to us. Between worship and doubt, remember to consider the faithful promise of Jesus is always with you.

C. Scott

Be obedient despite the doubt.

Guanacas - Colombia

Population: 700
Agriculture and livestock are the basis of their economy. They have adapted their lifestyle, but retain their animist religion. Only 4% have given their hearts to Christ. They speak Spanish.

Pray: For the Gospel to impact in the lives of the Guanacas.

Never Put the Cart Before the Horse

> *And so the Jewish leaders said to the man who had been healed, "It is the Sabbath; the law forbids you to carry your mat." John 5:10*

We can get ourselves into big trouble when we alter the order of things and a means becomes an end in itself. Religious practices are an excellent way to approach God, but when the ways and customs become more important than the will of God, we become spiritually dry. We lose freshness and religion becomes more important than relationship with Jesus.

We are constantly seeking more order and organization when it comes to the life of God in us and so, it's no surprise we become critical of church leaders and the decisions that are made within the church. If something seems out of place, whether it glorifies the Lord or not, we consider it a mistake. You need to understand God is not logical, His ways are not our ways and He can do things in ways we don't expect. It's sad to see the church of Laodicea described in Revelation 3:14 because they were so well organized they forgot to include the Lord in their church! Another example of God doing something in a way we do not expect is found in John 5. For 38 years, a man had been lying on his bed but because of Jesus, he was now able to walk! The Jewish leaders could not appreciate the miracle, nor rejoice with him, because he was breaking the law of the Sabbath. It's clear the leaders felt like they were walking with God, but instead were just walking with a paralyzed heart. Today, seek a relationship with God and not religion.
W. Altare

Are you aware of the correct order of things?

Jama Mapun - Philippines

Population: 51,000
The Jama Mapun are dedicated to fishing, boat building, and trade between the islands. They are faithful Muslims, strictly observing the 5 pillars of faith. Their language, Mapun, has some portions of the Bible translated.

Pray: For a translation of the New Testament to be completed.

movida

Moving lives

"Motivating young people to grow in their personal relationship with Jesus by training them to use their gifts and talents to better serve their local churches and in world missions".

MOVIDA
International

Moving lives

MOVIDA USA

MOVIDA Germany

MOVIDA
North America

MOVIDA
Europe

MOVIDA
Latin America North

MOVIDA Costa Rica

MOVIDA
Brazil

MOVIDA Ecuador

MOVIDA
Latin America Central

MOVIDA Peru

MOVIDA Bolivia

MOVIDA Paraguay

MOVIDA Chile

MOVIDA
Latin America South

MOVIDA Argentina

MOVIDA is training young people to better serve through...

Short-term Program

Is an opportunity for young people from North America and Europe to travel to South America and invest their time and talents in the kingdom of God. Whether in orphanages, hospitals, or a local church, the short-term program is a unique experience that transforms lives.

CIMA

During "CIMA" young people take part in workshops where they are; trained how the world can be reached with the Gospel of Jesus, taught biblical principals, and exposed to world needs. Through CIMA, MOVIDA motivates and equips young people to be mobilized for world missions and service in their local church!

Materials

MOVIDA uses their materials to mobilize people to pray and support world missions. The magazine UNIDOS and devotional book Explorer connect people with God's heart for the world!

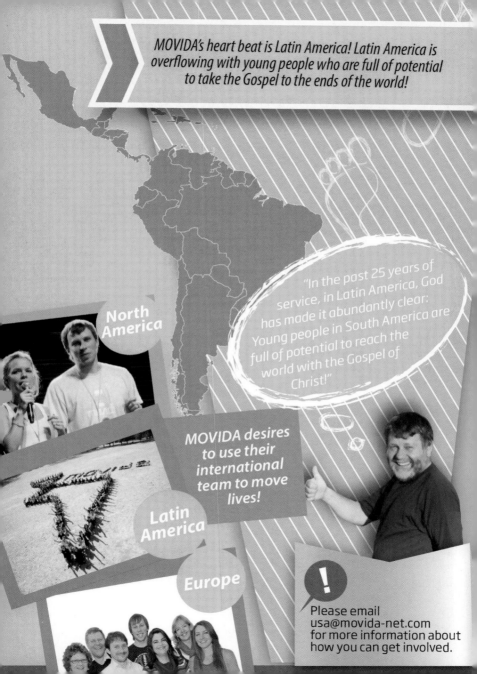

MOVIDA's heart beat is Latin America! Latin America is overflowing with young people who are full of potential to take the Gospel to the ends of the world!

"In the past 25 years of service, in Latin America, God has made it abundantly clear: Young people in South America are full of potential to reach the world with the Gospel of Christ!"

North America

MOVIDA desires to use their international team to move lives!

Latin America

Europe

Please email usa@movida-net.com for more information about how you can get involved.

The Law In Salvation

> *So the law was our guardian until Christ came that we might be justified by faith. Galatians 3:24*

The message of the Word of God revolves around two fundamental truths:
1. God is justice. He cannot overlook the sin of man and it has to be dealt with.
2. God is love. He is the grace that saves the sinner.

Often, we preach about Jesus, who is our incredible Redeemer and author of salvation, but rarely do we talk about the severity of sin and it's consequences. Thus, the common result is a lack of conviction of sin. As Oswald Smith said: "This modern theory of 'accepting Christ' without a deep conviction and true repentance of sin does not result in a genuine born again follower of Jesus."

We must be preach Law and Gospel, sin and salvation. You must give God time to act within each person, to convict sin, and to point out that without repentance, there is no salvation. The conviction of sin is the only proper prelude to saving faith.

O. Simari

Preach the entire truth of salvation!

Idaksahak - Algeria

Population: 2,100
The Idaksahak are a desert nomad people, which makes them very difficult to access. The men speak two languages: Tadaksahak, which is their native language and Tuareg, which they use for trade. There are some Biblical stories translated into their language. They are 100 % Islamic.

Pray: Through trade, they would have contact with Christians and those Christians would be bold in sharing Jesus.

The Right Motivation

> No one who puts a hand to the plow and looks back is fit for service in the kingdom of God.   Read Luke 9:57-62

After Jesus performed the miracle of feeding 5,000, there were many who said "I will follow" but Jesus made sure they understood the cost. Jesus explained to one person He owned no material possessions, not even the basics such as a "place to lay his head."

Jesus called one man to follow Him, but the man said he needed to first deal with family. Jesus wanted the man to follow Him and go preach the Gospel regardless of his family circumstances. The man was more than willing to follow Jesus, but he wanted to first deal with the problems he had. Jesus wanted first place in the man's life. Jesus knew the man would be entangled in thousands of arguments regarding his decision to follow Jesus once he got home. Jesus knew the man's trip home would most likely keep him from deciding to follow.

Jesus wants us to be willing to follow Him, even if He is not offering material advantages. He wants us to follow Him simply out of love. Our love should be first to Him and then to our family. Jesus desires for us to not become distracted by situations that change our desire or decision to follow Him! In life, there are many things that can be "done" to make it look as if one has returned to the path of God. But the real return happens when the right motivation is present and the whole heart is willing to put Him first.

M. de Rodríguez

Check your motives!

Haitian - Haiti

Population: 10,161,000
They constitute 94% of the nation's population. Numerous national disasters have led to a low quality of life and education. Although they are professing Catholics, voodoo and witchcraft are very popular within the population. Roughly 6% of the population believes in Jesus.

Pray: For God to destroy the chains of Satan entangling the Haitians.

The Danger Of Being "Religious"

> { *Thus, by their fruit you will recognize them. Matthew 7:20*
> *(See also John 8:31-47)*

When I entered into the mission field, it became very clear how people are dominated by sin and evil. Many of them were desperate to see their lives improved physically. The mistake we can make as missionaries is to give people the advice: "If you just stop doing bad things, everything in their life will get better." Often, people will learn how a missionary reacts to certain situations and develop a "Christian" attitude, with the goal of deceiving the missionaries into being helped. Missionaries are tempted to believe they are maturing in their faith, so they give them responsibility within the church. Do not be blind to deception. People who search only for earthly treasures will work well when they are with you, but once they are alone, they return to their old lives, which are dominated by sin. Missionaries see this happen time and time again within Christian churches.

Rather than approving or disapproving of their actions, you should work to help them distinguish right from wrong, by teaching them the Word of God. Then, these people will be able to realize what is pleasing to God and what isn't. Knowing God's desires allows people to experience a change of heart – a change of heart that is dominated by repentance and a newfound faith in their Creator.

N. Rivas

Do not make this mistake

Khatri - Afghanistan

Population: 2,400
The Khatri are a group from India. They are dedicated to trade and business. Their main religion is the Sikhism sect of Hinduism. Their language, Punjabi, has an entire Bible translation, as well as the Jesus film and other resources.

Pray: The Word of God penetrates into the hearts of each member of this ethnic group.

JULY

A Letter To Myself

{ *Teach us to number our days, that we may gain a heart of wisdom.*
Psalm 90:12

For a long time, I have maintained a "tradition" in my ministry with young people in Costa Rica and Chile. For me, it is almost a "ritual" to begin and end the year in the following way:

During the first meeting of a new year, I write out plans, goals, and objectives I would like to reach during the year. I find it incredible to start dreaming while standing before God and expressing to him: "This year I aim to...".

This activity motivates me to start the year with enthusiasm. At the same time, it helps me to set priorities. After writing the goals on a paper, I put them in a sealed envelope with my name on it. Then I store the envelope in a box in the church, so I can be reminded daily of the goals I long to reach.

During the last meeting of the year, I open up my envelope along with other members of my team. I often see smiling faces and hear: "Thank you Lord! With your help, I was able to accomplish my goals!" Other times, I see tears from team members who did not achieve the goals they had in mind.

I wonder: How has your year been so far? Has it been a year of growth? Have you reached goals you have set? What goals have you reached? What goals would you still like to achieve? Have you set goals in your spiritual life? Goals for your family? Goals in your profession?

I want to invite you to take a sheet of paper and write down your goals, plans, and objectives for this year. Take the paper and fold it, pray about it, and dream with God so that He may take you through a year of growth!

W. Núñez

At the end of this year, you can evaluate!

Kemei - China

Population: 1,500
The Kemei emigrated from Laos 60 years ago and were placed in the area of Xishuangbanna. They are animistic, burying their dead with pork, rice, vegetables, and a knife. They make contact with "spirits" through a "medium" and they have no Bible translation in their language of Kemiehua.

Pray: They will be set free from their demonic practices and they may come to know Jesus!

Bible in a year: Mark 11:1-14 / 1 Kings 1 / Hosea 4:11-5:3

Renew

> Do not conform any longer to the pattern of this world, but be transformed by the renewing of your mind. Then you will be able to test and approve what God's will is—his good, pleasing and perfect will.
> Romans 12:2

Satan, with all his hosts, works throughout this world to establish a way of life that is contradictory to the way of Jesus. Satan deceives by producing a world that seeks pleasure and fame above all else. Sadly we, the children of God, often value Satan's way of life more than the way of Jesus. Television, internet, money, movies, magazines, friends, and celebrities often try to lead us into a way of life that is not from God.

Today, fight to be obedient and reject Satan's mundane way of life. Focus on Christ and His Kingdom so that He may renew your way of seeing, feeling, and thinking. This will lead you to know God's "good, pleasing and perfect will."

Are you willing to pay the price? Are you willing to reject the foolishness of inappropriate TV, internet, and movies? Today, discipline yourself and teach your brain to know God! Make good use of your time, gifts, and resources! If you have the time to watch the news, surf on the internet, watch movies, or play football; but have no time to get to know God, then something is wrong!

F. Chinatti

Renew your mind!

Guaraní Ñandeva - Paraguay

Population: 1,990
The Guaraní Ñandeva are a small South American indigenous group. They have no translation of the Bible in their native language (also called Guaraní Ñandeva). They do have a small Christian community, but most Guaraní Ñandeva are animists. Missionaries, teachers, and Bible translators are desperately needed.

Pray: God will meet their needs and will bring the Gospel clearly to the Guaraní Ñandeva.

Bible in a year: Mark 11:15-33 / 1 Kings 2 / Hosea 5:4-15

July 3

My Messenger

{ *John wore clothing made of camel's hair, with a leather belt around his waist, and he ate locusts and wild honey... Read Mark 1:1-8*

What a privilege it is to be the messenger of the King of Kings and the Lord of the Universe! We may often think God's messengers live in luxury, but the life of John the Baptist was anything but luxurious. John was poor, lived in the desert, dressed in basic clothes, and ate wild food. Locusts were a main food in his diet!

John knew God had called him for a specific task and his lifestyle matched accordingly. The burdens and cares of this world did not break his character. He did not choose anything for his life that would be a hindrance or prevent him from fulfilling his mission.

The Apostle Paul had a similar lifestyle. He learned to live with less because he knew Jesus gave him the power and endurance to do so (Phil. 4:11-13).

Today, many young people have trouble surrendering to the will of God because they live captive to a lifestyle of materialism and consumerism. They have not understood the great richness of loving and serving God.

We are in this world to serve God and to extend His Kingdom. Jesus promises to give us all we need if we are willing to place ourselves in His hands and take His word to the ends of the earth. I am convinced that the reward of following and serving Christ will be infinitely greater than all the richness this world can offer!

A. Betancur

Are you willing?

Goanese - United Kingdom

Population: 12,000
The Goanese are immigrants from the state of Goa in India. They have been mixing with Englishmen for generations. The Goanese have the Bible in their own language and some have even become Christians. Sadly, their faith is often nominal.

Pray: The Holy Spirit will take control of the Goanese believers and their lives would be purified through Christ!

The First Prayer Request

> *This, then, is how you should pray: "Our Father in heaven, hallowed be your name, your kingdom come, your will be done on earth as it is in heaven." Matthew 6:9-10*

Within the context of this verse, the disciples wanted Jesus to teach them how to pray. This seems to be a strange request, but the lives of the disciples were about to be drastically changed – by teaching them how to pray, Jesus was preparing them for His absence.

Jesus first instructs them to come before God with reverence. He then teaches them to ask God's Kingdom to come on earth so that God's authority will govern on earth, just as it does in heaven. These thoughts beg the question: "Does the Kingdom of God govern your life?"

It is important for us to ask God to bring His Kingdom into our lives. We must ask Him to bring His Kingdom into what we hear with our ears, into what we see with our eyes, and into what we pursue with our energy. God and His Kingdom must reign in our hearts and be the controlling force of our feelings, thoughts, and actions!

It is clear that God's Kingdom rules in Heaven. We must pray that His Kingdom would also rule on earth. When God and His Kingdom govern your life, many people will come to the feet of Christ!

D. Travis

What kingdom governs your life?

Khotogoid - Mongolia

Population: 16,000
The Khotogoids live in Mongolia and have a strong Russian influence. 40% of Khotogoids are atheists, 30% are Buddhist, and 30% claim an animistic religion. Their language is Mongolian Halh, which has a translated Bible.

Pray: They would have access to a Bible, and God would use the Bible to give them an encounter with Jesus!

Bible in a year: Mark 12:28-44 / 1 Kings 4-5 / Hosea 7:3-16

Extending The Claim!

> Enlarge the place of your tent, stretch your tent curtains wide, do not hold back; lengthen your cords, strengthen your stakes.
> Isaiah 54:2

During the time of the Bible, it was common to use tents with large curtains that were staked to the ground with cords. If someone desired to increase the size of their tent, they would have to strengthen their stakes, lengthen the cords, and stretch the curtains wide. This wonderful picture highlights two important biblical principles.

1. Strengthening Stakes.

If you and your church desire to expand and reach more nations with the Gospel, or you desire to send more missionaries, then you must strengthen the local church. Missionaries need a strong church that has a clear vision, is healthy, and is committed to the service of God. If you desire to support missions, you must work to strengthen the local church!

2. Stretching Your Curtains.

The ultimate purpose of strengthening the local church is so that the church may complete the mission it was entrusted to. Do you work for a big, strong, healthy church? For what reason do you work? If the reason is not to fulfill the Great Commission, then your purpose is missing the intended goal. God has given the church a mission to bring the Gospel to the entire world and if the church does not fulfill its purpose, it has failed.

F. Rodríguez

Are you working to strengthen your local church? For what reason?

Ilchamus - Kenya

Population: 34,000

The Ilchamus live on the southern coast of Lake Baringo. They are hunters, but also gather wild fruits. Their language, Samburu, has a few audio Bible stories. Their main religion is animism. Approximately 0.5% of the population is Christian.

Pray: The Ilchamus believers may mature in Christ. Pray for their faith and ask that it will bring an impact to the entire community.

As The Poor Widow

> Calling his disciples to him, Jesus said, "I tell you the truth, this poor widow has put more into the treasury than all the others. They all gave out of their wealth; but she, out of her poverty, put in everything–all she had to live on." Mark 12:43-44

Being a widow in the time of Jesus was very difficult. If a woman was a widow and had no children, she normally lived in the streets with the homeless. Because of this, the words "widows and orphans" became synonyms with the words "homeless and helpless."

When we take a look at this verse in the Greek language, we see the Greek word "bios" is used to describe just what kind of offering the widow gave. The Greek word "bios" is translated to "live" (as in biology, biodegradable, or biography). The main meaning of "bios" is "life", but it can also mean "livelihood." When looking at the verse in its context and when we understand the full scope of the word "bios", we see a much deeper meaning to the sacrificial offering the widow gave.

She gave her entire life, all she had to live on!

Do you believe God can use you and your sacrifice just as He did this poor widow? The global plan of God, to reach the lost, is like a puzzle. Each person plays a unique roll just like every puzzle piece is unique. What is your role in God's global plan? Is your role to give an offering so others can go? This widow gave sacrificially; she gave an offering to the God Most High.

Your offering is not a reflection of how much money you have in your pocket, but rather how much faith you have in God! Do you give sacrificially to the Kingdom of God so His global plan may be reached?

A. Gulard

> Your offering can help take the Gospel to the ends of the earth!

Hitnu - Colombia

Population: 440
The Hitnu live in what is known as the Arauca area, which includes four communities located between the Lipa and Ele rivers. Little is known about this group because of their isolation.

Pray: The Gospel will reach this group in their native language.

The Storm

> *Be strong and courageous ... Joshua 1:9*

This was God's command to Joshua, and it is also God's command for you and me. Strength implies action, and courage involves attitude. These two things, with faith, are the basis for a successful life in Christ. It is imperative to remember to be strong and courageous in the midst of a trial, but it is not always easy to put this into action.

God never leaves us alone. God promises He will be with us. God says, "Do not fear" 365 times in the Bible. Once for each day!

God is faithful in keeping His promises. One of God's promises is that He will not allow you to be tempted beyond what you can bear (1 Corinthians 10:13). This, in simple terms, means the trials you are experiencing will not exceed your ability in Christ. God allows temptations and trials into our lives because He knows that through Christ's power, you will bring Him glory! If you are in the middle of something difficult, you can thank God because He is showing you that you are capable.

Is it possible to be happy in the midst of the storms of life? Yes! We can find joy in the midst of trials because we know they produce patience (James 1:2-4). We must endure to the end because God desires to complete the work He has begun in us!

We are not alone in the midst of a storm. God Himself is with us! He promises to guide us in the best way, even if it does not always seem to be. You can walk with God confidently. Be strong and courageous!

L. Ashmore

Do it!

Java Banyumasan - Indonesia

Population: 8,242,000
The Banyumasan are farmers on the island of Java. They are very prosperous when compared to their neighbors because of their fertile land and technologically advanced equipment. Their main religion is Islam. Only 2% of the population is considered Christian. They have a translated Bible in their native language.

Pray: For the spiritual maturity of local believers. Pray that they may be salt and light in their community.

Bible in a year: Mark 14:1-31 / 1 Kings 8 / Hosea 9:17-10:15

Lord, Send Workers!

> He told them, "The harvest is plentiful, but the workers are few. Ask the Lord of the harvest, therefore, to send out workers into his harvest field." Luke 10:2

This passage is very motivating. Jesus knows the size of the harvest in missions. He knows the lost in your neighborhood, in your city, in your nation, as well as the lost people in the world who have never heard His name.

In this passage, Jesus refers to the shortage of laborers for the harvest. He knows the opposition, the possible violence, the contentment, and the apathy that often keeps Christians from believing they need to go beyond their countries' borders.

But God has taken the weight of responsibility in missions. It is clear we are insufficient to accomplish the task, so we are forced to turn to Him and ask Him to send workers into the harvest field.

Have you experienced frustration in completing your role in the Great Commission? Take courage! Do not be disheartened by the great task because Jesus is in control. You cannot fulfill all the needs around you, which is why Jesus says, "Ask the Lord of the harvest." You must rely on, and rest in God. The Lord is with you!

M. de Rodriguez

Rest in Him!

Kikai - Japan

Population: 13,000
The Kikai live on Kikai Island, north of Okinawa. They typically work peacefully on the sea. Their predominant language is Japanese. Their main religion is Buddhism, with only 3% of people believing in Jesus.

Pray: The church, which has been planted, will continue to grow and will bring light into the community.

Bible in a year: Mark 14:32-72 / 1 Kings 9 / Hosea 11:1-11

Light In the Darkness

{ *This is my Son, whom I love. Listen to him! Mark 9:7*

Often in our lives, we feel attacked and must cling to a Bible verse for strength from the Lord. Life often presents dark circumstances, which make us unsure where to walk or what direction to turn. However, amongst the circumstances, God has promised not to leave His children nor reject them. In those difficult moments, it is important that we hear God's voice from Heaven. During Jesus' Sermon on the Mount, He said: "Do not worry, do not be afraid" (Luke 12:29-34). The prophet Isaiah also reminds us of the responsibility we as Christians fulfill: "I will also make you a light for the Gentiles, that you may bring my salvation to the ends of the earth" (Isaiah 49:6).

The disciples once received a word from the Lord saying: "This is my Son, whom I love. Listen to him." The path of the believer is guided by God's Word. "Your word is a lamp to my feet and a light for my path" (Psalm 119:105). Pronzato Alessandro once said, "While the lamp does not completely eliminate the night, we still walk with the light God has given us."

Through God's Word, we can find the path on which to walk. Through doubts, suffering, and pain, we must continually look toward God, who can do everything and who is saying: "I am here." Even with risk, we must follow Him and walk in faith.

C. Scott

Keep walking in faith!

Jakata - Afghanistan

Population: 1,400
Known for their military power, many Jakaya were recruited into the British and Indian army during World War I. Today, most are farmers or ranchers. Their language is Jakatí and they do not have a Bible translation. The majority of Jakata are Muslim.

Pray: The Gospel may reach the Jakata and they may have a Bible in their language.

Delight In The Lord!

{ *Delight yourself in the Lord and he will give you the desires of your heart. Psalm 37:4*

Often, Christians believe their "will" and God's "will" are in constant conflict with one another. Although we as Christians are fallible creatures, our "will" is not always opposed to the plan of God.

When our life is surrendered to Jesus and we begin walking in relationship with Him, He begins to transform us into His likeness (2 Corinthians 3:18). This means your heart begins to take on the same desires as His heart, His wishes begin to become your wishes, and His dreams begin to become your dreams.

God is madly in love with you and wants the best for you. As John Piper so eloquently puts it, "God knows when you are most satisfied in Him, He is most glorified in you!" Today, delight yourself in the Lord! He has formed you as a new creation (2 Corinthians 5:17). God has given you desires and dreams that are unique to you. The role you are playing in His Kingdom is valuable!

Are you delighting in the Lord? What are the desires of your heart?

S. Langemeier

Take delight in the Lord!

Irantxe - Brazil

Population: 250
The Irantxe live near the Cravari and Papagaio Rivers. Through many diseases, they have nearly been brought to extinction. Their religion is a mixture of animism and Catholicism, and they speak Portuguese.

Pray: Their hearts would be reached with the Gospel.

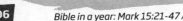

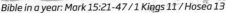

Bible in a year: Mark 15:21-47 / 1 Kings 11 / Hosea 13

A Bad Combination

> { *... if only you fully obey the Lord your God and are careful to follow all these commands I am giving you today. Deuteronomy 15:5*

A few days ago, I almost lost my father because he took the wrong medication, which caused an adverse effect on his body. His experience led me to think that every day of our lives, we make decisions that are either positive or dangerous. This makes me question: can these poor decisions be just as deadly as taking the wrong medication?

In our lives, as believers, we are exposed to the temptations of the world and are in constant battle against Satan. You, as a believer, must make the right decisions in order to walk in the path God has chosen for you. To do this, you must be attentive to what He whispers in your ear! Dangerous combinations of decisions can be as simple as being with ungodly friends and gossiping. Combinations of bad decisions can cause our relationship with Jesus to suffer. Sadly, by the time we listen to the Holy Spirit and realize we are making bad decisions, it is often very painful and difficult to turn back to the path of Jesus.

Taking the wrong physical medication happens because people do not consult a doctor. In the same way, we often choose not to consult God on our decisions, which can be very dangerous in our lives.

I encourage you to seek God's counsel every day. He has a plan for you that He ordained before you were even created!

G. Galindo

Spend time with God!

Gorani - Kosovo

Population: 25,000
The Gorani live in scattered villages in the mountains near the border of Albania. They profess to be Muslim, but their religion is mixed with many animistic rituals. 5% of the population belongs to the Orthodox Church. Their language is Serbian, which has a translated Bible.

Pray: For the Christian church to give a clear witness to their community. Pray that people would come to know Jesus as their savior!

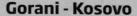

Where Do You Shine?

> *In the same way, let your light shine before others, that they may see your good deeds and glorify your Father in heaven. Matthew 5:16*

Many years ago, we sang a song in my church that I can still remember to this day. The lyrics were:

"Never wait for the moment of a great action, so that your light cannot go far away. From the big life problems to the little moments of attention, shine in the place you are! You can save a lost person with your light, shine in the place you are!" Sometimes we try to wait for the "big moments" to be impactful in the lives of others, or to share with them the light of Christ.

The reality is that the "big moments" in life are few and the "little moments" are plentiful! Often, we do not even recognize the "little moments", but it is in these moments that we have the opportunity to shine for Christ! In our house, in the university, at work, on a bus ride, wherever you are – you can shine for Christ!

We need to learn to put the same amount of effort in both the little and big moments of life. When we do this, others will recognize the Light of Christ and will be brought to God!

Before you step out of your house today, pray and ask God to remind you that you are being used as the light of the world. Pray that He would teach you how to be a light in all moments of life!

W. Bello

Shine where you are!

Kravet - Cambodia

Population: 7,200
The Kravet live along the border of Laos. Their language is Kravet and they have no translation of the Bible. Like most Cambodian groups, they are almost entirely animistic.

Pray: For missionaries to go to the Kravet and preach the Gospel. Pray their hearts would be open to receive the Gospel!

Bible in a year: 1 Corinthians 1:1-17 / 1 Kings 12:32-13:34 / Joel 1

The Full Message

> For I have not hesitated to proclaim to you the whole will of God.
> Acts 20:27

Spanish Pastor Don Vicente Tafalla used to say: "We do not know enough about this experience we call conversion. Often it seems like the 'Good News' stops after the lost person has a spiritual experience. Christians often make a relationship with Jesus look like a trap. We say our words and then wait and hope that the experience becomes real and genuine while never sharing the completeness of the Gospel."

The book of Acts says Christians need to fight to endure in four main areas:

1. To listen and learn the teachings of the apostles.
2. To have unity with brothers of the faith.
3. To take part in communion.
4. To worship God through prayer.

After becoming a Christian, have you sought after these things?

Sadly, many who come to salvation get stuck by not growing in their faith. Many spend their entire life as a spiritual baby because the completeness of the Gospel was never presented to them.

We must explain the fullness of the Gospel so that believers in Christ may experience the fullness of God.

O. Simari

Preach the entire message of the Gospel and do not hide truth from listeners.

Imragen - Western Sahara

Population: 23,100
The Imragen are typically fishermen or farmers. Their culture is very hostile to the gospel because the Imragen are devout Muslims. Their language is Hassaniya Arabic, which has audio stories about Jesus. There are no known Christians in this people group.

Pray: The Gospel of Jesus will transform their lives and missionaries will be called to the Imragen!

With The Armor

{ *Put on the full armor of God, so that you can take your stand against the devil's schemes. Ephesians 6:11*

When you became a Christian, you became a "child of God" and started living a supernatural life. Yes, a supernatural life, which means you are not just a mere mortal. God has formed you into a new creation and has adopted you, for eternity, as a member of His family!

God equips us with what the Apostle Paul calls "armor" so that we can be steadfast in our faith and fulfill God's purposes in our lives! As humans, we fight against invisible enemies. Often those enemies are our sinful nature, the dark ways of the world, dark spiritual forces, and anything else that keeps us from the will of God.

Are you aware that you are in a spiritual war? Every day there are forces of evil planning temptation and problems in your life. Their overall goal is to defeat you by robbing you of your joy in Christ, so that you will not be a witness to others.

I encourage you to put on the full armor of God and take a stand against the devil's plans of defeat. Through Christ's atoning sacrifice, the war has been won! Do not settle for spiritual defeat.

Pescador

Live your life in Christ!

Jamaicans - Jamaica

Population: 2,520,000
Jamaicans typically speak both Jamaican and English. Although Jamaicans have the opportunity to read the Bible in English, there is still no translation in their "heart language" of Jamaican. The church in Jamaica has grown to 30% of the population, but belief in Voodoo continues to grip their culture.

Pray: For the church to mature in their faith, and that they would receive a Bible in their native language!

Bible in a year: 1 Corinthians 2 / 1 Kings 15:1-32 / Joel 2:12-32

Like Jesus

> The Son of Man came eating and drinking, and they say, "Here is a glutton and a drunkard, a friend of tax collectors and sinners."
> Matthew 11:19

On Saturday mornings, while I studied at an institute for ministry, my wife and I agreed to deliver breakfast to a group of people living on the street.

The first Saturday we delivered the breakfast, I prayed and told the Lord, "I am not sure where I'm going, but I'm sure that you have sent me." When it came time to go, I grabbed my Bible and the meals, and took the first taxi I could find. After a 30-minute drive, I saw a boy sleeping on the street. I stopped to talk with him and found out his name was Peter. He explained that he was fourteen years old and was addicted to drugs. I gave him some food and decided to read the Bible with him. After our time together, I found other people in a similar situation. When I approached them, I noticed they were living in the drainage ducts of the city. I later found out these people were ostracized by society and were often called "moles" because they smelt nauseating, had horrible wounds and infections, and were addicted to drugs and alcohol.

On one particular Saturday, as we prayed with them, a few people began to shed tears. I could not help but notice that their prayers were sincere. I then decided to say something I will never forget. I said, "We have no friends, we are all rejected."

It's interesting how the religious criticized Jesus for His friends. Jesus was criticized for being a friend and living with those who were known as the outcasts of the Jewish society.
G. Rivas

Are you friends with the "outcasts" of your society?

Java Mancanegari - Indonesia

Population: 18,545,000

The Mancanegari grow rice, corn, soybeans, and tobacco on the island of Java. They live in fertile soil, which allows up to four harvests per year. Their religion is Islam. It is estimated only 3% have responded to the Gospel message. They speak Javanese, which has a translation of the Bible.

Pray: For a desire within their hearts to know the Word of God and have a relationship with Jesus!

Get Involved

> Then Jesus came to them and said, "All authority in heaven and on earth has been given to me." Read Matthew 28:18-20

Within this passage, we see how an "impossible" mission can be transformed into a "possible" mission. The impossible becomes possible because Jesus, the director of the mission, is sending His disciples out with authority. What about you? Are you involved in the supreme task Jesus has entrusted to His church?

If we are to be involved in God's mission, it is important to know God's heart. I grew up going to church. Although I did not understand my need to be forgiven, I always had a desire to be involved in the work of the church. Growing up, I had no understanding of the global mission of God. When I was 17, God changed my life. He opened my eyes to His patient and tender heart. When I began to know Him in a personal way, my desire and understanding to serve Him only grew! As my faith grew, I became aware of my responsibility to reach the world with the Gospel of Christ. Has your life been changed by the love of God? Do you have a desire to get involved in the mission Jesus has made possible? Nothing is more important than taking part in God's glorious mission to reach the world with the Gospel!

H. Ziefle

What are you waiting for?

Jahanka - Senegal

Population: 47,000

Jahankas are known to be strict Muslims. They earn their living by providing religious services for other Muslims. Their language, Jahanka, has some audio Bible stories.

Pray: Jahanka leaders would come to know Christ. Pray their influence would lead others into a relationship with Jesus.

One Body, Many Parts

{ *As it is, there are many parts, but one body.*
Read 1 Corinthians 12:20-25

It is easy to underestimate the power of different members in the Body of Christ. When we look at people, we often minimize their capability to serve. We judge them by their personality, background, economic status, physical appearance, talents, and spiritual gifts. In John 13:35, Jesus told His disciples, "By this, all will know that you are my disciples, if you love one another." Is the world recognizing you by your love for others? Do not allow pride, selfishness, immaturity, or sin to take root in your heart. Allowing these into your heart can cause division in the Body of Christ and can hinder the world from hearing the Gospel.

Wherever God calls you, make it your top priority to live in harmony with other believers. Let your love for others be a testimony of God's love to the world. When you love others, they will hear you proclaim the Gospel and believe your words.

T. Sandvig

Love the Body of Christ!

Japrería - Venezuela

Population: 200
They live north of the Sierra de Perija. Their knowledge of the Gospel is limited because the Bible has not yet been translated in to their native language of Japreria. It is estimated 4% are Christians.

Pray: For the Bible to be translated into their language.

Total Obedience

> And being found in appearance as a man, he humbled himself by becoming obedient to death—even death on a cross! Philippians 2:8

Why would Jesus go through so much sacrifice and humiliation? For humans, it's incomprehensible to understand the fullness of the sacrifice Jesus made. Jesus is the creator of everything and is adored by angels, but He voluntarily surrendered His status to come to earth. He willingly became human and experienced the same needs, constraints, and temptations as we do. It is incredible to think Jesus, the God of the universe, was a baby who needed a mother´s care and a father's provision.

Jesus willingly made this sacrifice because He knew it would result in salvation for sinners like you and me. He voluntarily surrendered His status, and fulfilled the task His father entrusted to Him. Jesus remained obedient through the most cruel, painful, and humiliating death.

The sacrifice Jesus made was for the right of humans to be declared righteous before God! Therefore, be sensitive to those who do not know Jesus. Live with passion, sharing His love with those around you. Live in obedience to God!

G. Vergara

What prevents you from surrendering total obedience to God?

Khoja - Kuwait

Population: 2,300

Khojas are immigrants from Pakistan. Almost 100 percent of the population is Muslim. Their language, Gujarati, has the entire Bible translated, but they continue to reject Jesus.

Pray: God would open their spiritual eyes so they recognize their need for Jesus.

Attitudes

> If anyone cause one of these little ones – those who believe in me – to stumble...If your hand causes you to stumble, cut it off...Have salt among yourselves, and be at peace with each other.
> Read Mark 9:42-50

This passage takes place after the disciples had finished arguing about who the greatest was (Mark 9:33-37). After arguing, Jesus tells them they are to be salt in the earth by respecting and living at peace with others. As Jesus spoke these words, salt was considered to be something that "preserved". To be salt meant to preserve peace within the community.

The Lord warns not to wrong others. He declares harsh implications when our actions cause others to stumble. Mark 9:38-41 speaks about the disciples wanting to stop a man from doing good because he was not part of their specific group. Jesus warns the disciples not to hinder the man just because he is not a part of their group. He then rejoices because of the good the man had accomplished.

Take the words of Jesus seriously. Do not hinder others from experiencing the love of God. Live at peace with those around you. Your responsibility, as a Christian, is to serve and love others!
C. Scott

Are you judging others or do you walk in love?

Boii – Czech Republic

Population: 100
They are a celtic tribe of Gallic background. Their main language is English and they are predominantly Roman Catholic. They fervently participate in Catholic festivities.
Some have accepted the Gospel, but they suffer from persecution.

Pray: Boii believers will be faithful to Biblical truth.

Let Us Pray Different

> Then you will call on me and come and pray to me, and I will listen to you. You will seek me and find me when you seek me with all your heart.
> Jeremiah 29:12-13

Do you know how important prayer is in your life? Maybe you do, but it will have zero effect unless you implement it into reality. When looking at the story of Daniel, a man God raised up to be one of the most important officials in King Belshazzar's empire, we realize time is a limited resource. Nevertheless, Daniel still chose to invest his time in prayer. Daniel did not change his priorities even when he became a ruler, but rather he continued to take time to seek God in private.

We are vulnerable when we don't take time to pray. Oswald Sanders once wrote, "The greatest men on the earth are the ones who pray. I do not mean those who talk about prayer, nor those who explain how to pray, but those who take the time to pray. Not that they have time. They take time from other activities they could be doing. That activity might be important and urgent, but it is less important and urgent than prayer."

Looking at Jeremiah 29:12-13 shows how valuable prayer is. You must see prayer as a dialogue with God, rather than a monologue of requests. When praying, you may sometimes be at a loss of words. Do not worry, it is during this time God often speaks to the heart! Psalm 5 says, "In the morning, Lord, you hear my voice: in the morning I lay my requests before you and wait expectantly." Our world seems to go faster and faster, but God's spirit is reflected in our lives when we make time to spend with Him!

W. Altare

A missionary heart is grounded in prayer!

Khoton - Mongolia

Population: 11,000
They are natives of Mongolia. The majority are Buddhists, but 20% still follow their ancient animistic religion. Their language, Kalmyk-Oirat, has an audio translation of the New Testament.

Pray: For the distribution of the audio Bible. Pray it will bring the Khoton to know Jesus.

Without Prejudice And Discrimination

> "Nazareth! Can anything good come from there?" Nathanael asked. "Come and see," said Philip. John 1:46

Within this passage, the disciples were being called by Jesus to join Him in the work of the Kingdom of God. During this calling, a confrontation of expectations was revealed. The culture, symbols, and worldview of Nazareth became the target of preconceptions, prejudices, and discrimination.

Being a disciple of Jesus meant to break these preconceptions and to proclaim the Kingdom of God with new values and feelings, motivated by love, from the presence of God in their hearts. Our society develops "expectations" marked by hierarchy and social class division, but each person has the right to form their own identity. We must resist any type of prejudice. Prejudice is the result of human sin. Jesus died and rose again so that we may have a full and abundant life. We must create conditions that invite all people to participate in the promised abundant life Jesus has offered.

Philip extended the invitation to Nathanael by saying, "Come and see." You can also invite people to break the expectations created by society. You can create a community of brothers and sisters and live together in the abundant life of Jesus Christ!

M. Gomes

Come on!

Java Osing - Indonesia

Population: 365,000
They value family and hospitality to travelers. They work diligently with farmland and livestock. Their religion is Islam, but they are also greatly influenced by Hinduism. There are a few Christians, but they suffer under great persecution. Their language is Javanese.

Pray: For the protection of believers so they may provide a strong testimony of God's Grace.

Living A Life Of Worship

> Then God said, "Take your son, your only son, whom you love–Isaac–
> and go to the region of Moriah. Sacrifice him there as a burnt offering
> on a mountain I will show you.' Genesis 22:2

In the time of Abraham, worshiping often meant to sacrifice an animal and present it as a burnt offering to the Lord. The first time worship is used in the Bible is in a context we would find hard to identify with. As a parent, Abraham was asked to sacrifice his own son to worship the Lord. When Abraham and Isaac traveled up the mountain, Abraham told his servants to wait while he and Isaac went to worship. Abraham believed God would provide a sacrifice. His decision to walk in faith, knowing God would provide, was a sign of his complete obedience to God.

Worshiping God is not confined to the four walls of a church. Worship often takes place in the midst of a difficult life circumstance. Abraham was asked to sacrifice his own son. He was being challenged to worship on a deep level. His obedience reflected his desire to obey God at all costs. Abraham's obedience was worship!

Worshiping is much more than singing praises to the Lord in your church. Worship is more than having a special place or set aside time to honor God. It is more than the ability to say a prayer you have memorized by heart and it is also more than lifting up your hands in admiration. Worship is a lifestyle. It is living in such a way for others to see and imitate!

M. Chiquie

Are you worshiping?

Inga - Colombia

Population: 23,000
They are located in an area known as Putumayo. From their cattle, the Ingas provide the majority of the milk for the country of Colombia. They are bilingual, speaking both Spanish and Inga. It is estimated only 3% are born again Christians. Many Ingas follow Catholicism mixed with their indigenous religion.

Pray: For the Inga's to have a deeper understanding of the Gospel.

Bible in a year: 1 Corinthians 9/2 Kings 1-2 / Amos 7

Are You Blind?

{ *...All I know is that I was blind but now I see. Read John 9:1-41*

Within this passage are two different types of blind people. One type was blind physically and the other was blind spiritually. The people who were blind spiritually were the Pharisees because they refused to acknowledge God had sent Jesus. The Pharisees didn't want to acknowledge the miracle Jesus had done through the blind man. This was because the Pharisees believed nothing should take place on a Sabbath, or it would be considered sin. Since the miracle had taken place on the Sabbath, they were furious.

The Pharisees doubted the reality of the miracle, so they often questioned and harassed the blind man. When he answered to the constant questioning and harassment he repeatedly said: "All I know is that I was blind, but now I see." To be spiritually blind is much worse than being physically blind. Although all evidence suggested what happened was as miracle, the Pharisees not want to acknowledge what God had done. They did not want admit Jesus was the promised Messiah sent by God!

It is important to realize the Pharisees were "religious" people. They thought they were following the God of the Bible. In our lives, we must fight against spiritual blindness. It is not always easy to want to believe the miracles God can do. Often, we are so caught up in our church structure, looking proper, and how we believe God functions that we don't see God's hand at work. Our heart is easily hardened. Jesus opened the eyes of the blind man and he was able to recognize and believe Jesus was the Son of God. The blind man not only received physical sight, he received a kind of sight more important: spiritual sight.

How is your spiritual sight? Have you let God work in your life so you can see His hand at work?
N. Rivas

Acknowledge the work of God!

Jebala - Morocco

Population: 1,127,000
They live as farmers and are one of the leading producers of wheat and barley. The Jebalas who live close to the Mediterranean are more prosperous and usually work in cities with multiple professions. They speak Moroccan Arabic, which has a New Testament translation. The majority follows Islam.

Pray: The Word of God would powerfully come into their hearts.

Bible in a year: 1 Corinthians 10 / 2 Kings 3 / Amos 8

Small Things For God

> It is too small a thing for you to be my servant to restore the tribes of Jacob and bring back those of Israel I have kept. I will also make you a light for the Gentiles, that my salvation may reach to the ends of the earth. Isaiah 49:6

Who is God speaking to in this passage? From verse 7, we know God is speaking to Isaiah, but through prophecy we know God desires to use all believers in His mission. This passage speaks to every servant of God who has been despised, hated, or has said: "My work has been for nothing. I have spent my strength for nothing" (verse 4). It is possible for God to leave you content in the small world you have created, but He desires to use you for His bigger plans! Today many pastors, elders, and churches feel small, weak, and poor. The majority of these people are seeing their mission with a small vision. Their plan and purpose is to serve only on a local or national level. It is common for this small scale of thinking to be considered noble and the best use of resources. In the eyes of God, serving only locally is a small thing. God has created his church to be the light of the world and salt of the earth! God has created believers to go and preach the Gospel to every person, to make disciples of all nations, and to be His witnesses to the ends of the earth. What is the size of your mission? Are you limiting the size of God's global mission? God has plans that are bigger than you!

F. Rodríguez

You can do it!

Kiorr - Burma

Population: 10,000
They originate from the Yunnan province in China, but were driven out for having a different culture. Their religion is Buddhism and their language is Kior. Very few Kiorrs have heard the Gospel. They do not have access to a Bible.

Pray: For Christian groups within Burma to share their faith with the Kiorr.

Giving For Missions

{ *Each of you should give what you have decided in your heart to give, not reluctantly or under compulsion, for God loves a cheerful giver. 2 Corinthians 9:7*

It is God's desire for everyone to give financially to missions! Giving is more than just a good idea; it is a command! When I was 16, I realized for the first time this verse applied to my life. During this time, God had given me a job working in a restaurant. While I was working I met a missionary family who had four children and were serving in Papua New Guinea. I knew the missionaries lived by faith and were supported through the gifts of believers. In my heart, I made the decision to support them with $20 per month. I knew $20 was not a lot of money, but I knew God would use the offering to help the couple in sharing Jesus with those who had not yet heard the Gospel! I knew because they were serving, people in Papua New Guinea would hear about the love of Jesus in their own language! It was such a joy for me to be able to give. It was an honor to be a blessing in their lives and ministry! I did not feel it was a burden or obligation because I knew God deeply loved the missionaries and the people in Papua New Guinea. Are you giving to missions? If you are not, I encourage you to start cheerfully supporting missionaries who are going to the nations!

MyT. Goddard

Invest your money wisely!

Izhorians– Sweden

Population: 14,000
Their first language is Ingrian. Many proclaim the Christian faith, but their faith is very nominal.

Pray: For spiritual awakening and a hunger to know the Word of God.

By Many Or By Few

> Jonathan said to his young armor-bearer, "Come, let's go over to the outpost of those uncircumcised men. Perhaps the Lord will act in our behalf. Nothing can hinder the Lord from saving, whether by many or by few. 1 Samuel 14:6

In this passage, Jonathan is investigating the size of the Philistine army. He crawls to the edge of a cliff and sees before him an innumerable group. He knows the army he is fighting in, Saul's army, has far less people and weapons. Jonathan realizes his army is inferior to the Philistines in every area but one.

Jonathan was the only one who understood the advantage his army had. In faith, Jonathan asked his armor bearer to go with him into possible danger. Jonathan told the armor bearer the Lord could win any battle, regardless of the amount of warriors they would face. He knew a victory from the Lord did not depend on the numbers or experience within his army.

In faith, the armor bearer agreed to go with him into the dangerous situation. Together, they believed God could deliver their enemies into their hands. While they were walking, the enemy initiated battle and the two responded and triumphed in the attack.

Do you feel disheartened? Do you feel you are facing overwhelming odds? God can take any misfortune and turn it into a victory! Trust in the Lord and let yourself be used by Him. He will direct your steps and protect you! The battle belongs to the Lord.

F. Chinatti

Be brave!

Java Pesisir Lor - Indonesia

Population: 33,999,000

They are the biggest people group in Indonesia. They live throughout the entire country. Traditionally, they are farmers or fishermen, but many are learning professions in the developed city. The majority are Muslims. It is estimated only 3% are Christians.

Pray: For the Gospel to reach more hearts among the Java Pesisir Lor.

Humility Before All

> Do not rejoice that the spirits submit to you, but rejoice that your names are written in heaven.   Read Luke 10:17-21

Jesus sent His disciples into the world to preach. He sent them with authority and the ability to overcome all power from the enemy. In Luke 10:19, Jesus promises His disciples they will be protected. He said to them, "nothing will harm you."

In ignorance, the disciples became proud and boasted about the fact spirits submitted to their commands. They foolishly forgot the authority was not their own, but rather given to them by Jesus. Jesus reminds the disciples the greatest joy they could have is having their names written in Heaven. Jesus knew salvation was the most important thing they could receive.

Like the disciples, the Lord desires to strengthen you. He desires for you to deliver His message of salvation to the world. When you deliver His message, you do not have to fear forces of evil. God has promised protection. When you are preaching the Gospel, you are fulfilling a responsibility. God desires to empower you as an instrument of His love! Today praise Jesus for salvation. Praise Him for using you to be a blessing in the lives of others!

M. de Rodríguez

Rejoice!

Koroshi - Iran

Population: 400
They strictly follow Islam. Their native language, Koroshi, has no translation of the Bible. No known missionaries are working among them. They urgently need to hear the Gospel of Jesus.

Pray: For the light of Christ to shine into the darkness surrounding the Koroshis.

Prodigals

> "My son," the father said, "you are always with me, and everything I have is yours." Luke 15:31

The parable of the prodigal son is about a father who loves unconditionally. It is important to understand unconditional love is often accompanied by suffering. For example, a parent's love is often unconditional, but when children reject their parents, great sadness is experienced. Unconditional love involves being patient and merciful when pain is encountered. Unconditional love accepts, celebrates, and welcomes those who return with a repentant heart.

The Heavenly Father wants His children to enjoy His affection, joy, and intimacy. He does not force His love, but is patient. The Heavenly Father longs for His children to get involved in His interests. He says, "My son, you are always with me, and everything I have is yours." The Father unites His children by being fair, loving, and bringing peace into relationships. He strives for His children to be free to love. Do you know the loving heart of the Father? He is always ready for you to come and celebrate!

C. Scott

How do you react toward "prodigals"?

Jiiddo - Somalia

Population: 42,000

They come from a town plagued by drought and famine. Almost all Jiidoo children are malnourished and dependent on international aid for food. Their religion is Islam. They do not have Biblical resources in their native language, Jiiddu.

Pray: International aid would connect the Jiiddos with Christians who would witness to them.

The Widow Of Zarephath

> *She went away and did as Elijah had told her. So there was food every day for Elijah and for the woman and her family.*
> Read 1 Kings 17:9-16

God cares for you, even when you doubt it. When you feel forgotten and alone with no clear direction, remember God is mindful of you and your situation. Life can be difficult and you will often find yourself in situations appearing impossible, but God is always with you.

In this passage the widow was in a very difficult situation. She lived in a town called Zarephath, which means "abundance". Nevertheless, she was in drastic need of basic necessities! To make matters worse, her area was experiencing a terrible drought. In her misfortune, all she had to eat was a little oil and flour.

One day, she began gathering sticks for a fire. She was preparing for what she believed was her last meal. As she was gathering the sticks, she met the prophet Elijah. He told her to prepare a meal for him and explained if she did, God would not allow her flour and oil to run out. He proclaimed that if she were faithful, her and her son would always have food to eat. Although it seemed contrary to logic, she obeyed and God responded with endless food for Elijah, the widow, and the widow's son.

The widow is a wonderful example of someone living in a difficult situation, but still having faith and trusting God! God rewarded her for her faith! Are you experiencing something difficult? Trust in the Lord and He will surprise you!

L. Ashmore

God will surprise you!

Kekchi - Belize

Population: 17,000
They have the Bible, Jesus film, and an audio of the New Testament translated into their language. Their church is large, but nominal. Their faith is mixed with their ancestral religions. They are in need of workers willing to disciple believers.

Pray: The word of God would be understood by Kekchi believers.

Bible in a year: 1 Corinthians 14:26-40 / 2 Kings 9 / Jonah 4

Always Give Your Best

> The warden paid no attention to anything under Joseph's care, because the LORD was with Joseph and gave him success in whatever he did.
> Genesis 39:23

Have you ever heard: "If God would give me the opportunity, then I would do my best", or "If I had more money, I would support others", or "If I had a job, I would wake up earlier and take advantage of my day"? We often make contingent statements claiming to improve our habits if we experience a hypothetical future.

Jesus clearly communicated those who live faithfully will "little" will be given the opportunity to be faithful with "more." Joseph is a tremendous example of this truth! Joseph was a dreamer, but he never dreamed he would be sold as a slave or put in prison. Nevertheless, he found himself confined in the walls of a cell. In such a situation, the majority of people would have given up, but Joseph remained faithful and gave his best with the little he was given.

While being in prison, he helped both an Egyptian leader and a prison guard. After remaining faithful through his difficult circumstances, God placed him in a position where he was able to be a blessing for the people who originally sold him as a slave.

God was with Joseph in the same way God is with you (Matthew 28:20). It is possible your circumstances are not as extreme as Joseph's, but it is still crucial to be faithful in your current situation. Are you are living in a place you do not like or studying a subject you do not enjoy? Remain faithful in your struggles!

H. Bascur

Give your best!

Javanese - Indonesia

Population: 15,454,000
They have the most Christians in Indonesia because they account to 8% of the total Indonesian population. Many are passionate Muslims. Some have rejected Islam and have a spiritual hunger for truth. The Bible is translated into their native language of Javanese.

Pray: God would touch their lives and open their hearts to the Gospel. Pray for special protection for those who are already believers.

The Glory Of God

> *This was the appearance of the likeness of the glory of the Lord...*
> *Ezekiel 1:28*

Welcome to "The Interview!" Today we will be hearing from the prophet who claimed to see the glory of God! Lets listen in....

- Hi there! I read in the Bible that you saw the glory of God. Is that true??
- Yes, I remember it like it was yesterday.
- Please tell us about it so we can know what God's glory is like!
- Okay, it is hard to believe, but I saw what looked like a hurricane, fire, and 4 glowing figures!
- Hey ummmm, I don't really understand, could you be a bit more specific?
- Of course, the four figures I saw looked like a man, lion, bull and eagle. The creature moved and it was faster than lightning. It had wheels, a vault, lightning, and something that looked like a throne. It had some human characteristics, but from the waist up it looked completely different than from the waist down! I also saw a very beautiful rainbow! And, well yeah... That was the glory of God!
- Hey man, what you are saying makes no sense at all! How can that be the glory of God?
- What do you want me to say?! This is what I saw! While my mind was trying to comprehend everything, I was so overwhelmed I fell on the ground and worshiped! God's glory is indescribable, it so big our minds can't fathom it. Instead of trying to fathom God's glory through my experience, why don't you just experience His glory for yourself? Jesus said: "Have I not told you that if you believed you would see the glory of God?"

Nothing is better then experiencing the glory of God! Today, experience and see God in your own life. Pray and ask God to give you your own personal experience with Him!

W. Núñez

See the glory of God with your own eyes!

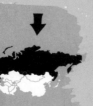

Kumandins - Russia

Population: 3,000
They live in the northern region of Eurasia, in the Ural Mountains. Their language is Russian. 70% of Kumandins believe an animist religion and the other 30% are considered atheists.

Pray: An interest to know God would begin to grow in their hearts.

AUGUST

Preparing For Missions

> { . . . Can we find anyone like this man, one in whom is the spirit of God? Genesis 41:38

When we think of missions, we often believe, under the guidance of the Holy Spirit, everything will harmoniously fall into place. We often believe God will show us the specific mission field, hand us the perfect academic preparation, provide us with secure finances, give us the ability to easily adapt to the new host culture, and produce a highly successful ministry. Sometimes, all these things fall into place, but often they do not.

Joseph did not hear a call from God, nor did he have time to prepare for his missionary journey. His brothers sold him as a slave to a country totally foreign to him. Joseph had many "ups and downs" in his life. He went from being the favorite son to becoming a slave. After working as a slave, he became a servant in the house of Potiphar. While he was a servant, he was sent to prison because of a woman's lies. After some time, he began to gain the confidence of his superiors and ended up helping a senior government official get out of jail. He then asked the official to intercede with the Pharaoh on his behalf. Joseph was convinced he would have freedom, but the ungrateful official forgot. Joseph spent another two years in jail.

When the time finally came, Joseph governed the entire country. He was also able to reunite with his brothers and forgive them for selling him into slavery (Genesis 37:39-45).

Do you want God to prepare you for the mission field? Expect the "ups and downs," and stand firm!

M. Eitzen

The result of following Jesus is wonderful!

Western Guarani - Paraguay

Population: 2,155
Also known as Guarayos. Guarayos have the whole Bible translated in their language. They have established churches with indigenous leaders and teachers, but they need more preparation to face the challenge of reaching their people.

Pray: For the leaders and Bible teachers as they prepare for service.

Bible in a year: 1 Corinthians 16 /2 Kings 12-13/ Micah 3

Jesus' Comprehensive Ministry

> *Jesus went through all the towns and villages, teaching in their synagogues, proclaiming the good news of the kingdom and healing every disease and sickness. Matthew 9:35*

This verse summarizes Jesus' ministry on earth. Jesus went through towns and villages, addressing people in their entirety: mind, spirit and body. Jesus addressed the mental aspect of people by teaching in their synagogues. He addressed the spiritual aspect by proclaiming the good news of the Kingdom and He addressed the material aspect by healing every disease and sickness. Jesus saw the importance of meeting all human needs. He knew a healthy relationship between man and God was crucial. Jesus understood people should be cared for completely, in all aspects of their life.

Our ministry, as Christians, must also be comprehensive. We must address mind, spirit, and body of those who are lost and broken. In addressing these three aspects, we allow for people to fully experience Jesus' love. The more comprehensive our service is, the closer we come to following the example of the Son of God!

F. Rodríguez

Is your ministry comprehensive?

Jofra - Libya

Population: 32,000
Jofras are nomads in the Sahara desert. They are dependent on animals for food, transportation, and raw materials for making clothing. Their language is an Arabic dialect and 99% are Muslim.

Pray: For God to open doors so they may have access to the Gospel.

Disobedience Is Not An Option

{ *If your right eye causes you to stumble, gouge it out and throw it away... And if your right hand causes you to stumble, cut it off and throw it away. Read Matthew 5:27-30*

Does Jesus really support doing outrageous things like taking a knife and removing part of the body? Removing limbs does not sound like something what Jesus would do. How can a passage like this relate to a healthy relationship with God?

All people struggle with sin, but God desires to help people overcome sin's power. God wants to mold and change us to become more like Him. The nature of God is holy, which is why He commands us to be holy. The Father, in His goodness, wants us to be like Him and walk in His ways! God desires obedience in your relationship with Him. He longs for you to surrender your life and soul. The closer you are to Him, the easier it is to follow His commands. When you are disobedient, your relationship with your Heavenly Father is hindered. When you are not walking in relationship with God, it causes sin to look more attractive and leads you on a path of darkness. Being united with the Lord and walking in obedience to Him will set you free from the power of sin. Being free from sin is the desire of the Father's heart, which is why Jesus uses an extreme parable to show how important remaining in relationship with Him is.

D. Travis

> It is better to remove the sin.

Karelians - Finland

Population: 11,000
Karelians are people of Russian origin who live in the province of Oulu. The majority of Karelians belong to the traditional Orthodox Church. Their language is Karelian, which has some portions of the Bible translated.

Pray: For a depth in their relationship with Jesus and for believers to boldly share their faith.

Do What I Say, Not What I Do

{ *Fathers, do not exasperate your children; instead, bring them up in the training and instruction of the Lord. Ephesians 6:4*

Those who have been called to be parents have been given a great blessing. With this blessing comes the great responsibility to be messengers of the Kingdom in the lives of children. Children can then respond to the message of the Kingdom in one of two ways: 1) by living according to the Word of God or 2) by surrendering to the desires of the flesh.

Jesus was a son who chose, each day, to honor the name of His Father. Jesus lived in accordance to the Word of God instead of the desires of the flesh. In my life, I stumble every day as a Father. It is a constant struggle against an attitude of isolation from God. I get angry with myself for "telling" my children instead of "showing" them what a life according to the Word of God is. It is my desire to be in the Spirit and walk in God's steps with not only my words, but also my actions. Children are the product of your investment into their lives. At the end of the day, children will reflect the behavior you have modeled before them. You have been given to them as a guide for living a life according to the Word of God.

Regardless if you have children, you should seek to revise your inner desires, which will also result in an exterior change. When your interior motives are in line with God's desires, your outward actions will reflect a message in accordance with the Word of God. Do not allow your message to be: "Do what I say and not what I do." You can choose to reflect a life according to the Word of God!

G. Galindo

Be intentional in your actions!

Kabaloan - Philippines

Population: 800
Kabaloans are a sub-group of the Agta ethnic group. They are the only group who still retain their tribal animistic religion. The majority of Kabaloans live in villages. Some have migrated to the city to work as laborers. Their language is Casiguran Dumagat, which has a translation of the New Testament.

Pray: Those who go to the cities would encounter Jesus and bring His truth back to their villages.

Knowledge Of God

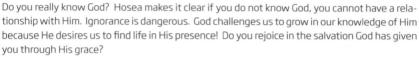

> My people are destroyed from lack of knowledge. Hosea 4:6

Do you really know God? Hosea makes it clear if you do not know God, you cannot have a relationship with Him. Ignorance is dangerous. God challenges us to grow in our knowledge of Him because He desires us to find life in His presence! Do you rejoice in the salvation God has given you through His grace?

John 17:3 says, "Now this is eternal life: that they know you, the only true God, and Jesus Christ, whom you have sent." Eternal life involves knowing God, but what does "knowing" Him mean? Does knowing Him mean attending church, being part of a small group, speaking with spiritual words, or praying continuously? These are all good things, but they do not mean "knowing" God. These things can all be accomplished without truly having a relationship with Him!

In Matthew 7:21, Jesus clearly says, "Not everyone who says to me, 'Lord, Lord,' will enter the kingdom of heaven...." This verse shows the church can house people who do not truly know God. Having a ministry or doing "good works" does not guarantee your place in Heaven! In order to know God, you need to have a deep personal relationship with Jesus! Do you truly know God? Do you know His Word and the desires of His heart? Eternal life is to know Him!

L. Ashmore

You can get to know Him more everyday!

Sorani Kurds - Kuwait

Population: 278,000

Sorani Kurds do not support their government. In Kuwait, they are rejected and excluded. They declare themselves Muslims, but they are nominal in their faith. Their language, Kurdish, has a translation of the New Testament.

Pray: God touches the lives of the Kurds and fills the gap in their hearts.

Eternal Riches

> But God said to him, "You fool! This very night your life will be demanded from you. Then who will get what you have prepared for yourself? This is how it will be with whoever stores up things for themselves but is not rich toward God." Read Luke 12:14-21

Jesus shared this parable to advise His disciples to "be on your guard against all kinds of greed; life is not about an abundance of possessions." Often, missionaries believe the major hindrance of their work is their lack of economical resources. Take courage! He who calls you will also provide for your needs! You do not need to fret about financial problems because God graciously distributes His resources to everyone according to His will.

When God blesses you with His riches, be a good steward of what He has provided. Use His blessings for the work of the Kingdom instead of hoarding it for yourself. It is a temptation to believe our tithes and offerings are the only finances the Lord owns. In this parable, God asks who will get the things you have prepared for yourself when you are dead? Money spent on material possessions will perish, but what we invest in God's Kingdom will last for eternity! Reflect on where you are investing your treasure.

M. de Rodríguez

Are you giving to the Kingdom of God?

Kyerung - Nepal

Population: 1,500

They are Buddhists. Their language is Kyerung, which has no translation of the Bible. They can read the Gospel in Nepali. They are friendly and are often willing to talk with people from different cultures and religions. Although they are open, no known Christians live among them.

Pray: For missionaries to share Jesus with the Kyerungs.

Do You Have A Passport?

> *Therefore go and make disciples of all nations, baptizing them in the name of the Father and of the Son and of the Holy Spirit, and teaching them to obey everything I have commanded you. And surely I am with you always, to the very end of the age.*
> *Matthew 28:19-20*

More than 2,000 ethnic groups around the world are waiting for you to travel to their country! Do you understand why? While the English language we enjoy has "a flood" of more than forty versions, these 2,000 groups are without "a drop" of God's Word in their own language!

Are you ready? Jesus left us a great responsibility in Matthew 28:19-20: "Therefore go and make disciples of all nations, baptizing them in the name of the Father and of the Son and of the Holy Spirit, and teaching them to obey everything I have commanded you. And surely I am with you always, to the very end of the age."

This great commandment involves facing tremendous challenges because it requires investing in new geographical locations, as well as discipling, baptizing and teaching others. For this to be accomplished, it is crucial to continue growing and maturing in your spiritual life. In order to disciple and teach others, you have to keep growing in your own faith in Christ. How can you expect to lead and teach others if you do not experience the wonders of being a child of God in your own life?

Is your passport ready? You can impact one of these 2,000 ethnic groups! They are waiting for you!

MyT. Goddard

Don't wait!

Kamayura - Brazil

Population: 500

They live in the State of Mato Grosso. Before marriage, they receive specific training. The males learn to fight and make tools, while the women learn to make hammocks and cook. They are Animists.

Pray: The Gospel would powerfully change their hearts!

Crossing Barriers

> Although I am less than the least of all the Lord's people, this grace was given me: to preach to the gentiles the boundless riches of Christ. Ephesians 3:8

Paul was given the task to preach. Like Paul, you have been given the same task to fulfill! Your task also involves being active in world missions, but if you want to take world missions seriously, you have to be willing for God to send you to a new geographical location. Out of this mindset, Hans Kasdorf said: "Missions is crossing borders with the Gospel".

When crossing borders, be prepared to face cultural barriers like: racial prejudices, language barriers, and new customs. Overcoming cultural barriers can be a difficult, but with the advancement of new technologies, we are becoming more mobile to reach the world! The airplane and Internet have made overcoming geographical barriers easier than ever, but there are still basic lessons that cannot be forgotten.

Coming into new cultures with a genuine and respectful mind is crucial to missions. Doing this will require much effort and great devotion, but it will help you connect with the hearts of people. Language barriers can also be difficult to overcome, but it is not reason to give up! Although there are many struggles a missionary must face, the greatest struggle often comes from within. Dr. Ricardo Esquivia, a Colombian lawyer, once told me: "Alfredo, the most difficult barriers for a church to overcome are the four walls of its own sanctuary."

Do not be "temple-centered". Have the courage to love others selflessly!

A. Neufeld

Do you have a barrier you can't cross?

Kachchi - Kenya

Population: 64,000
They are a group of immigrants who came from the Indian region of Uttar Pradesh. They have preserved their culture, Hindu religion, and language. Their language has some audio Biblical resources.

Pray: The Gospel will be attractive to their hearts and they will want to know Jesus.

Example Of Love

{ *Be merciful, just as your Father is merciful. Luke 6:36*

God's love is unconditional. His love is that of a true father and because His love is so perfect, it sets a high standard for everyone to love more selflessly! God is gracious and extends His arms equally to all. The Father's love gives freedom. His freedom means we have the ability to leave His house if we so desire, but because His love is so strong, He wraps His arms around us in forgiveness when we return and repent. His love forgives without being resentful or bitter. The Lord's love speaks with authority, but is compassionate and merciful.

Be merciful, as your Heavenly Father is merciful. Forgive others as He continues to forgive you. God celebrates life and is joyful when His children return home. You can always return home to your welcoming Heavenly Father. He longs to celebrate with you when you return! Jesus' model of love shows us how we should love. Follow His model and selflessly love others.
C. Scott

How is your love?

Kurmanji - Portugal

Population: 200 inhabitants
They are a Kurdish people group, who profess Islam. They have the New Testament in their language. There are some Roman Catholics among them, but many follow a very pagan religion. They have a great need to be changed by the Gospel.

Pray: Christians within Portugal would reach them with the Gospel.

Live In Your New Identity

> No longer will you be called Abram; your name will be Abraham, for I have made you a father of many nations. Genesis 17:5

Abram was 99 years old when God revealed Himself to him as the Almighty. After God revealed Himself, Abraham's heart was transformed and he was challenged to live a new life trusting in God. The challenge given to Abraham is the same challenge God is giving you! God's challenge is to walk faithfully in Him, as a perfect creation, with nothing to hide. Perfect does not mean mistakes will not be made. Perfect means taking ownership in being adopted into God's perfect family and thus, seeking to please your Heavenly Father in everything you do.

God made a covenant with Abraham by promising to make his decedents fruitful if Abraham walked faithfully. After the covenant, God changed Abraham and his wife's names and gave them new identities in the Lord. Like Abraham, God made a covenant with you. He made a covenant through Jesus to forgive you, save you from the punishment of sin, and to give you a new identity. The Father has promised to love you unconditionally and guide you with His Spirit. In return, you must put your faith in Him!

When you receive Jesus in your life, you become a new creation. Through the forgiveness of sins, God transformed you and gave you a new identity in Jesus! You were once a sinner, but now in Christ, you are a new creation! You're forgiven, loved, accepted, and adopted as a child of God. Your new identity is being capable, useful, holy, and righteous!

D. Duk

Enjoy your new identity to the fullest!

Kaili Unde - Indonesia

Population: 29,000
They live on the island of Palu Bay. They build their houses on stilts and have copra, cacao and palm plantations. They are devout Muslims, but many seek the help of "ancient healers". Their language, Kaili-Unde, has no translation of the Bible.

Pray: For a translation of the Bible to be made for the Kaili Unde.

Start With What You Have

> { *We have here only five loaves of bread and two fish! Matthew 14:17*

Often, we understand our calling to do good works and ensure the well being of others, but yet we tend to only focus on the things we feel we need. It is a constant temptation to choose to see only the things we do not have and forget everything we have received from Jesus. We easily forget the special gift we start with in our possession every morning: salvation! When we focus on what God has already given us and share it with others, we can be a blessing for many people.

Jesus was not a magician. He did not make a giant fish fall from the sky or loaves of bread grow from the ground. When He fed the 5,000 people with two fish and five loaves, He was simply relying on God's power. The passage tells of a child providing Jesus with the initial food. The child gave everything he had and Jesus used his offering to satisfy the hunger of thousands of people.

God will use your offering to take care of His people! You do not have two little fish and five loaves of bread, but rather you have the Almighty God! God never changes! He lives in you and has promised to never leave you nor forsake you!

J. Segnitz

Take what you have and start!

Lepcha- Bhutan

Population: 9,300
Lepchas live in thick forests in the south of Bhutan. Other ethnic groups in their nation discriminate against them. The majority are Buddhists. They speak their own language, Lepcha, which has a translation of the New Testament and the Jesus Film.

Pray: Biblical resources would be spread throughout the Lepchas.

God Sees You!

> For the eyes of the Lord range throughout the earth to strengthen those whose hearts are fully committed to him. 2 Chronicles 16:9

Have you ever noticed how God is present throughout the entire earth? He is not limited to a local church, city, country or even continent. God loves every country, ethnic group, family, and individual on earth.

God loves everyone in the word, but who will go and tell them about His love? Who will tell people God sent His son to die on the cross for their salvation? Who will tell them God knows their name? Who will tell them He passionately cares about them?

God looks at people individually.

Humans look at outward expressions. People will see you by the amount of money you have, what house you have, where you live, where you work, how many degrees you have, the clothes you wear, or the talents you possess. God looks at inward expressions. God sees your obedience, trust, faithfulness, and perseverance. God sees your heart! For God, you are not invisible!

David was faithful to the Lord when he was tending his sheep, carrying food to his brothers, and playing the harp for Saul. God recognized his faithfulness and rewarded him greatly. Are you being faithful in your life? Are you where God wants you to be? Often, when thinking about going into missions, people feel "insignificant" because of how big the task is. When people do not support you, when nobody believes you are worthwhile, remember God sees you! To Him, you are not invisible!

A. Gulard

The eyes of God are on you!

Ersu - China

Population: 20,000
They are of Tibetan origin. It estimated 98% follow Buddhism, but some Ersus have embraced Islam. Three Ersu languages exist, but they have no translation of the Scriptures. No known Christians live among them because they have not yet heard the Gospel.

Pray: God would reveal himself to the Chinese Ersus and that missionaries would go and translate a Bible.

His Work Of Art

> { *I praise you because I am fearfully and wonderfully made; your works are wonderful, I know that full well. Psalm 139:14*

I had never looked at paintings as an expression of their creator until I had the opportunity to meet Pablo Larrañaga. He is a prominent painter from Argentina who has won many awards for his work. Pablo has paintings exhibited in different galleries all around the world. As I listened to him talk about his paintings, it was very clear he was their creator. Each painting reflected a piece of his character. Every painting he created had meaning, purpose, and deserved a place of privilege in a gallery.

Comparing Pablo's paintings to Psalm 139:14 makes me think of God as the artist of our lives. I imagine God in His workshop creating details to make us unique. I imagine Him making a special place in His private gallery to show us off. I can picture God smiling as He creates each individual because He knows He has created an admirable and wonderful person!

You are His masterpiece, you reflect His character, and you have a purpose!

W. Núñez

> **See yourself with the eyes of God!**

Khasonke - Gambia

Population: 1,800
The majority live simple lives and are educated by their parents. They eat millet, rice, corn, goat meat, lamb and smoked fish. They are Muslims. They have an audio translation of the New Testament in their native language, Xaasongaxango.

Pray: For an understanding of the Gospel and encounters with Christ.

The Mission Of The Messiah

> *The Spirit of the Lord is on me, because he has anointed me to proclaim good news to the poor. He has sent me to proclaim freedom for the prisoners and recovery of sight for the blind, to set the oppressed free, to proclaim the year of the Lord's favor. Read Luke 4:16-19*

In Jesus' public presentation as the Messiah, He revealed the purpose of His ministry by quoting a prophet. He unveiled His ministry by showing it is for those who are suffering. After declaring His ministry, He was rejected by the people. They rejected Him because they expected a Messiah who would be a political figure and would free the Jews by force. Although people had specific expectations, Jesus had a strategy much different than what the people could grasp.

Jesus came not only to free the Jews from physical bondage, but also to introduce a new kingdom, the Kingdom of God. He came with miracles as evidence of the arrival of a powerful king. In Matthew 12:28, Jesus said, "But if I am casting out demons by the Spirit of God, then the Kingdom of God has arrived among you." Jesus came to proclaim His Kingdom and to powerfully set people free!

While on earth, Jesus shared two of the most important characteristics of His Kingdom. In Matthew 5:6-7, He said, "Blessed are those who hunger and thirst for righteousness... blessed are the merciful." Followers of Christ must exhibit justice and mercy because these characteristics are at the heart of Jesus. Today, you are called to live in His Kingdom. You are called to proclaim the Good News and to preach freedom to the suffering world around you. Be the hands and feet of Jesus!

A. Betancur

Let's fulfill our mission!

Lasgerdi - Iran

Population: 1,100

Iran is a country with many restrictions to the Gospel. Lasgerdis do not have a translation of the Bible or missionaries serving among them. They are all passionate Muslims.

Pray: The Gospel reaches the Lasgerdis and brings a radical change in their lives.

A Loving Servant

> { ... *Having loved his own who were in the world, he loved them to the end.* John 13:1

In this passage, Jesus knew the time had come for Him to leave this world and return to the Father. Even the last few hours of His life He spent investing in the lives of His disciples. Even though He knew His earthly life was going to end, He loved His disciples to the end. Jesus was clearly a person who loved. Jesus made time to spend with people. He made sacrifices to meet with His disciples in order to prepare them for what was to come. In Jesus' last moments, He was not selfish. He was not concerned about His suffering or the joy He would soon be experiencing. Jesus remained faithful and continued to teach and love others to the end.

The Father had given Him control over all things. Although He was given total power, He performed one of the most humble acts ever recorded. John 13:4-5 says, "so he got up from the meal, took off his outer clothing, and wrapped a towel around his waist. After that, he poured water into a basin and began to wash his disciples' feet, drying them with the towel that was wrapped around him."

Jesus was a servant to those who did not deserve it. He served those who would eventually leave Him. Jesus demonstrated that divine love never ends. Jesus was a person who loved to the very end!

C. Scott

Are you loving people?

Kalagan - Philippines

Population: 33,000
They live on the island Mindandao, which is located in the south of the Philippines. They are farmers and their main crop is corn. Most Kalagans are Muslim. Their language, Kalagan, has portions of the Bible translated.

Pray: For a translation of the New Testament.

The Perfect Compass

> "For I know the plans I have for you," declares the Lord, "plans to prosper you and not to harm you, plans to give you hope and a future."
> Jeremiah 29:11

Often throughout our lives, we feel discouraged and defeated. We feel as if we have no future because we do not have a clear compass to guide our path. However, we must never forget we have been given God's Word. His Word is like a spiritual compass guiding us to perfection.

God has a plan for you and He desires to show you that plan. He wants to remove the negative thoughts and replace them with His positive truth. God wants to assure you your future is full of hope. In His glory and greatness, He has promised to fulfill your deepest needs. You can confidently cling to Him because He is faithful.

Jesus Christ wants to release you from tomorrow's uncertainties. He wants to offer you His peace and give purpose to your life. Be assured, God gives you hope for the future! When you feel unmotivated and disappointed, do not put your eyes on the circumstances, but rather on God and His faithfulness.

M. Inciarte

God knows the ending of your story.

Kwinti - Suriname

Population: 200
They live on the Northern Banks of the Coppename River. They do not have Scripture in their language, but they have heard the Gospel in English. They lack mature native leaders.

Pray: The Bible would be translated into their language, so they can know Biblical truths.

The Road To Glorification

> For those God foreknew he also predestined to be conformed to the image of his Son, that he might be the firstborn among many brothers and sisters. And those he predestined, he also called; those he called, he also justified; those he justified, he also glorified. Romans 8:29-30

In this passage, Paul presents three stages of redemption: calling, justification, and glorification. In Romans 6:17-22, he speaks of more stages: obedience to the Gospel, liberation of sin, service of God, sanctification, and glorification (eternal life). Paul suggests if a conversion does not produce these fruits, there is reason to doubt the genuineness of the conversion.

Eternal life in Jesus involves sanctification and service; it ends with glorification. This does not mean salvation is a "work" we are required to do throughout our life, but rather, these are different stages experienced within salvation.

Justification and sanctification can be confusing. It is important to understand justification produces sanctification as a fruit. Paul writes against the idea that conversion is the end goal. He suggests salvation is not what someone experiences and then uselessly waits until death. He speaks as if walking with Jesus is a life process. The New Testament supports this idea by proclaiming salvation as a gift of pure grace. After salvation, other fruits will be manifested in their own time. God does not take us from the world when we are converted. He leaves us here so we can bear fruit, serve Him, and bring Him glory!

O. Simari

Show with your earthly life that you are on the way to eternal life!

Menia -China

Population: 1,400
They are a subgroup of the Tibetans, but their language, Ersu, is very different from the rest of Tibet's languages. It is estimated 95% follow Hinduism and the remaining 5% follow animistic beliefs. They have no translation of the Bible.

Pray: A Bible translating project would begin.

Redressed

> *Put on the full armor of God, so that you can take your stand against the devil's schemes. Ephesians 6:11*

Did you know we are in a spiritual battle? We have an enemy fighting against us every day and his name is Satan. Although we are in a battle, Christ has already won the victory through His atoning sacrifice on the cross.

When I was a child, we played with piñatas at birthday parties. I always loved it when the blind folded person broke open the piñata because candy and confetti rained down for me to enjoy. Often, I would get frustrated trying to break open the piñata because of how difficult it was to do without sight.

Working without sight is difficult. Trying to fight a battle blind is even more challenging. Often, we blindly overlook the divided families, broken marriages, corrupt parents, and hurting children in our world. Although Scripture warns us of the battle we are in, many people remain blind to the fight.

Do not fight the battle like a blind folded child hitting a piñata. Ask God to give you spiritual sight for the spiritual battles being fought around you. Clothe yourself with the armor of God and prepare for the battle! God is ready to declare victory!

Pescador

Are you wearing your armor?

Latvians – Latvia

Population: 1,326,000
Latvians have a translation of the Bible and other Christian resources in their language, Latvian. It is estimated 60% are Orthodox, Protestants, or Catholics. However, their faith is very nominal.

Pray: God strengthens the church and for the Christians to be a living testimony of the Gospel.

Real Love

> { *If you love those who love you, what reward will you get? Are not even the tax collectors doing that? Mathew 5:46*

The Mastanawas are an indigenous group who live near the Purús River. They are known to be aggressive and fight with machetes. When visiting the Mastanawas, I experienced their hostility on numerous occasions, but God in His grace protected us from harm. I find it interesting because some of the Mastanawas became our friends, but others in the tribe wanted nothing to do with us. I often found it difficult to form relationships because I sometimes felt the only reason they wanted to become friends was to satisfy their own needs.

While I was visiting, our team had a man who translated our conversations with the Mastanawas. One day, he became very angry with us and walked away. We didn't know what exactly happened, but we later found him hiding and drunk. The next day, I went to look for him. When I found him, I assured him he was still my friend and would always remain my friend, even if he had been drunk. After I said this, his eyes immediately began to shine and he began to trust our team again.

Jesus gave the commandment to love your neighbor. This means loving without judgment or prejudice. It is very easy to love people who love you, but it is difficult to love those who sin against you. Jesus challenges us to love everyone. He desires for you to love those who do not love you!

G. Rivas

> How is your love toward others?

Kikim - Indonesia

Population: 83,000
They are dedicated rice farmers who live on the island of Sumatra. They are faithful followers of Islam and reject all other beliefs. Their language, Malay Central, has a translation of the New Testament and the Jesus film.

Pray: Evangelism resources would be generously shared with the Kikim.

Three Clamors

> Then I heard the voice of the Lord saying, "Whom should I send? And who will go for us?" And I said, "Here I am. Send me." Isaiah 6:8

The word "clamor" means a fiery call for help. In the Bible, three different clamors are clearly proclaimed:

1. A clamor that comes from the earth (Acts 16:9).

Those who do not know Christ cry out for the Gospel. "That night Paul had a vision: A man from Macedonia in northern Greece was standing there, pleading with him, 'Come over to Macedonia and help us!'" Missions means giving others the opportunity to follow Christ.

2. A clamor that comes from Hell (Luke 16:27-28).

Those who die without Christ cry out for the Gospel to be presented to their relatives:

"He answered, 'Then I beg you, father, send Lazarus to my family, for I have five brothers. Let him warn them, so that they will not also come to this place of torment.'"

3. A clamor that comes from Heaven (Isaiah 6:8).

God calls His children to preach the Gospel: "Then I heard the voice of the Lord saying, 'Whom shall I send? And who will go for us?' And I said, 'Here am I. Send me!'"

Are you responding to the clamor? Be bold, so one day you may hear....

MISSION ACCOMPLISHED!

L. Díaz

Listen and respond!

Kiriri – Brazil

Population: 1,500

They live in the State of Bahia. They are animists and perform dances in which people become possessed. They have lost their native language and now speak Portuguese. They are unresponsive to the Gospel.

Pray: God breaks the barriers preventing salvation for the Kiriris.

Humble Servant

{ *Lord, are you going to wash my feet? John 13:6*

During the time Jesus lived, people washed their feet for personal hygiene. Slaves, women, or children did this task for other people, but in the days leading up to Jesus' crucifixion, something incredible happened.

The Gospel of Luke tells a story of the disciples having a dispute about who the most important was. The disciples were willing to argue with one another for a spot on the throne, but they never would have thought to argue over serving one another by washing each other's feet. Instead of serving, they sat down and ate while still being dirty. During all of this selfishness, Jesus did something unimaginable. He came to the disciples, humbled himself and began to wash their feet. He washed even the feet of Judas, who would soon betray him. Although Jesus had all the power in the world, he selflessly washed the disciples' feet.

Jesus did not allow his supreme authority to change Him. He remained humbled and served others. Be confident in your identity in Christ. Do not be defined by your hunger for power.
C. Scott

Are you a servant to others?

Khe - Burkina Faso

Population: 3,000
They live in the south of the country near Sierra Leone. They are farmers and breed chickens. They are animistic. Their language, the Khe, does not have a translation of the Bible. A small and weak church exists, but it is estimated only 3% of the population are believers.

Pray: The church grows and is strengthened in the Lord.

Passionate Commitments

> About midnight Paul and Silas were praying and singing hymns to God, and the other prisoners were listening to them. Acts 16:25

Today, people say Christians do like to make commitments, but the reality is people like to make the commitments which in line with their heart's desires. No one enjoys going to a party they are obligated to go to and no one enjoys giving gifts they are obligated to give. Commitments are a good thing, but it is difficult to endure the suffering of an obligation you do not enjoy.

When commitments are full of passion, energy, and pleasure, they are easy to fulfill. For example, if you are married to someone you passionately love, it is easier to stay committed to the relationship. Another example would be why thousands of people fill sports stadiums around the world every week. They do not fill the stadiums because they are obligated to support a team, but because they are full of passion!

It is a pity when church meetings are seen only as an obligation instead of a passionate commitment to the Lord. Obviously, passion is not a permanent emotion, but a driving force in life. The truth is, passion is contagious! When you surround yourself with people who are passionate for the Lord, you become passionate yourself. The world is full of passionate missionaries like Paul and Silas. They are passionate to reach the lost with the Gospel of Jesus! How do you think the prisoners responded when they saw Paul and Silas' passion for the Lord?

W. Altare

The Lord deserves my greatest passion, not my obligation.

Mugali - Nepal

Population: 7,300
The Mugali live high in the mountains. They normally build their houses with wood, stones, and 3 floors. They are Buddhists. They do not have a translation of the Bible in their native language, Mudom.

Pray: Missionaries would break the geographical barrier and reach them with the Gospel of Christ.

Passion For God

> Phinehas son of Eleazar, the son of Aaron, the priest, has turned my anger away from the Israelites. Since he was as zealous for my honor among them as I am, I did not put an end to them in my zeal.
> Numbers 25:11

"People choose their death by choosing how they live." This phrase is true because the choices we make define our lives. Living in this reality means we must be careful in the decisions we make each day. Our choices will not only affect our future, but the legacy we leave behind.

Have you ever considered what affect your decisions will have on your future children? Phinehas was a dedicated, passionate man of God. He lived in reverent fear of God and out of that fear, brewed a hate for sin.

At one point during history, Israel was so involved in sin, idolatry, and sexual immorality that the wrath of God began to sweep through the nation and kill the leaders and people. In the midst of the suffering, a shameless Israelite appeared with his Midianite wife at the Tabernacle. Phinehas was so outraged by their disrespect for God that he speared both the man and his wife to death.

God was so pleased with Phinehas' passion that He stopped the killing of the leaders and people. God then proceeded to make a promise of eternal priesthood for Phinehas' children. God promised his name would be remembered for generations. Your zeal for the Lord can change history! Your passion can change a society and be a tool in saving people from eternal damnation. Have the courage to be passionate for the Lord!

G. Vergara

Does your passion for God lead you to hate sin?

Maghrebi - Israel

Population: 348,000
They are Jews who speak modern Hebrew. They have an entire translation of the Bible, but they do not consider the New Testament part of God's Holy Word. They reject Christians. It is estimated only a few have recognized Jesus as the Messiah.

Pray: The entire Bible would be seen as God's Word and that Jesus would be accepted as the Messiah.

Show Me How To Pray

{ *When you pray, say: Our Father in heaven, hallowed be your name, your kingdom come. Read Luke 11:1-4, 13*

In this passage, Jesus is teaching His disciples how to pray and talk with God. In His instructions, He describes how to address the Father, what the disciples should ask for, and reassures them their prayers are being heard. This helps us understand our prayers should express our devotion to God. Praying involves acknowledging God's beauty and recognizing His holiness. After expressing devotion, we should pray for God's will to rule our lives. Our prayers should reflect His heart towards those who do not know Him.

We are so privileged to have a Heavenly Father who is powerful and generous. We should not fall into the temptation of keeping Him only for ourselves. We must pray for the Gospel to be known all over the earth. Our prayers should include intercession for missionaries, lost people, and believers. Our desire should be for the Kingdom of God to come on Earth!

Jesus cares about all needs. He cares about providing for your daily food and other material necessities. He desires all to experience forgiveness. Pray with confidence! Pray with clear desires because you are praying to a Heavenly Father who loves you!

M. de Rodríguez

Have you learned how to pray?

Letuamas - Colombia

Population: 700
The Letuamas live in the Amazon. They are fishermen, farmers, and some are miners. Their language, Tanimuca-retuara, has a translation of the Jesus-film. It is estimated only 0.3% believe in Jesus.

Pray: For the Letuamas to see the Jesus film and for their hearts to be captivated.

Essential Requirement

{ *... Purify yourselves, for tomorrow the Lord will do great wonders among you. Joshua 3:5*

In this passage, God delivered a great challenge to His people. He challenged them to sanctify themselves. God knew without sanctification, it would be impossible for the Israelites to have victory in the battles they would face when entering the Promise Land.

God is holy and does not achieve His work through unholy instruments. He knew purification was necessary for His plan to be put into action. After His people were purified, God knew they would experience victory.

Do you want to experience victory with the Lord? Do you want to lead others into a relationship with Jesus? You must be cleansed from sin and walk with the Holy God. God will not use you if you are not justified before Him. What does your life look like? Do you need to fall on your knees and be purified before God? God knows your past, present, and future. You cannot deceive Him. Do not let sin hinder you from becoming His holy instrument. When you become purified you will experience blessings and victories!

M. Gomes

Start on your knees!

Korowai - Indonesia

Population: 3,900
They live in the forest. They are hunters, gatherers, and grow bananas. They raise pigs, but use them mainly for sacrifice during religious rituals. They are pantheists and animists. They have not yet heard of Jesus.

Pray: For the Bible to be translated into their language, Korowai. Pray they may experience freedom from their spiritual darkness.

Camp Together

> Then the cloud covered the tent of meeting, and the glory of the Lord filled the tabernacle. Exodus 40:34

What an incredible sight this must have been. Imagine you were present when the big cloud, representing the presence of God, came and covered the tent. What an incredible experience! The tent in this passage was the place where God met Moses. After Moses and God met, Moses returned to the people to give the commands and requests God had said.

John 1:14 says, "The Word became flesh and made his dwelling among us". The original meaning of this passage is: God "came to make is tent" among us. What a beautiful image we are given! God Himself came to make His permanent presence with His people. This means God is close to you and is not just passing by. He wants to have a part in your life by sharing in the fights and victories. God wants to live in the midst of your reality! What an unexpected action from a King! In the middle of our weakness, He comes, is present in our lives, and gives us hope! Are you desperate for God to intervene? Do you need guidance in your life? God is here! He is placing His permanent tent in the middle of your circumstance and fighting with you!

H. Bascur

Turn to Him!

Lithuanians - Lithuania

Population: 2,748,000

They are a native Baltic group from Lithuania. They have had a Bible translation in their language, Lithuanian, since 1998. Their predominant religion is Roman Catholic, but some have converted to the Lutheran Church and other evangelical denominations.

Pray: Lithuanians adopt the Bible as the standard for their faith.

Example Of Service

{ "No," said Peter, "you shall never wash my feet." Jesus answered, "Unless I wash you, you have no part with me." John 13:8

Jesus was a man who reinvented social order. From a human perspective, there is no logical reason for a King to humble himself and wash feet, but Jesus was not on earth to live by standard expectations. Through Jesus' selfless love, He broke social class barriers and touched many lives.

The selflessness of Jesus was something Peter could not understand. He could not comprehend why Jesus would humble Himself by doing such an unrewarding task. Peter felt unworthy to be washed by Jesus. Like Peter, no one is worthy of the selflessness of Christ, but Jesus does not base His service on what people deserve. Jesus bases His service on grace and mercy.

It is difficult to understand why Jesus would serve and make sacrifices for people who do not deserve it, but Jesus is gracious. He serves humbly and sets a new standard for serving, leading, and discipling others. Through the selfless acts of Jesus, you can learn to love others! Are you willing to serve as Jesus did?

C. Scott

Are you graciously serving?

Kobiana - Guinea Bissau

Population: 700
Their beliefs are animistic. They perform spiritual rituals and have a system of sacrifices. Their language, Kobiana, has parts of the Bible translated. They have some audio Bible recordings, but it is estimated only 1% are Christians.

Pray: For a spiritual awakening in their hearts, so they may come out of spiritual darkness and into God's light.

What Is That In Your Hand?

{ *Moses answered, "What if they do not believe me or listen to me and say, 'The Lord did not appear to you'?" Then the Lord said to him, "What is that in your hand?" "A staff," he replied. Exodus 4:1-2*

In this passage, we see Moses full of fear, doubt, and weakness. Moses was uncertain about the future, but God surprised him by asking a simple question: "What is that in your hand?" Moses replied with a simple answer, "A staff".

From a human perspective, the staff was only a tool Moses used in the desert to care for his father-in-law's sheep. God saw much more within the staff. God saw how the staff would become part of Moses' life during the 40 years he would live in the desert. He saw how the desert would be used as a learning environment to mold Moses' character. He saw how Moses had learned humility, self-control, and other virtues while tending the sheep with his staff. God knew Moses possessed what was needed to lead and teach the Israelites.

When you are overwhelmed by your challenges, remember Moses. The difficulties you are facing in your family, church, school, or workplace should not be feared. God can use the situations in your past to fulfill His future plans! He can use you to lead others into a dependent relationship with Him.

A. Corrales

> What you have in your hands is much more than you think!

Kraho - Brazil

Population: 2,000
They are animists. They believe the sun and moon are the creators of the world. They live near big cities and mix their native culture with modern life. They have no translation of the Bible in their native language, Kraho.

Pray: They are led to Christ through contact with people in the cities.

God Calls, You Respond!

> The Lord had said to Abram, "Go from your country, your people and your father's household to the land I will show you." Read Genesis 12:1-8

At the time God called Abram, he was comfortable living with his family. However, when God calls somebody, He always does with a purpose and expects it to be obeyed. In our lives, God calls us to experience salvation and to receive forgiveness from sins. God calls us to have a personal relationship with Jesus, but He also calls us to get involved in the work of His Kingdom. In Abraham's life, he was not always obedient to God's call, but when he failed, he always strived to get his heart lined back up with God's plan for his life. It is easy to become distracted from God's calling, but it is crucial to make decisions that lead you back to God and His purpose. Are your friendships, feelings, projects, sins, forms of entertainment, conversations, or bad habits preventing you from following God's call on your life? If the answer is yes, you must flee from them so you are not hindered and led to ruin. God has called you for a purpose! He desires you to obediently carry out the purpose He has for you. Flee from anything disrupting your communion and obedience to God!

D. Duk

Will you do it?

Muka - Brunei

Population: 300
They are known as fishermen and boat builders. Their economy is dependent on the production of palm, wet rice, coconut, and rubber. 100% of the Mukas are Muslim, but they are friendly to Animists and Christians in Brunei. They have no translation of the Bible in their native language, Central Malanau.

Pray: God touches their hearts so they would surrender their life to Jesus.

When We Look To Heaven

> Fixing our eyes on Jesus, the pioneer and perfecter of faith. For the joy set before him he endured the cross, scorning its shame, and sat down at the right hand of the throne of God. Hebrews 12:2

During the Olympic Games, many different facial expressions can be seen from the competitors. Athletes often express emotions of pain, sadness, joy and frustration. Although the expressions are often very different one another, one expression seems to never change. When athletes win or lose, they look to the sky.

Looking into the sky suggests athletes understand life is bigger than themselves. Not all athletes would acknowledge the existence of God, but their actions suggest human nature recognizes something supernatural reigns over the universe. The totality of God exceeds our understanding. His majesty leaves us looking to the sky, giving Him glory, and crying out for a piece of connection.

What do you do after a victory? What is your reaction when you receive bad news? Most people look to the sky and search for a sign of gratitude, relief, wisdom, or comfort. Fix your eyes on Jesus because He is the one who leads you to the Father. Through Jesus, your faith is perfected and you receive salvation. Recognize His greatness by raising your eyes to Heaven and searching for His great love!

G. Galindo

Raise your eyes to heaven!

Letemboi - Vanuatu

Population: 1,000
They live in the south of Malekula. Approximately 30% are Catholics, but they mix their beliefs with their ancestral animistic religions. They have no translation of the Bible in their native language, Letemboi.

Pray: They would know the Gospel in their own language.

First Sowing

> Those who sow with tears will reap with songs of joy. Those who go out weeping, carrying seed to sow, will return with songs of joy, carrying sheaves with them. Psalm 126:5-6

One day, God opened up a store selling anything anyone could ever want. When the news got out, a man hurried to the store and enthusiastically said to God, "Sir, I know your store sells everything I could ever want! Could you please sell me all of the joy in the world? I would also like my city to be converted to Christians and want to see no more poverty in the streets!" "I'm sorry my friend" responded God. "I do not sell fruits in my store, only seeds! I do not sell finished projects, but rather tools to work with! If you want to receive all of your requests, you will have to work first!"

Does this allegory speak to your heart? Often, people despair and crave for immediate action in their life, church, or community. God, however, puts us in a position of persistent work. We are called to sow, fertilize, water, and wait for God's fruit to grow. The Lord inspires us to not only work for the fruit, but also to sacrifice for it. Sacrificing will include giving maximum effort and experiencing unwanted pain. May the Lord fill you with strength and perseverance as you fearlessly spread His Word. Have courage as you face challenges and difficulties.
M. Chiquie

Are you sowing?

Koti - Mozambique

Population: 96,000
They live in the district of Angoche. They are fishermen, farmers, and merchants. A small community of Christians lives among them, but their understanding of Jesus is minimal.
The majority of Kotis profess Islam. They have some evangelistic audio-visual resources in their native language of Koti.

Pray: Bible translators and Bible teachers would invest in the Kotis.

SEPTEMBER

The Mission

> The Lord said to Moses, "How long will these people treat me with contempt? How long will they refuse to believe in me, in spite of all the signs I have performed among them?" Numbers 14:11

When looking at the history of Israel, we see God's chosen people, but unfortunately, we often do not understand their place in history. When we look at their story, we can see parallels to our own hearts. While wandering in the desert, Israel experienced the presence of God in supernatural ways. However, they often hardened their hearts against God and did not desire to follow and serve Him. In their stubbornness, they would reject the authority of God and overlook His provision and guidance.

Perhaps, as you have read this book, you have come before God and made your heart right with Him. Sadly, millions of the people you are surrounded by are simply not interested in Him. Some people do not want to accept that God is real. Many simply walk through life without depending on God because they claim there is no afterlife. Moses always prayed for these kinds of people. He was a mediator before the throne of God and prayed so they may avoid their destruction. What about you? What are you doing for those around you? Are you interceding for them? Do you take time out of your day to talk with people who are living in the moment and running out of time? God has given us this mission!

L. Ashmore

Are you remaining faithful to God's mission?

Malayali - United Arab Emirates

Population: 575,000

Malayalis are indigenous to India. They profess Hinduism and it is estimated only two percent believe the Gospel of Jesus Christ. They speak Malayalam, in which the entire Bible has been translated.

Pray: For the Malayali church to be strengthened and to be a light in the darkness.

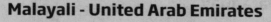

Must I Serve Him, Too?

> *For he knew who was going to betray him, and that was why he said not everyone was clean.* John 13:11

Despite knowing what would soon take place, Jesus served and washed the feet of the one who would later betray Him (John 2:25, 6:64, 70). What would you do if you met someone in a group who was like Judas? Perhaps you would refuse to serve the person, even if they had done something far less severe than Judas' betrayal.

Judas had heard the message of Jesus, but it did not change him. Paul later writes to the Corinthians about the folly of the cross (1 Corinthians 1:23-25), a plan for salvation that seems foolish to the world, but is really wiser than the wisest of human plans. He writes how the message of Jesus is a stumbling block to Jews and foolishness to Gentiles. Paul wrote this because he knew the love of Jesus appears contrary to human reason. For example, most people, when exposed and vulnerable to the enemy, would not continue to wash the feet of someone who would soon betray them.

Following the example of Jesus, who washed the feet of ALL His disciples, means abandoning our right to choose who we want to serve. Although Jesus knew it was Judas who would eventually betray Him, Jesus selflessly served him anyway. Are you a person who serves all people, or are you a person who picks and chooses who you want to serve? Do you experience the grace of God and share it freely with others, no matter what they've done? Are you willing to serve your enemies, even if serving them means humbling yourself and exposing yourself to rejection? Judas was about to leave and fulfill his betrayal, but nevertheless, Jesus was willing to serve him and wash his feet. Through Jesus' choice to serve, Judas experienced Jesus' love in a way that strongly impacted his life.

C. Scott

Serve everyone equally!

Maká - Paraguay

Population: 1,120

Through the selling of their crafts, the Makás are the best-known indigenous people of Paraguay. They live in central Paraguay, near Asuncion. Several Christian churches have been established among them and the New Testament is getting ready to be printed in their language. New Tribes Mission missionaries are currently working on translating the Old Testament.

Pray: For the strengthening of the Maká believers, that they will be a light in their community.

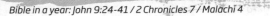

Beautiful Works

> { *Jesus said to them: "Why are you bothering this woman? She has done a beautiful thing to me." Matthew 26:6-13*

In this passage, Matthew shows Jesus spending time in the house of a leper, a choice that was not culturally acceptable during this time period. Furthermore, Jesus ignored other social norms by allowing a woman, who had a questionable reputation, to touch Him while she poured oil on His head. The disciples reacted to this behavior in frustration and acted as if they cared about the poor. In their frustration they declared the anointing of Jesus was "wasting" the valuable oil. Jesus immediately corrected them, claiming the beautiful act of the woman would be remembered forever. As we serve our Lord, we will also be remembered. Our actions, our character, our sacrifice, our attitude, our words—all will be remembered. Jesus wants our service to be honorable to Him. He desires our acts of service to not be conformed to the cultural habits of the world. If we choose not to serve Him, and remain culturally acceptable to the world, our poor choices and deeds will also be remembered. How do you serve? Are you trying to please God or the world?

D. Travis

Serve Him with beautiful works!

Nung - Vietnam

Population: 990,000

Living in the high mountains of Vietnam, Nungs are active planters of corn and rice. Their beliefs are animistic and Taoist. Marriage arrangements are made in the adolescent stage of life. The Nung language has just a few translated Bible passages.

Pray: For the Word to be translated into their language so that it will bring life to the Nung people.

Motivation To Pray

> Surely the arm of the Lord is not too short to save, nor his ear too dull to hear. Isaiah 59:1

The Lord's hand can reach any tribe, race, or nation in the world. His hand is capable of reaching people no matter how far away they are, how immersed in a false religion they are, how closed they are to the outside world, or how many missionaries they have killed. The Lord's hand can reach all people!

The ear of the Lord is not deaf. He will listen to those who talk. Are you praying for the salvation of the lost? Do you care about where the millions who have not yet heard the Gospel of Christ will spend eternity? Do you pray for the people who are without a translation of the Bible? Jesus prayed, "Father forgive them, for they know not what they do," and God answered His prayer on the day of Pentecost when three thousand people repented. John Knox prayed, "Give me Scotland or I die." God answered his prayer and gave John the country of Scotland. George Whitefield prayed, "Oh Lord, give me souls or take my soul." God answered his prayer and used him to save many souls.

Why don't we pray? Many Christians think that everyone will go to heaven. The Bible is clear about salvation and damnation. Hell exists and is a reality for people around the world. Do you lack compassion? Do you understand people die and go to hell every day? Often we don't believe it is possible for God to truly adopt the lost into His family and redeem the broken. We lack faith in God's sovereignty. Is there a country or ethnicity for whom you don't pray for because you think it is impossible for them to know Christ? Praying for the lost is a sign of humility. God does not always give His children what they ask for in prayer, but prayer is a sign of love for God and for other souls. Prayer is a sign of trusting in His power and His ultimate plan. Since God's ear is not deaf, I pray for the lost! A. Gulard

Do you?

Livonian - Latvia

Population: 20
This small people group lives in the western part of Latvia. They speak the Liv language, which is only spoken by a few people. They have a translated New Testament. Twelve Livonians are known Protestant Christians.

Pray: For God to strengthen the faith of these believers, so they can leave a legacy of faith to the people groups around them.

Virtual Personality

> The eye is the lamp of the body. Therefore, if your eyes are healthy, your whole body will be full of light. Matthew 6:22

Unquestionably, we live in a highly technological age. The technology that revolutionized the communication world has also led to changes in behavior and personality. For example, a boy between 9 and 14 years of age spends an average of 6 hours a day using an electronic device. What does this mean in a daily schedule? It means less time outside, faster time spent eating meals, and less time spent with parents.

Today, in the 21st century, the daily routines of people involve communicating their feelings through a number of virtual realities. Social networks give people the opportunity to be more vulnerable, spontaneous, witty, and even daring with their personal thoughts, feelings, and experiences. However, this virtual reality is not in line with the real world, where people are much more harsh and abrasive with their words and deeds. The virtual world has caused people to loose their authenticity, often presenting a completely different persona compared to who they really are.

Moreover, these behaviors have led to addictions of sins like pornography. People who have problems with alcohol and drugs are easily identified in the real world because of their demeanor, smells, looks, and behavior. But those who are trapped in virtual vices can hide their sins from those living in the real world. People trapped in virtual vices can go to church, sing, pray, and serve all while their life is being hid in a secret and dangerous world. Live every day asking the Lord for His strength to be manifested in your weakness. Do not let your life be filled with darkness from what enters your eyes. Pray for people who are trapped in a virtual world of sin.
W. Altare

With clean vision comes a pure heart.

Lubu - Indonesia

Population: 49,000
Lubus live in isolated villages on the island of Sumatra. Their daily life consists of cultivating rice. They have no basic amenities. They are known for practicing witchcraft and spells. They speak Lubu and have no translation of the Bible.

Pray: For the Lubu to be freed from the influence of evil.

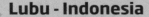

The Eternity Of God

> Who has done this and carried it through, calling forth the generations from the beginning? I, the LORD—with the first of them and the last of them—I am he. Isaiah 41:4

God owns time. He does not work within a limited time frame like humans do. People are only able to function in the present. People are constrained to living life by reacting to the events taking place around them. It is impossible to go back in time or move forward into the future. But how does God interact with time?

God has existed and will exist for eternity. This means He was present before the creation of the world. He suffered through the sin of Adam and Eve and wept during their banishment from the Garden. He witnessed the parting of the Red Sea, saw Joshua and his people enter the Promised Land, and has been forever present in the history of Israel. God watched in horror as His Son was crucified and He rejoices at the growth of His church today. No event has ever escaped His eyes. He is not only the God of today, but He is eternal and knows the future.

Have you ever felt anxious about what is to come? Do you know God is in control of your future? Put your trust in Him instead of worrying. Have peace because He is an eternal God and has amazing plans for your life.

L. Ashmore

Do you dare to trust Him?

Matagalpa - Nicaragua

Population: 42,000
Matagalpas are an indigenous Caribbean group. The majority of Matagalpas are fishermen. They have lost their native language and now speak Spanish. They can read the Gospel, but they have not responded positively. It is estimated only 3% follow Jesus.

Pray: For a transformation in the hearts of the Matagalpas.

What Is Still Missing?

{ *Jesus went through all the towns and villages... When he saw the crowds, he had compassion on them, because they were harassed and helpless, like sheep without a shepherd. Matthew 9:36*

Jesus had a very active and successful ministry. He healed the sick, raised paralytics, resurrected the dead, and acquired many followers. On one occasion, over 5,000 people gathered to hear Him preach. Any pastor would want to have a ministry as successful as Jesus'. But as He visited the towns and villages, Jesus saw multitudes of people who were scattered, like sheep without a shepherd.

Today, a lot of pastors have successful ministries. They have created large churches and have filled them with activities and services. However, if you walk through any city or town you will realize a great spiritual need still exists. Jesus never stopped to admire His success. Jesus focused on having compassion on those who had not yet been shepherded. Where is your vision? Is it to be successful, or is it focused on what needs to be done? If you are looking at what you have already accomplished, you are in danger of becoming inactive. Focus on what needs to be done and the people that need to be reached. Doing this means having the same mindset as Jesus. Are you proud of your success or are you troubled for those who have not yet been reached?

F. Rodríguez

Keep the vision of Jesus.

Kuranko - Sierra Leone

Population: 339,000
They are a branch of the Mandinka tribe. They live in both Sierra Leone and Guinea. They consider childhood impure, so they are "purified" during puberty. Their beliefs are animistic. They have a complete translation of the Bible in their native language, Kuranko. It is estimated only 0.4% are Christian.

Pray: For the Word of God to touch their hearts and transform their lives.

The Power Of God

{ *Did I not say that if you believed, you would see the glory of God?*
Read John 11:17-44

When we live comfortable lives, I believe we gradually stop believing God has power. When we have everything at our disposal, it is difficult to see God's power. It is more than likely we have all the food we need, have houses for shelter, go to the hospital when we are sick, and have our family and church for support. In reality, we have everything we need.

Often, we pick and choose when we see God's glory. It's easy to see the power of God when a life is transformed (which is most definitely the right thing to do). But I believe we fail to believe in God's power in every situation. How would life change if we did not ignore His power? For example, what if someone was sick? Our natural tendency is to go to the doctor, but what if our first response was to turn to God and pray to Him to fix the situation?

When I first arrived on the mission field, God challenged me with this very question. Upon arriving, He challenged me to trust and have the faith that He had the power to heal. This same topic is what Jesus spoke of with Martha, "Didn't I say that if you believed you would see the glory of God?"

Sometimes we find ourselves in need. We realize our knowledge, experience, or resources are not sufficient for what we are facing. In this moment, we understand there is only one place to turn: God. Sadly, this moment of despair is often the only time we look in faith to Him. Is God your last resort? When you come to God, nothing you share can surprise Him. He has the power to intervene in any situation in your life, but it requires having faith!

N. Rivas

> Only then you will see
> the glory of God.

Okinawan - Japan

Population: 980,000
The Okinawan are originally from the Okinawa islands. They speak Okinawan and Japanese, but their native language has no translation of the Bible. Entire extended families live together and the older women have great authority in the family affairs. It is estimated only 2% of the population are Christians.

Pray: For Okinawan believers to share their faith and be a good testimony.

How Do You Serve?

> When he had finished washing their feet, he put on his clothes and returned to his place. "Do you understand what I have done for you?" he asked them. John 13:12

"You call me 'Teacher' and 'Lord,' and rightly so, for that is what I am." Through this act, Jesus set an example of how we should serve one another. He taught by being a servant Himself. In this passage, Jesus emphasized He is the Lord and Master, but He still lived humbly surrendered and gave an incredible example by teaching how to serve. This act of servanthood tends to contradict how most perceive the way masters and teachers should act. Few authority figures lead by example. However, Jesus led by example and modeled meekness, humility, service, and brotherly kindness. In Jesus' perfection, He expects His followers to live exhibiting these same traits. The example of Jesus encourages believers to pay attention to His behavior and strive to imitate it. "I have set for you an example, that you should do as I have done for you... Now that you know these things, you will be blessed if you do them." John 13:12-17

How are you serving others? Do you serve your neighbor with love, humility, respect, gentleness, and kindness? Jesus has given us an example of service!

C. Scott

Are you going to serve?

Macushis - Brazil

Population: 28,000
The Macushis live near the border of Venezuela and Guyana. Their main activity is cultivating fruits and vegetables. They have the New Testament in their language, Macuxi. A small church has been started among them, but it is weak.

Pray: For workers to disciple the church.

Differences Among Us

{ *Be devoted to one another in brotherly love. Honor one another above yourselves. Romans 12:10*

In our lives, it is inevitable that we will go through difficult times. Some difficulties arise during discussions with people who have different viewpoints from our own. Having confrontations is extremely difficult, but what makes confrontations even more challenging is when they involve friends. Unfortunately, even when we take time to work through conflicts, we do no always find a clear solution.

When we are in the middle of conflict, we can either choose to fight and prove our point or choose to depend on the Spirit for guidance. Whenever Jesus went into villages and was faced with confrontation, He always answered wisely because the Holy Spirit guided Him. Because He was guided, Jesus always spoke wisely when He dealt with conflict among His disciples.

Have you ever had a challenging conversation with a close friend? Did you find it difficult to reach a solution? Take the first step and rid yourself of your selfish desires. Give the Holy Spirit a chance to work through you. When you have this attitude, it is easier to work through differences with the people you love. If you allow the Spirit to work through you, the love God has poured into your heart can help you overcome any obstacle and can cover a multitude of sins. G. Galindo

Decide to love!

Moghal - Afghanistan

Population: 300
Moghals are originally from India. They are made up of various clans. Their native language, Urdu, is almost extinct. They are Muslims and no known Christians live among them.

Pray: For missionaries to go to the Moghals so they can be reached with the Gospel.

If You Don't Know Why, Wait For The How

> *And we know that in all things God works for the good of those who love him, who have been called according to his purpose. Romans 8:28*

We love to hear testimonies about the beautiful things God has done, but we tend to put so much emphasis on these things that we forget difficult situations and trials still happen. Today, I want to share with you different trials I've had to face. When I lived in Chile I was attacked, stoned, kicked, and beaten. When I was in Peru, the community rejected me. When I was in Argentina, I was wrongly accused of carrying drugs on a bus. When I was in Bolivia, I was assaulted, robbed, and left without a penny. At one point during my life, I was in Uruguay and could not be with my family after they had experienced a terrible earthquake in Chile. In Mexico, I was fed rat and when I was in Paraguay, I had unjust problems with the police. Throughout all of these trials, I could not understand why God would allow me to experience these things.

How do you feel about the trials in your life? I don't want to discourage you, but are you wondering why God has allowed certain things to happen to you? Honestly, I do not have an answer for why you are in a difficult situation. But I do know in every difficult situation, God is with you! In my life, it has always been evident God is near because He has always delivered, cared for, guided, helped, and healed me.

I encourage you to trust God. A certain situation may be beyond your control, but I guarantee your situation is not beyond the control of God. I encourage you to pray and let God know you don't understand why you are in your current situation. Ask Him for care, love, and guidance through your difficulties. It is okay if you don't understand the situation, but it is important to trust and see God extend His hand and deliver you from your trails!

W. Núñez

> Do not ask why,
> but wait for the how.

Mari Hop - Papua New Guinea

Population: 1,100
Mari Hops live in four villages in the province of Madang. Their religion is animistic. Their language, Mari, has no translation of the Bible. They have heard the Gospel in the neighbors' languages, but they have no firm understanding of salvation.

Pray: For Bible translators and for Mari Hops to be more responsive to the Gospel.

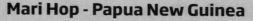

September 12

Let Us Run The Race

> Therefore, since we are surrounded by such a great cloud of witnesses, let us throw off everything that hinders and the sin that so easily entangles. And let us run with perseverance the race marked out for us, fixing our eyes on Jesus, the pioneer and perfecter of faith. For the joy set before him he endured the cross, scorning its shame, and sat down at the right hand of the throne of God. Hebrews 12:1-2

Throughout our daily lives, many people watch us. The more we claim to follow God, the more "witnesses" will watch what we do. Two different types of witnesses exist: those who run alongside of us, experiencing the same race, and those who are on the sidelines watching us run. For this reason, we must shed all things entangling us in sin. When we shed the things slowing us down, it becomes easier for other witnesses to run with us. This is because we become free and have nothing holding us back.

In order to run with perseverance, we must be focused. Situations will occur when we will be tested, but we have to trust God has our heart in His hands. God knows our daily circumstances. To have our eyes fixed on Jesus, the author and perfecter of our faith, means always placing our trust in Him. You can be confident because He is responsible for renewing your strength. Jesus is the perfect trainer in your race. The best way to run this race and handle its challenges is to rely on the hand of God!

D. Duk

Do not let go of Him!

Mandaean - United Kingdom

Population: 1,000

Mandaeans are originally from Iran and Iraq. They have lost their native language and now speak British English. Their religion is based on baptism in "living waters". Many are Muslim and still follow very strong death rituals. Although they have heard about Jesus, they have rejected the Gospel.

Pray: For God to free Mandaeans from their dark rituals and that they would accept the Gospel as truth.

To Both Those Who Want and Don't

{ *The people to whom I am sending you are obstinate and stubborn. Say to them, "This is what the Sovereign Lord says." Read Ezekiel 2:3-5*

Ezekiel had just had a vision of the glory of God. The Lord had taken the initiative to talk with Ezekiel and to send him to preach to the children of Israel. Ezekiel's mission was to deliver a warning of divine judgment, to preach repentance, and to proclaim salvation from divine punishment. God warned Ezekiel that the children of Israel were obstinate and stubborn, but He was willing to send a messenger if they would listen.

This situation is very similar to our present day. We live in a secular environment where people prefer pleasures, riches, fame, and power. They prefer this self-seeking lifestyle over seeking the things of God (Matthew 6:33).

Sometimes we use the excuse: People around us have hard hearts and don't believe. Why should we preach the Gospel to them? When Ezekiel was dealing with this same situation God said to him, "But they will know a prophet among them." The Lord wants us to proclaim the message, not only to those willing to hear, but also to those who do not want to hear. In doing this, people will not be able to say, "I never had an opportunity for salvation." Do not stop! Preach all you can!

M. de Rodriguez

You always have an opportunity!

Matapi - Colombia

Population: 200

Matapis spend their time gathering food, working with agriculture, and fishing. Their beliefs are animistic and they worship sacred plants. They have adopted the Yucuna language, which has a translation of the New Testament. It is estimated only 3% have positively responded to the Gospel.

Pray: For the Spirit of God to transform the Matapis.

September 14

To All Nations

> Then Jesus said to her, "Woman, you have great faith! Your request is granted." And her daughter was healed at that moment.
> Read Matthew 15:21-28

Let's recreate this situation: A Canaanite woman sees Jesus as He passes by and she cries out for His mercy because her daughter is being tormented by a demon (v. 22). Jesus does not immediately answer her, but instead allows the silence to purify her faith. The disciples then ask Jesus to send the woman away, which upset her, so she followed them screaming.

Jesus then turned to His disciples and said, "I was sent only to the lost sheep of Israel." The Canaanite woman responded by falling at Jesus' feet and begged, "Lord, help me." Jesus responded by saying, "It is not right to take the children's bread and throw it to the dogs." The woman then said, "Yes, Lord, but even the dogs eat the crumbs that fall from their master's table." Jesus responded, "Woman, great is your faith! I'll give you what you want!" In that very moment the Canaanite woman's daughter was healed.

Jesus was sent to the children of Israel, but that did not stop Him from going beyond borders. The Canaanite woman was a Gentile, but she had the faith to ask Jesus to heal her daughter. Because of her faith, her daughter was healed. Jesus eagerly recognizes faith. This story of the Canaanite woman was not the only healing request granted to the Gentiles (Luke 7). What moved Jesus? What is common among these stories? Faith!

Faith is universal. It is not limited to a certain group of people and it does not apply to only those who we identify with. God's salvation for humanity is revealed through Jesus Christ to all nations. M. Gomes

May God bless you in this endeavor!

Lele - Guinea

Population: 42,000

The Lele live in Yombiro, Kassadou, and Tangalto. They are mainly farmers and traders. The predominant religion is animism, but 40% profess Islam and 5% profess Christianity. The Lele's language has some audio Bible stories.

Pray: For the church to grow stronger and be a powerful testimony to the community.

Bible in a year: John 16:4-33 / 2 Chronicles 24 / Psalm 81

September 15

Obeying The Call

{ *The Lord had said to Abram, "Go from your country, your people and your father's household to the land I will show you." Genesis 12:1*

The Biblical principle found in Genesis 12:2 is one of divine blessing: "I will bless you, and you will be a blessing." When these words were said to Abram, a concept of giving and receiving was revealed. Abram was the first man mentioned in the Bible who received a call for a global and comprehensive purpose. Because the request from God was unique, it required great faith. For Abram's big move, God had a promise and divine blessing in mind. Often God's promises are conditional and dependent on agreements. For Abram, God's command to go to an unknown land was given before God promised him he would become a great nation. Many people falsely assume Abram immediately obeyed, but this was not the case. Genesis 12:1 states, "God had said." The grammatical form shows this was not the first time God had commanded Abram. The word "had" implies the message had been repeated and God had already invited Abram to his calling. Acts 7 also indicates Abram lived in Haran and then entered the land God had given Him. When God works in your life, He begins a process that never ends. God continues to call until his commands are obeyed. God has divine blessings for you, but sometimes, in order for your faith to grow, you will receive a command before the blessing. Receiving commands before blessings allows you to practice obedience and helps you learn to trust God. Learn to have peace with God and His commands!

H. Ziefle

Are you being obedient to God's call?

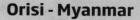

Orisi - Myanmar

Population: 108,000
Orisis practice Hinduism mixed with animism. Some Orisis practice witchcraft in their villages. Their language is Oriya, which has a translation of the Bible since 2004. It is estimated only 0.2% are Christians.

Pray: For the Word to captivate their hearts and for them to surrender their lives to Christ.

Always

> So do not fear, for I am with you, do not be dismayed, for I am your God. I will strengthen you and help you, I will uphold you with my righteous right hand. *Isaiah 41:10*

I clearly remember the night when God spoke to me through His word and called me to be a missionary. In the moment I accepted the call without question, but four years later, when I was well established in secular work, I began to have doubts. I knew during this time God was calling me to quit my job and start preparing for the mission field.

I had fears of leaving everything I had achieved, not having a secure salary, and having a life full of uncertainties. I struggled with my fears until June 2006, at 11:45 PM. At this specific time God showed me, through His Word, a promise that still sustains me today: "I will uphold you with my righteous right hand" (Isaiah 41:10). During that night I decided to drop everything, quit my job, and trust that God is faithful.

Now that I have served a few years as a missionary, I can say with absolute certainty God is faithful. Slowly, God is taking away every fear because He continues to provide for my every need. I pray God helps you trust Him so that you can make decisions based on faith in Him.

G. Rivas

Get on your knees in prayer!

Marshallese - Nauru

Population: 100

Marshalleses come from the Marshall Islands and are one of the ethnic minorities in Nauru. They have both a translated Bible and the Jesus film in their language. Almost all claim to be believers, but their lives do not show faith in Jesus. They need to return to a commitment with Christ.

Pray: For Marshalleses to be strengthened in their faith and to reach others for Christ.

Divine Glory

> Jesus prayed for his disciples and said: "...May they also be in us so that the world may believe that You sent me. I have given them the glory you gave me, that they may be one just as we are one." John 17:21-22

The word "glory" is usually associated with splendor, magnificence, and majesty. It implies recognition for doing something important. What kind of glory did the Father give Jesus? What kind of glory does Jesus want to give us?

In this passage John describes another concept of glory. In the world, people usually seek personal gain or self-glory (John 5:44, 7:18). In the Gospel, the ultimate example of glory is Jesus Christ giving his life on the cross. Many search for glory from one another, Jesus selflessly offers Himself for the glory of others. "For even the Son of Man did not come to be served, but to serve, and to give His life as a ransom for many" (Mark 10:45).

God gave Jesus glory by sending Him as a human we could relate to. God became man in the person of Jesus Christ and John explains that through His sacrifice we have seen God's glory. Jesus' act of coming to earth exhibits servanthood. Jesus left everything He had ever known and entered a broken world. Because Jesus was willing to sacrifice, true glory was shown. In His humility, Jesus identified with the issues and problems people face. His example encourages sacrifice for others and leads us to seek their well-being. God's glory has nothing to do with man's idea of praise and prestige. Being a joyful servant is what brings God glory. This is the type of glory Jesus desires to give!

C. Scott

Search for the glory of God.

Miraña - Peru

Population: 600

Mirañas are located on the border of Brazil and Colombia. The women farm for the family, and the men hunt and fish. They are animists and believe all things have a spirit. They have the New Testament in their language.

Pray: For the Word of God to open their eyes so they can see and know Christ.

Much In Little

{ *We have here only five loaves of bread and two fish. Matthew 14:17*

In the story of Jesus feeding the five thousand, Jesus started the miracle by receiving just five loaves of bread and two fish from a child walking by. This amount of food was the normal amount used to feed one person for one day. If someone was in great need, this small amount could be shared between two people, but it was clear this amount could never be used to feed over five thousand people. However, when this small amount was placed in the Master's hands, it miraculously became enough food for the five thousand men, wives, and children.

Regardless of the size of your current obstacle, it is important you understand your God is bigger than what you are currently facing. God's power was reflected in the disciples when they contested, "We only have five loaves of bread and two fish." If God was reliant on the disciples' perception, the story would have ended in hunger and frustration, but God was bigger than their situation. He used a child who was willing to give up what little he had so it could be put it in the Master's hands for His use. No amount is too small for God to multiply and reveal His power. If you identify the strengths and gifts God has given you, no matter how big they are, and commit to letting Him use those strengths through you, a new story of your life will be written! It will be a story written with the pen of Jesus and it will give God glory!

F. Chinatti

Let God write your story!

Makwe - Mozambique

Population: 29,000

Makwes live in the district of Cabo Delgado. Although their native language is Makwe, almost all Makwes can understand and speak Swahili. They are engaged in agriculture, fishing, and trade. Their religion is Islam. Some audio resources are available for evangelism.

Pray: For God to open their hearts and minds to the love of Jesus.

Persistence In Prayer

> So I say to you, "Ask and it will be given to you; seek and you will find; knock and the door will be opened to you." Luke 11:5-12

In my beloved country, Chile, the person who insists and insists on something until it happens is called a "catete". I personally find it hard to be constantly persistent because I do not want to bother someone by constantly asking questions. In my prayer life, I used to think, "If God heard me ask the first time, why should I keep insisting? He already knows what I need." However, when we look in the Bible, we see that this type of thinking and logic is not how God works.

As I was reading Jesus' parables in Luke, I noticed an attitude of persistence that I had never noticed before. As I began to study the Greek grammar in Luke 11, I noticed the context implied that the person who is doing the asking has an attitude of persistence. This got me thinking I should adopt an attitude of persistence when it comes to my requests and prayers to God. If we can be persistent in praying for God's will to be done, as it is described in the first part of Luke 11, then why wouldn't God answer our prayers and open doors for us? Do you have concerns or questions regarding missionary service? Are you preparing for missionary service? What do you need from your Good Father? What have you asked for? What are you looking for? Do you feel left alone knocking on the door? I encourage you to persevere! Your Father wants you to be a "catete." Respectfully trust God will provide, in His perfect timing, for what you are crying out for.

T. Sandvig

Do not faint!

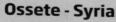

Ossete - Syria

Population: 61,000
The Ossete live in an ancient village in the Caucasus region. The majority are Orthodox Christians, but many profess Islam. They speak Osetin, which has an audio recording of the New Testament.

Pray: For the Christian church to have a revival and to regain a life of powerful testimony.

Losing To Win

> But whatever were gains to me I now consider loss for the sake of Christ. What is more, I consider everything a loss because of the surpassing worth of knowing Christ Jesus my Lord, for whose sake I have lost all things. I consider them garbage, that I may gain Christ.
> Philippians 3:7-8

Money. Fame. Success. Possessions. Pleasures. Often we view life as a race to acquire these things. We live convinced that happiness is what defines people and we forget what really matters.

In Philippians 3, Paul tells us he had all the qualifications to be considered successful in the eyes of people. He was highly religious, had a good social status, was politically respected, and was culturally relevant. But Paul decided to shed all of that and considered it a loss, so he could follow Christ and live according to the purpose of the Lord.

The call God has given you is far more valuable than anything the world can offer. Real success is not having a college degree. It is not about having a successful career, a beautiful house, or a fancy car. The most valuable thing in this world is to become what God has created you to be and to do what He wants you to do. Your goal in life should not be to achieve worldly prosperity, but to fulfill the plans God has for your life. Jesus went through suffering and death to give you life - a life not to be wasted pursuing things of the world. In the eyes of the world, you might be missing out on the pleasure of material things, but in the eyes of God, you are gaining everything. All of the suffering and pain Jesus endured was to give you life. What will you do with it?

G. Vergara

In your life, do you care more about what the world says, or about what God says?

Mirandes - Portugal

Population: 10,000

The Mirandes live on the southeast border between Portugal and Spain. They are dedicated Roman Catholics by tradition, but very few are born again in the Holy Spirit. They do not have the Bible in their native language, but they know of the Gospel from European Portuguese.

Pray: For the Word of God to penetrate their hearts and for them to truly convert.

Bible in a year: John 20:1-18 / 2 Chronicles 31 / Psalm 87

Teach Me, O Lord!

{ *Teach me your way, Lord, that I may rely on your faithfulness; give me an undivided heart, that I may fear your name. Psalm 86:11*

As a full-time Christian worker, I have served the past eight years in Paraguay. As I serve, I find myself constantly coming back to Psalm 86:11. At one point or another, every Christian worker who desires to be effective in ministry comes to understand what it means to die to themselves and become a student. Part of dying to oneself involves making sacrifices. It is a sacrifice to have discipline and learn a new language. It is a sacrifice to leave home and travel to a new place. It is a sacrifice to live where the culture is unfamiliar and everything is a challenge. However, if you can continue to die to yourself and rely on the Lord's faithfulness, God can work through you and do amazing things. Even people with years of Bible training or mission experience acknowledge there are always new things to learn and to be applied in life. Christian workers, armed with several college degrees, can have adequate knowledge. But they can only become truly useful in the hands of God when they find humility in Christ.

Regardless of your age or your number of important titles, you must be a humble student everyday. This must take place so the Lord can be glorified in your life and ministry. This concept of humility and having an undivided heart will always apply, no matter if your service is in your own town, in your own country, or somewhere around the world.

MyT. Goddard

Practice humility!

Manjúi - Paraguay

Population: 520
Also known as the Choroti, the Manjúis have both Christian and animist beliefs. Many take part in a literacy program, which is bringing new perspectives to life. The translation of the New Testament is in its final phase.

Pray: For missionaries among the Munjúis, for the Bible translation, and for the Christian faith to be well taught.

Full Armor

> Therefore put on the full armor of God, so that when the day of evil comes, you may be able to stand your ground, and after you have done everything, to stand... Ephesians 6:13

Our sovereign God knows His enemies very well and that is why He commands us to take up the only thing that is effective against them, armor. In Ephesians, Paul compares this armor with the armor of a Roman soldier. Paul writes it is a personal decision to put on the Godly armor or to battle without it. It is up to you to obey or disobey.

Unfortunately, our human nature is constantly looking for ways to rebel against the divine, and that is why we often opt out of putting on the armor of God. Instead, we rely on our own strength and grit. Evil is always looking for ways to devour the weak, and it manifests itself in many ways: illness, death, depression, disorientation, confusion, loneliness, frustration, betrayal, grief, sadness, abuse, and violations of any kind. We simply cannot stand against the weight of the world through our own strength. Sadly, most people deal with adversity by turning to friends, psychologists, drugs, witches, or horoscopes. After they find no answers, they are left wondering why they cannot achieve their desired results.

I encourage you, with all of my heart, to put on the FULL ARMOR of God. It is the spiritual coverage you need when standing and fighting against life's dark adversities. In every situation stand firm and know God is with you.

Pescador

Have you put on your armor today?

Mamprusi - Ghana

Population: 272,600
Mamprusis moved to Ghana from Togo. Their social status is very low and they have an extreme need for basic services. Only 15% of the male population receives education. Their main religion is animism, while 15% are Muslim, and 4% are Christian. They have the New Testament and Jesus film in their language, Mampruli.

Pray: For the Gospel to be widely distributed and accepted throughout the Mamprusis.

Saved To Be Holy

> For we are God's handiwork, created in Christ Jesus to do good works, which God prepared in advance for us to do. Ephesians 2:10

Salvation isn't just about avoiding Hell, the forgiveness of sins, or about personal justification. Often we think of salvation as a solution to all of our problems. Salvation, however, is much more than that. When we look at Scripture, we see we have been saved to be holy, which means salvation requires sanctification. While the conversion experience happens at a specific point in time, sanctification is a process that stretches into eternity as God intervenes in our lives. It is through His intervention we are transformed. Sanctification takes place every day, every moment of our lives. If you have committed your life to Christ, you have received not only salvation, but have begun the process of sanctification. You can live your life confidently seeking God's calling and plan.

Sanctification is what Paul had in mind when he wrote Philippians 2:12, "Continue to work out your salvation." God sets sanctification in motion for each person. Sanctification is a call to implement what God has called us to be. God did not save us because of our works, but we are being transformed to do the good works God prepared for us to complete.

O. Simari

Live out your salvation by tending your sanctification.

Pacoh - Laos

Population: 18,000
In their language, "Pacoh" means mountain. They live isolated in remote mountains near Laos. The Gospels of Mark and John have been translated into their native language. Sadly, only 15% of the population is literate and can read the translations. Their religion is animistic.

Pray: For the Gospel to be recorded on audio and for it to be distributed to the Pacohs.

First Things First

> Therefore, if you are offering your gift at the altar and there remem-
> ber that your brother has something against you, leave your gift
> there before the altar. First go and be reconciled to your brother; then
> come and offer your gift. Matthew 5:23-24

If you read this devotional book on a daily basis, more than likely, you have a strong desire to serve God. Everything you do for God is an offering. Some believe that an offering is only asso-ciated with money, but it is so much more than that. An offering also includes your time, kind-ness, sacrifices, and service.

Jesus teaches us to deal with relational conflict in a Godly way before bringing an offering to God. He commands us to leave our offering at the altar and repair broken relationships. Have you experienced a time when you tried bringing an offering to God in the midst of a struggling relationship?

Do you know the enemy is constantly trying to attack your ministry? One of his most effective tactics in destroying your ministry is damaging your relationships. Jesus prayed fervently to the Father for unity because He knew the importance of it.

Too often we immerse ourselves in our material offerings and neglect our relationships. Notice in the passage, Jesus did not talk about who is right or wrong, but rather He talks about who has the responsibility to go and be reconciled in the conflict. There is a reason we are not able to sleep when we are in conflict. This is because God created us to be in unity with one another and to work through conflicts that cause divisions in our hearts. The Lord has commanded us to be unified!

W. Altare

Go. Unify. Offer.

Masama - Indonesia

Population: 2,400

Masamas are a Malaysian group living in Sulawesi, Indonesdia. No portion of Scripture has been translated into their language, Andio. Their main religion is Islam, but some retain their ancient animistic religion. It is estimated only 3% have heard the Gospel, which was presented by Catholic priests.

Pray: For a start of a Bible translation so the Masama can know Jesus.

True Glory

> { *...To see my glory, the glory you have given me... John 17:24*

Jesus encourages us to discover a kind of glory we are not accustomed to. It is a glory that comes from washing one another's feet (John 13:12-17). It is a glory rooted in love and service. "A new command I give you: Love one another. As I have loved you, so you must love one another. By this everyone will know that you are my disciples, if you love one another" (John 13:34-35). This divine glory involves listening to God and listening to people. It is a glory of serving, living meekly, humbly learning to forgive, and learning to be forgiven. This glory asks the question: "What would you like me to do for you?" (Mark 10:51)

The majesty and beauty of this divine glory manifests itself in a unique way (Isaiah 52:13-15, 53). It does not focus on achievements or large numbers that draw attention. The glory does not struggle for power, control, or the applause from an audience. It is does not delight in self-exaltation, selfish ambitions, or self-righteousness. In Jesus Christ, this glory is magnified. Through His service, forgiveness, and reconciliation we can see this glory at work. Long for this glory so you can become fully intimate with Christ. Through the power of the Holy Spirit you can live in this glory. Do you desire it?

C. Scott

Follow the model of Christ.

Mocho - Mexico

Population: 200
Mochos live on the border of Guatemala and Mexico. It is estimated 30% have received the Gospel, but they continue to rely on foreign missionaries for teaching and aid. They need to establish local leaders with solid Biblical training.

Pray: For the raising up and training of pastors within the Mochos, so the Gospel can be regularly taught in their own language.

Just A Glass Of Water

{ *And if anyone gives even a cup of cold water to one of these little ones who is my disciple, truly I tell you, that person will certainly not lose their reward. Matthew 10:42*

In Matthew 10, we read the instructions Jesus gave the twelve disciples when He sent them out in pairs of two. Jesus warned His disciples some people would warmly receive them and others would coldly reject them. He discussed the rewards for the people who would welcome the disciples with open arms. "Anyone who welcomes you, welcomes me, and anyone who welcomes me, welcomes the one who sent me. Whoever welcomes a prophet as a prophet will receive a prophet's reward, and whoever welcomes a righteous person as a righteous person will receive a righteous person's reward" (Matthew 10:40-41). Jesus adds to His statement by saying even if a glass of water is given to the disciples, the act will not go unrewarded.

God continues to send missionaries around the world. Missionaries today are still in need of warm care, just like the disciples of Jesus' time. You may be tempted to think you are not capable of supporting a missionary because you do not have enough money or resources. Jesus' words to his disciples teach us that no matter what we give, it will be used for the glory of the Kingdom and will be rewarded by God. You can support missionaries by simply providing them with accommodation, food, a jacket, or money. Whatever it is, your sacrifice will glorify God's Kingdom. Be assured, your offerings will be rewarded by your Father in Heaven!

F. Rodríguez

Do you support missionaries?

Pear - Cambodia

Population: 1,500
Pears live in houses made of bamboo in the woods. They live from fishing, hunting wild animals, and subsistence farming. They are animists and perform many sacrificial rituals they believe please the spirits.

Pray: For the Pear people to be set free from the power of darkness.

Guarding The Walls

> { *Son of man, I have made you a watchman for the people of Israel; so hear the word I speak and give them warning of me. Read Ezekiel 3:17-21*

In ancient times, cities were protected with high stonewalls. Watchmen would stand in towers on top of the walls and watch for an approaching enemy's attack. The watchmen's duty was to view the surrounding and sound the alarm when danger was spotted. If the watchmen did not sound the alarm when they spotted danger, the city would be destroyed and the watchmen would pay for their neglect by being put to death.

God told Ezekiel, "I have made you a watchman, when I say to a wicked person, 'You will surely die,' and you do not warn them or speak out to dissuade them from their evil ways in order to save their life, that wicked person will die for their sin, and I will hold you accountable for their blood." As children of God, we must announce the danger of the damnation of sin. Paul wrote to Timothy, "Preach the word; be prepared in season and out of season; correct, rebuke, and encourage–with great patience and careful instruction" (2 Timothy 4:2). Paul also said, "Watch your life and doctrine closely. Persevere in them, because if you do, you will save both yourself and your hearers" (1 Timothy 4:16).

God has not called us to be diplomatic against the forces of evil, but to proclaim their danger with patience, perseverance, and knowledge of the Word. Preach truth as the Bible says and do not worry about being popular.

M. de Rodríguez

Be a true watchman!

Manya - Liberia

Population: 64,000
The Manyans live in northeastern Liberia, near the border of Guinea. They are known for their food: rice with very spicy sauces. Their religion is Islam, but they have mixed it with their native beliefs. Some audio Bible translations exist in their native language, Manya.

Pray: For the Word of God to spread throughout Liberia and for the Manya to bear fruit.

The Grace Of God

> { Although I am less than the least of all the Lord's people, this grace
> was given me: to preach to the Gentiles the boundless riches of Christ.
> Ephesians 3:8

God specializes in using the impractical. Paul knew this fact very well. He knew God's grace poured into his life, not only to save him, but also to use him to preach the wonderful message of salvation to the Gentiles. God takes pleasure in using people that are seen as incapable. He loves leading them to do things no one else would do.

God called Abraham and sent him to a new land. God instructed Jonah to go preach to a city of bloodthirsty sinners. Sara was old, yet God promised her a son. God commanded Elijah to ask a poor widow for food. God spoke through a fiery bush to an 80-year-old shepherd named Moses and said he would be used to set people free from slavery. Jesus took illiterate fishermen and turned them into fishers of men. The Apostle Paul was a fierce persecutor of Christians, but he was thrown from his horse, blinded, and was transformed into one of the world's greatest missionaries.

All these people have two things in common: they were all insignificant and they all found grace in the eyes of God. Do you fall into these categories? Can God choose one ordinary, flawed person and make that person into a brave missionary who will make a difference in the world? I am convinced God continues to call insignificant people to take the Gospel to the nations! Will you be one of them?

A. Gulard

In God's grace, go and
preach to the nations.

Sau - Afghanistan

Population: 4,200
The Sau are Muslims in both religion and culture. No known Christians live among them. Their native language, Savi, has no translation of the Bible. More than half of the Saus currently live in Pakistan as refugees.

Pray: For God to manifest His love and to bring the salvation of Jesus Christ to the Saus.

The Test Will Come

{ *Some time later, God tested Abraham... Genesis 22:1*

God had promised Abraham a son and by the time we read Genesis 22 the promise had been miraculously fulfilled. God graciously gave Abraham a child and blessed him immensely. However, after Abraham received a son, God came and tested his obedience. Surprisingly, this test involved Abraham sacrificing his only son. Abraham was obedient and did everything God told him to. He did not think, even for a moment, that this proclamation was not from God. He knew God was leading this difficult test and therefore, Abraham confidently obeyed.

Can you imagine how Abraham felt as he walked up the mountain to sacrifice his son? He was probably wondering why God was taking away the promise He had made. When God asked Abraham to sacrifice his son, all of God's promises were being challenged. But Abraham was radically obedient and God preserved His promise and stopped Abraham before he made the sacrifice. God allowed Abraham to keep what he loved, but it required testing his heart. Because Isaac, Abraham's son, had become so important to Abraham, he risked taking the place of God in Abraham's life.

Do you have something important in your life? A boyfriend, girlfriend, profession, job, parents, or possession? Remember God can test your heart and take away anything at any moment. What will you do? How will you respond?

D. Duk

Follow the example of Abraham!

Dutch - Netherlands

Population: 12,698,000

This entire country, whose language is Dutch, has an entire translation of the Bible. Many Dutch believe God exists, but the majority wants no relationship with him. They are financially wealthy, but spiritually poor. It is estimated only 4% of this massive population are Christians.

Pray: For God to release the Dutch from the deceitfulness of riches.

Foolishness?

> Then the Lord said to Joshua, "See, I have delivered Jericho into your hands, along with its king and its fighting men. March around the city once with all the armed men. Do this for six days." Joshua 6:2-3

In this passage, God promised Joshua that He would deliver Jericho into the Israelites hands after they marched around the city for six days. I am sure when this request was made, the majority of the Israelites wondered why they should waste their time walking around the city. From a human perspective, the normal way of conquering Jericho would involve intense battles, strategic planning, and powerful force. Why would God make such an unusual request?

When God makes a promise, He makes it so He can receive maximum glory. From a human standpoint, it is foolish to think the Israelites could conquer a city by walking around its walls, but from God's perspective, the plan is true brilliance. Isaiah 55:8-9 says, "For my thoughts are not your thoughts neither are your ways my ways," declares the Lord. "As the heavens are higher than the earth, so are my ways higher than your ways and my thoughts than your thoughts."

God's promises are divine, but because they can look "foolish" in the eyes of the world, we often look idiotic as we wait for a promise to be fulfilled. Can you image how the Israelites felt as they walked around Jericho for the first time? Before God's promise was realized, I am sure they felt pretty silly. But after they remained faithful and God fulfilled His promise, they triumphed over their enemies and God was forever glorified. Are you looking like a fool waiting for a promise to be fulfilled? Don't worry, God is faithful and will fulfill the promises He has made!

S. Langemeier

Keep walking in faith even if you look foolish!

Nonama - Panama

Population: 3,600

Nonamas work with agriculture. They have a strong sense of ethnic identity, which comes from their animistic and pantheistic religions. It is estimated .5% believe in Jesus. The Gospel is being spread through the Jesus Film in their native language, Woun Meu.

Pray: For God to use the Jesus Film to bring salvation to these people.

OCTOBER

Dehumanized Society

> *Therefore, as God's chosen people, holy and dearly loved, clothe your-selves with compassion, kindness, humility, gentleness and patience.*
> *Colossians 3:12*

We live in a consumer society where the technology industry surprises us every day with something new and innovative. As a result, we get fixed to the idea of always having the newest or trendiest item and if we don't, we often feel dissatisfied.

Statistics say 80% of waste is technological equipment we throw away because it is considered outdated. Often, technology devices are thrown away before we even figure out how to use the cool features and functions that originally caught our attention.

Sometimes we tend to have that same attitude towards the people in our lives. However, we have to understand people are not mass-produced, but instead, they are original and unique creations of God. We must adopt the attitude of compassion, kindness, humility, gentleness and patience toward everyone that comes into our path. How often do we feel like a certain person isn't living up to our standards? Do we value all of the beautiful qualities God gave them or are we quick to judge and become easily dissatisfied?

Paul refers to us as God's chosen people, holy and dearly loved. Because we are dearly loved, we are called to love. We must convey the love of God to all those in this world who are 'dehumanized'. We are to shine in the darkness, give comfort in times of sorrow, strengthen the weak, and bring hope in the midst of despair.

W. Altare

Do not lose your
humanity!

Samtaos - Thailand

Population: 100

About 12,000 Samtaos are spread over four countries in Asia. However, a tribe of 100, in Thailand, has lost contact with other Samtaos and has established their own culture, religion, and dialect. They have been visited by Christian missionaries, but few believe the Gospel.

Pray: The Word is sown in their hearts and they will bear fruit.

Good News

> *Although I am less than the least of all the Lord's people, this grace was given me: to preach to the Gentiles the boundless riches of Christ.*
> *Ephesians 3:8*

In this verse, Paul uses two words that define the Gospel: "boundless riches". Even though Paul was in jail facing a death sentence while writing to the Ephesians, he was still able to see joy in preaching the Good News.

Evangelism is not effective if we leave out the positive message of the "Good News." The whole point of the "Good News" is to explain how good it really is. Obviously, there will be times where we have to discuss hard issues and tragedies of sin when we are evangelizing, but we must look to God and find joy in the tough times.

Every day we hear bad news. In fact, about 90% of the news around the world is based on tragedies or moral evils. This should provide us with even more motivation to bring light into this world through evangelism. Evangelism is about sharing the fascinating news that God's riches are more than enough and his promises for us are true. Christ has paid our debt and has invited us to be a part of his royal family where His riches are boundless. In a world of bad news, it is such a joy to be able to announce the Good News of salvation, forgiveness, and reconciliation with God!

A. Neufeld

Are you sharing the Good News?

Masna - Mauritania

Population: 2,100
They are fishermen and farmers who live on the Atlantic coast. They adopted Islam in the sixteenth century and do not allow other religions within the culture. Their language is Prosee Hassaniya, which contains several resources for evangelism.

Pray: For a spiritual awakening and that they will see God's grace and receive Christ.

Who Trains Harder?

> No, I strike a blow to my body and make it my slave so that after I have preached to others, I myself will not be disqualified for the prize.
> Read 1 Corinthians 9:24-27

One of the most important and popular Olympic events in Paul's time was boxing. Back then (and even to this day), if a boxer wanted to beat an opponent, he had to train many hours and discipline his body constantly. Paul says the Christian life is like a boxing match.

As Christians, we face many difficult opponents throughout our lifetime, but none can compare to the ultimate opponent: ourselves. Often, we let our flesh and our bodily desires overwhelm us, and although our bodies are not bad in and of themselves, the Bible warns us not to let the flesh tempt us spiritually and lead us into sinfulness.

In His perfect love, God created our bodies, and He gives us a second chance through the cross to die to ourselves and to our selfish ways. But like any worthy adversary, our flesh is always present within us and can overwhelm us if we are not alert and strong in God.

Paul was aware of the battle we fight daily with our 'old bodies', and he speaks in many of his letters of training himself to be strong in the Lord to overcome his bodily desires. Instead of giving into temptation, he disciplined his body to do what was right in the sight of the Lord. In this way, he teaches us that fighting bad habits and developing good ones is a key to success in the Christian life. Furthermore, Jesus challenged his disciples to develop the habit of prayer as a way to overcome our fleshly desires. "The spirit is willing, but the flesh is weak."

You and I need discipline to serve God and to bring His message to the world. Practice self-discipline, because its reward will never fade, and with it, we can reign victorious over our old, worldly adversary!

A. Betancur

Discipline your body!

Nunkak Macu - Colombia

Population: 1,500
Their main activities are hunting and fishing. They live in the Amazon. Seven percent of them are Christian. This has been achieved due the distribution of an audio New Testament which is in their language, Cacua.

Pray: There will be continued distribution of the audio Bible.

Realities Of The Mission Field

> Then he said to his disciples, "The harvest is plentiful but the workers are few. Ask the Lord of the harvest, therefore, to send out workers into his harvest field." Matthew 9:37-38

Jesus saw the crowd's needs, He saw they were sheep without a shepherd, and had compassion on them. He then used the illustration of a field that has a huge harvest but a lack of workers to harvest it. He used this illustration to further explain how lost people are. These verses show us some realities that are still valid today:

•There is a lot to do. One third of the world's population has never heard the Gospel of salvation through Jesus Christ. There are many open doors, needy hearts, and thirsty souls who are still waiting for a truth to fill their lives.

•The laborers are few. Less than 5% of missionaries go to places not yet reached. Furthermore, there are many projects that cannot be completed due to lack of workers.

•Jesus wants people to go to the mission field. The mission of the church is only part of the mission of God. World evangelism is a project of God, and He is calling people to join His project.

•Prayer is the fuel of missions. When you pray to God, you become more spiritually connected to His plan. Jesus asks us to pray to the Father for more missionaries. Prayer is the first and foremost step in the missionary movement.

Knowing this reality, what will you do? Pray to God, and ask for more workers.

F. Rodríguez

Let yourself be moved for Him if He wants to send to you!

Nanubae - Papua New Guinea

Population: 1,600
They live in the East Sepik Province. They are involved in numerous tribal cults and witchcraft spirits. None of the Bible has been translated into their language; however, it is estimated 1% have already heard of Jesus. They need missionaries!

Pray: For a Bible translation project to start and bring spiritual liberation to the Nanubae people.

Bible in a year: Revelation 4 / Nehemiah 5:1-7:3 / Psalm 99

With Eyes Of Faith

> *The Word became flesh and made his dwelling among us. We have seen his glory, the glory of the one and only Son, who came from the Father, full of grace and truth. John 1:14*

The Gospel of John is a Gospel of surprises. One of the biggest surprises was the way Jesus was brought to this earth. Many did not expect the Son of God to arrive as an average man from the house of a carpenter. The people of this day had other expectations of how the Messiah would arrive, even though the entire Old Testament pointed to His coming. Perhaps it was the false expectations that caused the world to overlook His glory (John 1:10). Even though Jesus came down in human form, humans did not receive Him. When Jesus walked the dusty roads of Palestine, one would have thought He should be walking in the air or transported in the latest model vehicle escorted by a choir of angels. It was quite the opposite; while some paid Him no attention at all, others resorted to giving Him dirty looks as he passed by. Jesus performed miracles, but many who watched Him saw nothing (John 6:30). Eyes of faith were needed to see Jesus. The key issue is to realize: we choose what we see.

Many religious people failed to see Jesus for who He really was because they did not have eyes of faith. What does it mean to see His glory? We will see His glory when we choose to serve, when we choose to seek the good of others while keeping eyes of faith, and when we choose to be filled with grace and truth. It is loving mercy. God will reveal Himself and his mercy to those who chose to have eyes of faith.

C. Scott

Do you see the glory of God?

Ta'oih - Vietnam

Population: 21,000
They are dedicated to the cultivation of rice, cassava, beans, sweet potatoes and other crops. They are experts in hunting and taming elephants. They believe in spirits and worship their ancestors. Their language does not have a Bible translation.

Pray: For Christian workers to translate the Bible and to teach the Gospel.

Bible in a year: Revelation 5 / Nehemiah 7:4-8:12 / Psalm 100

In The Hands Of Jesus

> They all ate and were satisfied, and the disciples picked up twelve bas-
> ketfuls of broken pieces that were left over. Read Matthew 14:15-20

Too many ministries never reach their full potential for the sole reason of "not having enough funds in the budget to fulfill their plans." How many times have we heard Christian workers say, "We cannot afford to do that"? The tension that was in Matthew 14 is similar to situations that happen in ministry today.

In this story, five thousand families came to listen to Jesus. After a long day, they started to become hungry and the disciples wanted to send the people away to go get food from the surrounding cities. Jesus stuns His disciples when He says, "give them some food yourselves". The disciples insist they don't have enough food to feed everyone. Jesus commands them to bring Him the small amount of food they did have. They bring Him five loaves of bread and two fish and put them in His hands. Jesus raises the food up to heaven and blesses it. With just five loaves of bread and two fish, five thousand men with their wives and children were fed.

Note: only the first five loaves and the two fish are first touched by Jesus (v. 19). The food didn't start multiplying until it was in the hands of the disciples. After all were fed, each disciple had a basket full of food leftover. You may not understand it at the time, but we'll never know if we have enough to feed the world if we do not put the resources in the hands of Jesus and then trust Him to work through us.

D. Travis

Give it all!

Matmata - Tunisia

Population: 9,600
They live isolated south of the Jerba Island. All professions are based around the sea, which is also their main source of food. Their language is Nafusi, which has no resources of evangelism. Their religion is Islam and they faithfully follow the five pillars of faith.

Pray: For someone to start a project of Bible translation in their language.

Obedience

> Then lie on your left side and put the sin of the people of Israel upon yourself. You are to bear their sin for the number of days you lie on your side. Read Ezekiel 4:1-17

Ezekiel is a prophet like no other. God instructed Ezekiel to do some difficult acts in order to bring the message of God to the stubborn people of Israel. Even before his first sermon, Ezekiel had to perform an extremely tough illustration (Ezekiel 4:1-3). He had to lie day and night, for over a year, on one side of his body and on one arm (v4-6), all the while being tied with ropes so that he could not roll over (v8). If that wasn't enough, he was instructed to eat and relieve himself from the same place, and ration his food and water intake each day (Ezekiel 4:9-13). In this way, Ezekiel was announcing God's threatening message to Israel.

I doubt anyone today would follow these crazy instructions to proclaim the Word of God. However, Ezekiel DID! He was a man who literally followed every instruction that God gave him. He suffered for the sake of obedience in delivering the message that God wanted to give. How far are you willing to go in obedience to publicize God's salvation? Has God ever asked you to do something difficult like He asked Ezekiel to do? Sometimes, we feel like we are sacrificing so much by simply spending a few years preparing at a Bible school, or a few hours in prayer, or walking a few miles to reach the lost. God expects obedience at any cost, all to bring the message of the cross.

M. de Rodríguez

Be obedient!

Shabak - Iraq

Population: 30,000
They live mostly north of Mosul, on the border of Turkey and Syria. They have no gospel witness or Bible translated into their language, nor do they have any missionaries or established churches. One hundred percent of the population professes Islam.

Pray: For the knowledge of Jesus to reach the Shabak.

Prepared In Advance

> For it is by grace you have been saved, through faith—and this is not from
> yourselves, it is the gift of God— not by works, so that no one can boast.
> For we are God's handiwork, created in Christ Jesus to do good works,
> which God prepared in advance for us to do.
> Read Ephesians 2:4-10

God, in His mercy and love, made us alive with Christ even when we were far from Him because of sin. By His grace, we have been saved! Because of the resurrection of Christ, we have the opportunity to sit in a heavenly place with God. It is through Him we can see the incomparable riches of His grace because of the kindness He poured out on us through His only son, Jesus Christ.

When we receive the salvation of God, we are given rights, but also responsibilities. Verse 10 tells us God has prepared a package of good works for us to do: works we can thank God for preparing for us in advance. These works often include showing the love of God to others and being a channel of blessings for them to be saved! Do you keep in mind that God always has work for you? Through love, He has prepared the way and it is your responsibility to move. Look around and discover where and how you can serve God.

D. Duk

Get to work!

Norwegians - Norway

Population: 4,476,000
Despite intense weather conditions in Norway, Norwegians live a quite modern and affluent lifestyle. Their religion is Protestant, but they currently struggle with new doctrines that lead them away from the Bible. Their language is Norwegian.

Pray: The Norwegian believers turn back to sound Biblical doctrine.

Many Ethiopians

> Philip ran up to the chariot and heard the man reading Isaiah the prophet. "Do you understand what you are reading?" Philip asked. "How can I?" he said, "unless someone explains it to me?" So he invited Philip to come up and sit with him.   Acts 8:30-31

Philip saw an opportunity to explain the Bible to this new Christian. There are millions of people in the world who are just like the Ethiopian who Philip met. Sadly, they won't have the opportunity to meet with Philip. In fact, a huge number of people die every day without ever reading a single verse of the Bible in their language. Over 340 million people do not have the Bible translated into their native tongue. There are still many places in the world with no church, no missionaries, no Bible, and not even a single Christian. There are thousands of Christians who are being beaten, tortured, imprisoned, stripped from their families, and sometimes killed for their efforts to try and spread the Good News.

We must not ignore the fact that many Christians are striving hard and risking their lives to get the Word out to people who have never heard it before. This is where our responsibility comes in. We must be disciplined in praying for those who make sacrifices like Philip did. However, when we are also presented with the opportunity to be with a new Christian, we should take the time and patience to feed into that person. Let's practice the attitude of Philip. Lord, how can we make Your name and salvation known in all the earth?

The Bible teaches us the fundamental purpose of man is to glorify God. Therefore, we need to ask ourselves: How can I best exalt His name? How can I glorify Him? Charles Spurgeon once said, "The greatest joy of a Christian is to give joy to Christ." What gives joy to Christ? How will the lost people of this world know and understand His Word without someone to explain it to them?

A. Gulard

Be like Philip!

Mby'a Guarani - Paraguay

Population: 14,324
Their language is Guarani and they have a complete translation of the Bible in their language. There are several churches among this group, but some communities don't have anyone witnessing to them. Mission agencies are working to train indigenous leaders and teachers from the churches.

Pray: For the work of mission agencies and for the existing Christian communities.

You're Late Again

> "Lord," Martha said to Jesus, "if you had been here, my brother would not have died. But I know that even now God will give you whatever you ask." John 11:21-22

Many times throughout our lives, we feel like saying to God, "You're late again." It may be when we don't get a job we hoped for, a family member becomes sick or dies, or a special opportunity falls through. Sometimes, we get so desperate to hear an answer and when we don't receive clarity as soon as we hope, we believe God's too busy dealing with something more important than our issue. When scenarios don't happen the way we expect, we blame Him for being late. However, I challenge you to look within your heart and think of all the times God made you wait and then gave you something greater than what you originally asked for. Sometimes God does the total opposite of what we ask for, but in the end, it yields an incredible blessing.

We must have hearts like that of Martha, who despite knowing her brother had been dead for four days, was sure Jesus could resurrect him by simply asking God... And Jesus did! With God, nothing is impossible. The same God who raised Lazarus from the dead two thousand years ago is your God today. The next time doubt creeps in, remember that God is powerful! He is above every name, above all power, and He loves you! His timing is perfect and in His timing, He will give you what is best!

M. Inciarte

Trust in Him!

Mandaean - Australia

Population: 3,700

It is a Syrian immigrant community. They speak Mandaic, but use mostly English. Their religion is based on the baptism in "living water" and communion with angels. No known believers live among them and no missionaries are currently reaching them.

Pray: For God to place a follower of Jesus among this people group.

Travel To The Past

> To the Jews who had believed him, Jesus said, "If you hold to my tea-ching, you are really my disciples. Then you will know the truth, and the truth will set you free." John 8:31-32

Personally, my past doesn't always bring up good feelings or memories. In fact, when I look back on my childhood, I remember many moments of being afraid and anxious. Last week, I had a flashback from when I was growing up. I remembered just how afraid, anxious, and sad I used to be. After about an hour of remembering, I became so engulfed by my past memories and feelings, I began to feel like an 11-year-old girl all over again. Then, all of a sudden, God spoke to my heart and reminded me I was FREE.

How many times have you felt trapped by your past situations? How often do fear and anguish take over your body and mind? Even though it may not be fun to re-live the past, I am thankful the Spirit can set us free and heal us from our old memories. Sometimes we go through situations that aren't easy, but in His grace, God is able to deliver us. Through His grace, He takes us to where He wants us to go and develops us into who He wants us to be. If for any reason, you are experiencing past regret, ask God to remind you of the freedom in which you now live. Remember, you live in His grace and love!

G. Galindo

Do not let the past imprison you!

Tayal - Taiwan

Population: 80,000
They live in the northern mountains of Taiwan. They have heard the Gospel in Japanese and it is estimated 9% believe in Jesus. Tayals have a great need for Biblical teaching because their native religion often creeps into their relationships with Christ. Their native language is Atayal.

Pray: For missionaries and Bible teachers to teach sound doctrine among the Tayal.

Without Anxiety

> Rejoice in the Lord always... Do not be anxious about anything, but in every situation, by prayer and petition, with thanksgiving, present your requests to God. And the peace of God, which transcends all understanding, will guard your hearts and your minds in Christ Jesus.
> Philippians 4:4-7

How often do we find ourselves in situations where we are stressed, anxious, or fearful? Sometimes the most stressful situations come when working in teams. Paul knew working with other people would lead to stressful situations because sin is in our human nature. Therefore, Paul emphasized how important it is to present our requests to God. Stress and conflicts are guaranteed to arise in our countries, churches, and mission fields. They are guaranteed to happen simply because we are human and face differences with one another. However, we must be disciplined in giving our stressful situations to God.

God does not like to see His missionaries suffer through anxiety or tension in ministry, but sometimes it does happen and it always happens for a reason. It is easy to worry about whether or not enough financial support will be raised (Matthew 6:25-34) or to be anxious when faced with threats of persecution (Matthew 10:17-21, 1 Peter 4:12-16, 5:6-7). When doing God's will, many distractions will come our way. Paul, in his wisdom, advises us to step back during these trials and lay them in the hands of God.

I tend to reject "formulas" in the Christian life, but I notice an important sequence in Paul's words to the Philippians. When faced with tests, pressure, or persecution, we must focus on DECIDING to praise and rejoice in the Lord. Rather than being scared or anxious, we must present our requests to God and GIVE THANKS ... BEFORE seeing the response or outcome. In this way, God will work in our hearts and take care of the discouragement and doubt.

T. Sandvig

Follow this formula!

Mijikenda - Kenya

Population: 328,000
The Mijikenda are made up of nine tribes. They majority of Mijikendas are Muslim. By adopting this faith, they escaped slavery and started a profitable trade with the Arabs. They have the New Testament in their language, Kigiryama.

Pray: The Word of God becomes more desirable than materialism.

Wise Decision Making

> *But when he saw the wind, he was afraid and, beginning to sink, cried out, "Lord, save me!" Matthew 14:30*

Each walk with Jesus is different. Some have been following Jesus for years, others may have only known Him for a few months, and a few may have just recently made the decision to follow Him. Those who have been following Christ for a while know the path isn't always easy. Millions around the world have accepted this incredible challenge and, like Peter, have stepped out of the boat. Although many have stepped out of the boat, many have also began to sink.

Peter began to sink when he focused on the circumstances around him. It is interesting the circumstances Peter experienced were the exact same when he decided to step out of the boat and onto the water. Instead of trusting, he looked away from Jesus and let the circumstances control his situation. The moment he focused on his circumstances he began to sink. If you make decisions based solely on the circumstances around you, you will be tempted to doubt.

When Peter made the decision to step out of the boat and start walking on the water, he did so while looking straight into the eyes of Jesus. If you expect to follow the path God has prepared for you, you have to make the decision to keep our eyes on Christ.

J. Segnitz

Set your focus only on Jesus!

Ofaye - Brazil

Population: 62
They have lost their native language and now speak Portuguese. They live in the State of Mato Grosso do Sul. Their religion is animism, and the sun is their god. They have not had contact with the Gospel because they do not allow missionaries into their territory.

Pray: God would open doors for the Ofaye to hear the message of salvation.

Do Not Underestimate The Enemy

> *In order that Satan might not outwit us. For we are not unaware of his schemes.* 2 Corinthians 2:11

When I traveled to Cameroon in 1998, I got to the airport, felt the heat on my face, heard the mosquitoes buzzing around, and I felt so happy to be there! There was absolutely nothing in the new environment that made me uncomfortable. Everything was beautiful and perfect to me. I felt like I was finally home.

From the beginning, I was eager to share the Gospel, but I still didn't know French (the language spoken in Cameroon). Nevertheless, I didn't fear interaction and I began to visit our neighbors. I noticed instantly they took a liking to me. One even showed me how to make a traditional outfit. Shortly after, I began to participate in a church. I helped out with Sunday school and even got to evangelize in a village called Ayos Etoud.

I constantly surrounded myself with children and the people often welcomed me into their homes and offered me meals. I really wasn't prepared for what would come next. One day the pastor said to me, "Ivette, be careful what you eat. There is a witch nearby and she's not happy with your work in the village." Initially, I didn't pay much attention to the advice of the pastor. That is, until one day, I began to feel ill because I had unknowingly eaten something prepared by the sorcerer. I was so sick that I had to leave the village that I loved.

Several people and I began to fervently pray to God and soon I recovered. When I returned to the village, the people were shocked to see me because some believed I had died. However, the situation proved my God was more powerful than the power of a witch. Ever since this experience, I pray to God not fearing the power of evil, but not ignoring it either.

I. Santander

Do not let the enemy have an advantage!

Moor - Mauritania

Population: 3,380,000
They are distributed throughout the country's Atlantic coast. In their area, they control the trade of salt and gold. They profess Islam, but are of the sect Malikite. Their language is Hassaniya.

Pray: The Word of God comes into their hearts.

Jesus In The Boat

{ *Lord, save us! We're going to drown! Matthew 8:25*

As the journey quietly began with good weather, the boat was a good place to sleep and rest, so Jesus laid his head down and slept. As he slept, an uncontrollable storm gradually formed and threatened to sink the boat.

The disciples woke him up and said, "Lord, save us! We're going to drown", to which Jesus replied, "You men of little faith, why are you so afraid?" Then He rebuked the winds and sea and it was "completely calm" (Matt. 8:26).

After two thousands years, the daily storms of life continue and new disciples come and go, but Jesus is still the same yesterday, today, and forever (Heb. 13:8). Is the Lord in your boat? If Jesus is in your boat, you should have no fear of storms. Jesus can immediately calm your storm or simply turn your boat into a submarine! He promised in Isaiah 43:2, "when you pass through the waters, I will be with you." Our problem is we often remain "men of little faith." Time and time again, we lose the opportunities to persevere through the storms of life and share with the world about the life Christ gives.

Have you wondered how people without Christ face the storms of life? From the "boat", the words of the Master still echo, "Go and preach the gospel to every creature." Invite people into the safety of the boat and show them the love of God. The world is waiting for you! Christ Himself is coming for their salvation (2 Peter 3:9)!

F. Chinatti

Therefore, go!

New Zealanders - New Zealand

Population: 2,823,000
Their language is English. They have all resources for evangelism. The established church faces the typical problems of secularism and nominalism. They need to go back to the Bible and devotion to Christ.

Pray: For a spiritual awakening among Christians and for the Gospel to reign in their lives.

Three Attitudes

{ *When Jesus saw him lying there and learned that he had been in this condition for a long time, he asked him, "Do you want to get well?"* *John 5:6*

In this passage, Jesus meets a crippled man who hasn't been able to walk for 38 years. Jesus asks the man, "Do you want to get well?" The crippled man's response was, "I have no one to help me into the pool when the water is stirred. While I am trying to get in, someone else goes down ahead of me." (John 5:7)

The crippled man highlights a common problem within the church: a lack of support and sympathy. Because he received no support from those around him, his faith was limited. Jesus came and had compassion on the man and he was instantly healed. What is interesting about this story is Jesus chose to heal on the Sabbath. During this time period, healing on the Sabbath was forbidden. Most people in this circumstance would have been worried about breaking the law, but Jesus did not worry. He boldly focused on justice, mercy, and humility. Sadly, the authorities watching Him focused only on the law, rules, structure, and power.

It's important to remember the quality of leaders is determined by how they treat the needy (Ezekiel 34). Today, many people are in need of compassion and healing. Do not ignore God's voice when you feel compassion for someone. How many people do you know like the crippled man? How many people do you know who are in need of compassion and support? Why are they remaining in their broken condition? Be compassionate and supportive!
C. Scott

> Practice justice, mercy, and truth.

Shahari- Oman

Population: 36,000
They live in Dofar and have devoted their lives to Islam. They speak Shehri, which has no Biblical resources. Christian influence is desperately needed, but it is difficult for missionaries to come into contact with Shaharis.

Pray: The truth of the Gospel would reach the Shaharis.

Enlarged

> *So if you think you are standing firm, be careful not to fall!*
> *1 Corinthians 10:12*

I always found Chuck Norris jokes to be really funny. The jokes portray him to be indestructible, all-knowing, and all-powerful. For Chuck, nothing is impossible. "He can kill two stones with one bird." "He can make an onion cry." "When Alexander Graham Bell invented the telephone, he had two missed calls from Chuck." "In 10 years, Chuck will be 10 years younger." "He can hack in to any intelligence network using only a calculator." "He can draw circles using a ruler." "Monsters tell stories about Chuck around a campfire." "He can count from infinity to zero." It's as if Chuck Norris is a combination of every superhero. What is most striking about Chuck Norris is the arrogance and self-confidence put into an ordinary, imperfect man. The idea is Chuck can do anything without anyone's help.

Sadly, this is how many Christians see themselves. They tend to believe they can do everything on their own. Because they think they can do everything independently, little thought and effort is put into praying and reading God's Word. It then becomes easy to fall into the temptation of living life without the fellowship of other Christians.

Paul urges you to always be on your guard. In 1 Corinthians 10:12, Paul suggests even when you feel moments of victory or closeness with God, you should be careful not to fall. Do not let your heart be filled with pride by believing you have a piece of "Chuck Norris" inside of you. Be dependent on God!

W. Nunez

It's up to God.

O'odham - Mexico

Population: 1,700
They come from the Sonora desert. They speak Tohono O'odham and have an audio version of the New Testament. They are faithful Roman Catholics and reject anyone who leaves the church. It is estimated only 1% of the population has a personal relationship with Jesus.

Pray: The Word of God would speak to their hearts and transform their minds.

Bible in a year: Revelation 17/ Isaiah 1-2 / Psalm 108

The Double Perspective Of Salvation

> *In his great mercy he has given us new birth into a living hope through the resurrection of Jesus Christ from the dead, and into an inheritance that can never perish, spoil, or fade. This inheritance is kept in heaven for you, who through faith are shielded by God's power until the coming of the salvation that is ready to be revealed in the last time.*
> *1 Peter 1:3-5*

The double perspective:

1. Salvation is immediate and present: "I tell you, now is the time of God's favor, now is the day of salvation" (2 Corinthians 6:1-2, Acts 4:12, Acts 13:26).

2. Salvation is for our future: each day brings us closer to the day of our glorification. This is why Paul says we were sealed by the Holy Spirit "for the day of redemption." (Ephesians 4:30)

If we can live each day with these two perspectives in the mind, the plan of salvation becomes more meaningful and proactive. We know this life is a race that has an unavoidable finish line. Our goal should be to proclaim salvation until the day we reach that "finish line." There is no reason we should reduce the Gospel to a cold, mechanical formula. To speak about a relationship with God is to speak about a relationship with your best friend.

The Gospel teaches people are born again through the death and resurrection of Jesus Christ. On this earth, you are in a permanent state of waiting to receive your full gift of salvation, but today, through the sacrifice of Jesus, you have been saved from the punishment of sin! The best is yet to come!

O. Simari

Live each day with faith, waiting for the glorious day of your redemption!

Portuguese - Portugal

Population: 9,872,000

The Portuguese are the largest people group in Portugal. The majority profess to be Roman Catholics. Many only take part in religious festivities. It is estimated only 2% live a life dedicated to Jesus. They need to be re-evangelized with the Gospel.

Pray: For the Word of God to give new life and to create a spiritual awakening.

Bible in a year: Revelation 18/ Isaiah 3-4/ Psalm 109:1-19

Responsibility Of An Ambassador

> God was reconciling the world to himself in Christ, not counting people's sins against them. And he has committed to us the message of reconciliation. We are therefore Christ's ambassadors, as though God were making his appeal through us. We implore you on Christ's behalf: Be reconciled to God. 2 Corinthians 5:19-20

Every once in a while, I'll hear a vicious rumor that horrible diseases like AIDS and cancer were created in labs to control the world population. I have even heard the rumor that cures for the horrible diseases exist, but are kept secret from the world. If these rumors were ever discovered to be true, the world would turn into chaos and the people responsible would be held accountable for the billions of lives lost.

Should we have the same ideology for salvation? Should Christians be held accountable if they have understood and accepted the message of salvation but withhold it from others? As followers of Christ we have a great responsibility. We have the responsibility of being ambassadors of the world's greatest cure, salvation. Salvation is a message every person needs to hear and it is our blessing to be able to share it. The message is full of hope and eternal healing for the lost souls of the world walking towards their eternal death.

Most Christians believe the responsibility of sharing God's message of salvation is a choice. However, God has called and entrusted Christians to share the wonderful treasure of eternal salvation. When you ignore this calling, it is as irresponsible as deliberately spreading cancer or AIDS. "If anyone, then, knows the good they ought to do and doesn't do it, it is sin for them" (James 4:17).

G. Vergara

What are you doing with the message entrusted to you?

Toku-no-shima – Japan

Population: 5,000
They live on the southern islands of Japan. Their native language is dying because most people speak only Japanese. Many Toku-no-shimas have little education and are considered second-class citizens. They have access to the Gospel in Japanese.
Pray: The Gospel would bring value to their lives and they would understand Jesus desires a relationship with them!

Out Of The Boat And Walking By Faith

{ *"Lord, if it's you," Peter replied, "tell me to come to you on the water."*
Read Matthew 14:22-33

In this story, the disciples saw a man walking on the water, but believed he was a ghost! When Peter realized it was Jesus, he said, "Lord, if it's you, tell me to come to you on the water." Jesus then replied, "Come." Peter responded by stepping out of the boat and walking on the water toward Jesus.

I can't imagine what was going through Peter's mind as he took those first steps out of the boat. In verse 30, we see while he was walking, he became fearful: "But when he saw the wind, he was afraid and, beginning to sink, cried out, 'Lord, save me!'" What happened to Peter? He didn't think twice about stepping out of the boat and onto the water, but after a few steps he fixed his mind on the impossibility of the act. When he began to focus on the impossibility, he subsequently lost his focus on Jesus. Jesus in His mercy, immediately reached out His hand, caught Peter, and said, "You of little faith, why do you doubt?"

Peter left the comfort of the boat to walk in faith towards Jesus. While walking, he started to doubt the safety offered to him by the Creator of the Universe. In your specific calling, are you willing to leave the boat and walk by faith towards Christ?

MyT. Goddard

Have you stepped out of the boat yet?

Mwani - Mozambique

Population: 112,000
The Mwani people adopted Islam because the Arabs invaded Africa and made all non-Muslims their slaves. They can read the Quran in Arabic, but the majority of Mwanis do not understand the meaning of what they are reading. Evangelism has proved to be challenging.

Pray: The Mawanis are reached with an audio Bible in their native language.

Presentation

> He answered, "I am a Hebrew and I worship the LORD, the God of heaven, who made the sea and dry land." *Read Jonah 1:8-9*

After being interrogated by a flood of questions, Jonah responds by saying he is Hebrew. What is interesting is when Jonah is asked about his identity, he begins to describe God. Who do you say you are when questioned by others?

In our society, it is common for people to find their identity in the offices they hold or the titles they possess. In reality, those things are no reflection of who we are before the throne of God. Little is heard about a pastor in a small village or a missionary in an unknown place. This is because the majority of people are drawn to places where they can receive recognition for their accomplishments. Instant credibility is given to those with the title of "doctor", "engineer" or "pastor of a mega church". In our world, credibility is dependent on titles. Although I don't have anything against the previous titles, I pray Christians will always give more credibility to a life reflecting Jesus' servant heart.

When asked the question, "Who are you?" I would love to hear somebody say, "I am a Christian and I fear the Lord." This answer echoes the same answer Jonah gave over a thousand years ago. "I worship the Lord, the God of heaven, who made the sea and the dry land."

G. Rivas

Who do you say you are?

Nivaclé - Paraguay

Population: 28,000

They are part of the Matacoan linguistic family and have the New Testament in their native language, Nivaclé. They live in the Paraguayan Chaco and work mainly with agriculture. Many are animists and are heavily involved in sorcery. Crimes are paid for by blood revenge.

Pray: For the missionaries working among them and for wisdom to communicate the Gospel.

Compassion First

{ *Get up! Pick up your mat and walk. John 5:8*

In the gospel of John, we read about Jesus healing a man who had been crippled for 38 painful years. After the healing, one would expect to hear a joyous reaction from the religious leaders. Instead, they told the man, "it is the Sabbath; the law forbids you to carry your mat." (John 5:10) For 38 years, this man had not walked, but the religious leaders were more concerned about him using his newfound legs to "work" on the Sabbath than joining him in praising God for the miracle.

Caring for the people you lead is the key to leadership. The religious leaders believed keeping the rules was more important than celebrating a person's healing. Sadly, this crippled man was invisible to the religious leaders until he broke one of their laws. They had no interest in the needs of their people. While people continued to cry out for help and healing, all they heard was the law. The law started to take such precedence in the leaders' lives, it began to overtake the voice of God. As the voice of God was extinguished, they increased their efforts to kill Jesus (John 5:16-17).

Following the example of Christ is very risky and can cause challenges. You will face opposition and betrayal, but if you want to serve the living God, the only way is to follow this daring example of Christ! Like Jesus, bring compassion to places where there is none!

C. Scott

Are you being compassionate?

New Caledonian Javanese - New Caledonia

Population: 11,000
They are located in Noumea, on the southern tip of the island. Their religion is Islam. The women dress in black and suffer from discrimination. They have no translation of the Bible in their native language, Javanese. No known Christians live among them.

Pray: For a translation of the Bible, so they can hear the Gospel in their language.

Servant Obedience

{ *So Abraham went, as the Lord had told him. Read Genesis 12:1-9*

This particular passage shows the obedience of Abraham and the faithfulness of God. Although Abraham often wavered and made mistakes in his life, the faithfulness of God remained with him every step of his journey.

We see the four stages in which Abraham showcased his strong faith in the Lord:

a) Believing (v. 6): He left everyone and everything - his land, family, house, and inheritance to wander into a strange and distant land. He believed in the invisible God!

b) Obeying (v.4-6): A faith that doesn't move us is not true faith. The faith of Abraham moved his feet and made him tread the path of obedience.

c) Thanking (v. 7 -8): God led Abraham with a flashlight. God always chose to reveal just a few steps ahead to Him, never the entire plan. Why? He did this so Abraham would depend on Him and not himself (Hebrews 11:8-13).

d) Evangelizing (v. 8 -9): "He invoked the name of the Lord," meaning Abraham publicly declare d the attributes of God.

This is what it means to be a missionary! Abraham took part in accomplishing the mission that God has also called us to accomplish. We can learn how to walk in the faith God calls us to by simply reading about the journey of faith Abraham took. Are you walking in faith in the Lord every day, despite your circumstances? Are you taking steps of obedience? Are you grateful in all circumstances and uncertainty?

L. Díaz

Let us fulfill our mission with faith and obedience!

Neho - Ivory Coast
Population: 14,000
They are immigrants from Liberia, but have settled on the coast of Cote d'Ivoire. Their religion is animistic. Each family worships a particular spirit and each village worships a specific deity. A Christian church exists among the Nehos, but the members are all foreigners. Their language, Neyo, has several Bible audio stories.

Pray: For God to give the church strategies to reach the natives.

Incorporated Technology

{ *And over all these virtues put on love, which binds them all together in perfect unity. Colossians 3:14*

ICT is an acronym that stands for "information and communication technologies." New technologies used to communicate with people around the world are being developed and pioneered constantly. It is now possible to talk with loved ones who live thousands of miles away, for free. But although new technology is invented every day, it's good to remember the original communication "technologies" God gave us.

One of these "technologies" is the "look" we give others. One look can say so much. You don't even have to say words for something to be said because looks can accurately communicate your feelings. A look can show approval, rejection, encouragement, discouragement, guilt, anger, and even love.

Another communication technology God has given us is our ears. Although our ears pick up many sounds throughout the day, we often choose what we want to hear. Sadly, many people in the world feel like no one hears them. Sometimes, all people need is someone to listen to them.

Hearing is related to yet another communication technology given by God: speech. Speech can be dangerous because if it is abused, it can result in you not hearing others. Excessive talking is a temptation that results in words being said without actually saying anything.

We all need to hear inspiring words at some point in our lives. God reminds us the mouth speaks out of the abundance of the heart. This should be the reason why you fill yourself with the word of God! Isaiah 50:4 says, "The Sovereign Lord has given me a well-instructed tongue, to know the word that sustains the weary. He wakens me morning by morning, wakens my ear to listen like one being instructed." God desperately wants you to use your senses for His glory! To see, hear and speak with love!

W. Altare

Use your senses for the love of Christ!

Ruthenes - Ukraine

Population: 517,000
The Ruthenes are considered Balkans. Their main religion is Roman Catholic, but they only practice their beliefs during some festivals and on family occasions. Their native language is Rusyn, which currently has no translation of the Bible.

Pray: For a revival among the Ruthenes and for their love of God to extend beyond tradition.

A Follower Of Jesus

{ *So they pulled their boats up on shore, left everything and followed Jesus. Read Luke 5:1-11*

Peter was one of Jesus' disciples. We see in the Gospels and the book of Acts how God used Peter in extraordinary situations. If we take his example seriously, our lives can be tremendously challenged. Peter was a man who walked on water, but he was also a man who denied his relationship with Jesus. It is easy to suggest Peter is like many Christians today because he was a follower who experienced many ups and downs.

One of the biggest lessons we can learn from Peter's life was how he became a follower of Jesus:

Verse 5: Peter's faith was practical. In this passage, we see how he instantly obeyed Jesus' advice. Verse 7: He shared the blessings he received. Verse 8: He recognized the greatness of Jesus and his own condition of sin. Verse 9: He marveled at the greatness of God's work. Verse 11: He left everything and followed Jesus.

What does it mean to leave "everything"? Peter left his job and was no longer a fisherman, he left his family and walked from town to town with Jesus, leaving his prosperity behind. As a follower of Jesus, what are you willing to leave? Are you following Jesus wholeheartedly? Do you have things you should leave to become a better follower of Him? Take a few moments in prayer and ask the Lord!

M. de Rodríguez

Leave everything and follow Him!

Dhavad - India

Population: 1,700

They mine iron and use it to make tools. They are very poor and this has hindered them from mining iron on an industrial level for trade. The majority of Dhavads follow Islam.

Pray: Through their poverty they will experience God's provision and recognize Jesus as their savior.

The Budget According To Jesus

> But Jesus answered, "You give them something to eat." They said to him, "That would take more than half a year's wages! Are we to go and spend that much on bread and give it to them to eat?" Mark 6:37

One particular story in the book of Mark tells of 5,000 men, plus their wives and children, who gathered to hear Jesus speak. But there was one problem: no food was available and the stomachs of the thousands of people began to growl with hunger.

While the disciples proposed the people be sent away to the nearby villages to buy food for themselves, Jesus said, "Give them something to eat." Back in that time, enough food for all those people would have cost more than 200 pence, which is more than a half-year's salary. After calculating the "budget", the disciples decided: "We cannot take care of this project." But Jesus asked, "How much food do we have?" After discovering they only had five loaves of bread and two fish for the thousands of people, Jesus said, "Bring them to me." He took what little food they had, gave thanks to His Father, and passed it out to the crowds. After everyone had taken what they needed and ate until they were satisfied, the Scriptures tell us twelve baskets of bread were left over!

This is very similar to what often happens in churches. We have been given the Great Commission by Jesus, but we calculate how much everything will cost, we prepare a budget and say, "We can't. Sending missionaries will just have to be postponed until we feel we can afford it." However, what we fail to realize within our churches is that the Great Commission is a command, not something to be done only if the budget allows it. All Jesus asks is that we give what we have into His hands and let Him multiply it. Instead of thinking about what you don't have, think about what Jesus can do with what you do have! Today, ask yourself the question, "What do I have to give to Jesus and do I have the faith that He will multiply it?"

F. Rodríguez

Think about it!

Sinhalese - Oman

Population: 10,000
The Sinhalese are indigenous people from Sri Lanka. Most Sinhalese follow Buddhism, but it is estimated 1.2% are evangelical Christians. The New Testament has been widely circulated through audio. They have the Jesus film in their native language.

Pray: The proclamation of the Word of God continues to bear fruit among the Sinhalese.

There Will Be Difficulties

> { *They had such a sharp disagreement that they parted company.*
> *Read Acts 15:36 - 16:10*

Often times, we think ministry is a problem free work environment with nothing but harmony between one another. Reality is quite the opposite. Paul, one of the greatest missionaries of the Bible, had to jump several hurdles during his ministry. If you are unfamiliar with this passage, read carefully about the obstacles he had to overcome to continue the mission:

1. Paul and Barnabas completely disagreed about John Mark. It ended in separation. Barnabas went with John Mark, and Paul went with Silas.

2. Paul later invited the disciple Timothy to join his ministry, who happened to be half Jew and half Greek. Because the town they were going to knew Timothy was half Greek, Paul had him circumcised to make ministry smoother.

3. The Spirit of Jesus prevented Paul from entering the region where he planned to go. He then received a vision from God telling him in which direction he should go.

Are you having difficulties in your ministry? No matter how much effort you put into serving the Lord, do you experience conflicts with other believers? Are there people in your team who are not so easy to get along with? Does God ever change your plans at the last minute?

We must be determined to carry forth with the work of God, despite the troubles we run into. God let's us go through difficulties while working with other people to make us stronger and capable of accomplishing the tasks He sets before us. Don't give up!

M. Gomes

Keep going!

Nialetic - Eritrea

Population: 98,000
The Nialetic are a subgroup of the Nara people. They live in cone-shaped houses and their villages look like beehives. Their economy is dependent on agriculture. They are Muslims in name, but follow an animist religion and practice polygamy. Their language, Nara, has no translation of the Bible.

Pray: For missionaries to live among them and translate the Bible into their language.

The Time Will Come

> Commit your way unto the LORD; trust in him and he will do this.
> Psalm 37:5

When I was nineteen, I felt led to go to Africa. As I prepared for this journey, I experienced many ups and downs, which I believe was just a way for God to mold me for the ministry He called me to. Sometimes, I felt a great deal of impatience and wanted to do things my way instead of letting things happen with God's perfect timing. I even remember one particular instance when I had pulled away from God and before I knew it, I had become easy prey for the enemy. However, in His mercy, God faithfully pulled me back and allowed me to repent and see His will for my future ministry.

During ministry preparation, God is especially interested in our character, humility, patience, and willingness to serve. This stage of my life was not easy and it was only by God's grace that I was sustained. I would encourage everyone who is called into full time ministry not to take the stage of preparation lightly. Do everything you can to better equip yourself for the service of God: study a profession, participate in seminars, go to camps, and serve with short-term missions teams. Learn skills that can help you serve the needs of people. Be diligent in learning so you can be prepared when doors are opened to share the Gospel. Have faith that God's timing for you is perfect because before you know it, it's time to GO.

God has great plans for your life. He wants you to use all your gifts and talents for His glory, but you have to trust Him! God's timing is perfect and you must learn to wait on Him.

I. Santander

> God knows the
> right time!

Pacahuara - Bolivia

Population: 20
To preserve this ethnic group, the government decided to integrate them into the Chácobo ethnicity. As an act of resistance, they have retained their culture and language. Their religion is animistic and they practice sorcery. They are unreached by the Gospel.

Pray: For missionaries to preach the Gospel to the Pacahuara.

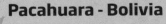

Bible in a year: 2 Thessalonians 2 / Isaiah 27-28 / Psalm 118

God Insists

> So he left the land of the Chaldeans and settled in Harran. After the death of his father, God sent him to this land where you are now living.
> Acts 7:4

In this passage, Stephen is referring to Abram and how God called him to lead his family to the Promised Land. God had promised he would be a blessing to all nations, but that doesn't mean Abram was fully obedient along the way. In the Scriptures, we see evidence that Abram delayed obeying God. It says Abram dwelled for a while in Haran, which was not the Promised Land. Perhaps, the death of his father could have been the main cause for this delay in obedience.

This can also happen to us. In different points in our lives, God will give us certain instructions and we have the choice to obey, obey under own circumstances, or not obey. Unfortunately, Abram half obeyed. He delayed his journey and when he finally decided to go, he took his father and his nephew Lot, which later caused him a great deal of trouble.

The interesting thing is God could have left Abram alone in Haran. However, when Abram's father died, God reminded him he had not yet reached the goal he was given. Just like Abram, you might have lost sight of the call from God by making cultural, family-related, or economical excuses. Don't be surprised when God calls you again and gives you the same message He already spoke. When God has a purpose for a person, He keeps calling until there is a response.
H. Ziefle

Stop running from God!

Trieng - Vietnam

Population: 18,000

They eat rice and cassava, but also raise poultry. They are animistic and their religious leader is usually a warlock. They have heard the Gospel in Khmer, but their native language is Trieng. It is estimated five percent are Christian.

Pray: For the Bible to be translated into Trieng, so more hearts can be reached.

Choosing To Serve

{ *After that, he poured water into a basin and began to wash his disciples' feet, drying them with the towel that was wrapped around him. Read John 13:5-10*

This example of Jesus is unique. Sadly, we often think twice before serving in a way that won't be noticed or gain recognition from others. It is a temptation to want to be well known, but when the goal is only to be well known, it is easy to become dependent on recognition and refuse to listen to a possible call from God. When you are dependent on the recognition from others, it can be difficult to believe God if He calls you to go to a new place where you know no one and have to start from scratch. But do not forget the example of Jesus!

Jesus stepped off His throne, left His home and position as King, and came down to earth to wash the feet of His disciples. Jesus showed He was willing to serve on any level. Although Jesus was a humble servant, we often feel sweeping a floor or cleaning a toilet is humiliating work for a leader. If you want to be a true disciple of Christ and a leader of the flock, follow the example Jesus set as a servant leader! You need to be willing to serve anywhere, whether it is in a place you are well known or in a place where you are unknown. Jesus taught His disciples through service!

N. Rivas

Are you willing to serve like Jesus did?

Oloha - Solomon Islands

Population: 50
The Olaha people are an ethnic minority group in their Catholic Christian state. The majority is nominal in their faith. They have heard the Gospel verbally, but have no translation of the Bible in their native language. Many young Olohas have migrated to Australia.

Pray: They would receive a Bible translation in their native language.

Bible in a year: 1 Timothy 1 / Isaiah 31-33 / Psalm 119:33-64

Sacrificially

> Calling his disciples to him, Jesus said, "Truly I tell you, this poor widow has put more into the treasury than all the others." Mark 12:43

It was Easter time in the Temple of Jerusalem. Jesus had sat down across from the offering box and started watching various people put their money into the temple treasury (v 41). "Many rich people threw in large amounts. But a poor widow came and put in two very small copper coins, worth only a few cents" (v 42). Jesus sees this, calls His disciples over, and says, "They all gave out of their wealth; but she, out of her poverty, put in everything–all she had to live on" (v 43-44).

Right before this event (v 38-40), Jesus had been talking to H-is disciples about watching out for the teachers of the law who "devour widow's houses and for a show make lengthy prayers." I don't think it's any coincidence that we see a drastic contrast in the comparison between the two types of givers. Jesus states the widow gave comparatively more than anyone else because she gave sacrificially. Even though the amounts of giving will be different between the rich and poor, their willingness to give joyfully and sacrificially should be the same. However, it seems as though many rich people have a hard time giving "everything", just as the widow did. Jesus desires us to give sacrificially, no matter what our circumstances are or how much we have in our bank accounts.

C. Scott

Follow the example of the widow!

Pemon - Guyana

Population: 500
They live on the border near Brazil. They have had many influences in their religion, but still believe in the one true God. They fear spirits and demons. They are engaged in agriculture and their main food is yucca.

Pray: God would free them from demonic oppression.

NOVEMBER

There Is No Age

> Then the Lord said, "Rise and anoint him; this is the one." So Samuel took the horn of oil and anointed him in the presence of his brothers.
> 1 Samuel 16:12-13

When David was anointed king of Israel, he was a young man and the smallest member of his family. During this time, most people saw him as just a boy who looked after a flock of sheep. This makes me think there is no certain age for a call from God. God does not expect us to be important people or to have a special title. He looks at our heart and sees if we are obedient. God speaks to us when we have a deep desire to know His word and when we learn to listen to Him. Often God has a specific calling for a specific ministry. It is possible for Him to call you to the specific task of going and spreading the Gospel in a certain culture. God will prepare you throughout your life so that you can fulfill your calling. At the age of 19, I received the call from God to be a missionary in Africa. During this time, I was learning how to listen to the voice of God. I was afraid, but I told God, "If you're calling me, then prepare me for this job." I then fervently started to pray for Africa. After 13 years of preparation, the time was right for me to leave, just as God had planned. Has God called you to a specific mission field? Do you feel a burden to pray for a specific place? In His time, God will fulfill His call for you.
I. Santander

Are you willing to go?

Oromo - Egypt

Population: 3,100
The Oromo measure their social status by the number of animals they own and the number of children and grandchildren they have. They are herders, but place high value on warfare training. The majority of Oromos are Muslims, but some still make sacrifices to their native god, Waqa.

Pray: For God to free them from the darkness of idolatry.

The Missionary Strategy Of Jesus

> *Therefore, go and make disciples of all nations, baptizing them in the name of the Father and of the Son and of the Holy Spirit.*
> *Matthew 28:19*

God's plan to redeem the world included sending Jesus to the earth with two main purposes. First, He was to die on a cross and rise from the dead after three days, paying the price for the world's salvation. Second, Jesus was to prepare a group of disciples and send them out to preach. Jesus chose twelve men to be His disciples. He prepared them and sent them out in pairs of two with the responsibility of preaching. He then commanded them to go into all the world and make disciples of all nations.

While Jesus was on earth, large crowds often followed Him. On one occasion, over 5,000 men with their wives and children followed Jesus. He knew the only way to be loyal to such a demanding group was to individually disciple people. His goal was for discipleship to be perpetuating, meaning disciples would create more disciples. At the beginning of His ministry, He had only twelve disciples. Later, seventy disciples are mentioned and after the resurrection, a hundred and twenty disciples gathered together (Acts 1:15). The model Jesus gave was the foundation of the early church. Therefore, Paul told Timothy everything he learned should be taught to men who will also teach others (2 Timothy 2:2). From this example, we clearly understand Jesus created an effective strategy to make disciples. Do you understand how important discipleship is?

F. Rodríguez

Are you a disciple?

Shelta - Ireland

Population: 26,000
Sheltas are known as travelers. Their native language is Shelta. They have no Biblical resources in their native language, but most have heard the Gospel in English. A high majority would consider themselves Christians, but their faith is nominal.

Pray: For Biblical truth to be taught.

Treasuring The Word

> *I have hidden your word in my heart that I might not sin against You.*
> *Psalm 119:11*

We are in an age of speed. We want everything fast: fast food, fast cars, and fast Internet. Our desire to be fast has caused us to treat our relationship with Jesus as something that must quickly happen. We think we can treat our relationship with him like a formula and get the results we desire. We expect to quickly achieve a deep, personal relationship with Jesus.

But it does not work that way! The author of this Psalm understood what a relationship with God required. The author says he has "hidden" the Word of God in his heart. Why do we hide things? Normally, we hide things because we believe they are valuable. Hiding prevents things from getting lost or stolen.

Hiding the Word in your heart means spending time reading it, meditating on it, and memorizing it. Hiding God's Word does not happen instantaneously, but requires perseverance and dedication. It is not enough to only read a passage or spend a few minutes thinking about it. Hiding the Word in your heart means asking the Holy Spirit to guide you into understanding. It involves hearing the voice of God and avoiding distractions by preparing your heart.

Do you want to live a life that pleases God? Do you desire to know right from wrong? Hide the Word of God in your heart. Set aside time each day and learn God's Word.

W.Bello

Get started today!

Rashaida - Eritrea

Population: 46,000
The Rashaida live on the coast of the Red Sea. Women cover their entire body except for their eyes. Their religion is Islam. In 2000, there were seven known Christians, all of which were soldiers. Their language, Arabic Hijazi, has some audio stories of the Word of God.

Pray: For the maturity of the believers and a boldness for their faith.

Steadfast In Adversity

> *"You would have no power over me unless it had been given you from above,"* Jesus answered. John 18:28-19:16

This passage clearly shows the majesty of Jesus as he stood before Pilate. Contrary to expectations, Jesus did not defend himself. Instead, he was confident and believed God had control over all things. As Jesus stood before Pilate, he bore witness to God's truth and waited to fulfill his purpose. Jesus' calmness exhibited his deity and close relationship with God.

How is your faith in your present circumstance? Often, it is a temptation to be afraid or nervous when you are unsure about future outcomes. Feelings of loneliness can cause you to feel isolated and defenseless. But have no fear! Although you are weak, God sees your need and brings comfort to your unstableness. You can have confidence in your personal relationship with Jesus because he is at the throne of the Father, interceding on your behalf. You are connected to the plan of God and can say with confidence, "You will have no power over me unless it has been given to you from above." Regardless of your circumstance, remain steadfast.

N. Rivas

Are you living in communion with God?

Pisabo - Peru

Population: 510

The Pisabos speak Spanish and Pisabo. They collect wild fruits and hunt small animals. They are peaceful and have good relationships with the Mestizos. They are animists. They believe deities are living and violent. Some Christians live among the Pisabos, but it is unknown how many.

Pray: For the Peruvian church to reach out to the Pisabos.

Bible in a year: 1 Timothy 5:21-6:21 / Jeremiah 3-4 / Psalm 120

Do Not Be Afraid

{ *I tell you, my friends, do not be afraid of those who kill the body but after that can do no more. Read Luke 12:1-12*

Jesus taught His disciples many things. On this particular occasion, Jesus taught his disciples not to fear hypocritical people like the Pharisees. He suggested the Pharisees only have power to damage the body, but God has the power to damage the body and soul. Therefore, our goal must be to remain pure in the sight of God.

Jesus makes a sharp contrast between God and the Pharisees (v. 7). He states, God is capable of being more "dangerous" than the Pharisees, but He does not share their aggressive attitude. God is careful with His creation and cares for even the smallest creatures.

Christians are very careful around people who are hostile to the message of God. As we try to avoid offending people, we often overlook God's command to have no fear!

Christians' first priority should be not to offend God. God deserves reverence, glory, respect, and admiration. He is all-powerful, but cares for and loves you. Jesus boldly invites you to be courageous in communicating the message of salvation. Proclaiming the message of salvation has no boundaries or excuses. Although situations can be dangerous, the world is waiting for the good news of salvation.

M. de Rodríguez

Be brave!

Tseku - Bhutan

Population: 7,200

Tsekus are a Buddhist group from Bhutan who live in the Himalayan Mountains and follow the Tibetan culture. They have not heard the Gospel in their native language. Tsekus are in urgent need of a Bible translation.

Pray: For the Tsekus and Tibetan groups to hear the Gospel.

Not Afraid To Talk About God

{ *She said to her mistress, "If only my master would see the prophet who is in Samaria! He would cure him of his leprosy." 2 Kings 5:3*

The story of Elisha healing Naaman, a prestigious and powerful leader from Aram, often goes unnoticed. The story takes place after Naaman had won a battle and captured a young Jewish girl. After the girl was captured, she was sent to a distant land to become the slave of Naamans wife. Becoming a slave meant living in a new place without her family, friends, or culture.

Naaman suffered from leprosy, which at the time was incurable. The disease caused him to be desperate because he wanted to be cured. The Jewish servant girl was convinced only God could heal Naaman, but it was not easy for the girl to speak boldly to her master because he did not fear God. She knew if she spoke boldly to him and he did not respond positively, it could result in her death. She chose to speak powerfully by stating only the God of Israel could heal Naaman of his disease. Naaman trusted the girl and sent for the prophet Elisha. Elisha came and healed Naaman, which resulted in him acknowledging God as the one true god.

If the girl had been silent about her faith, Naaman would have never known the Lord. Regardless of your status, you will always have opportunities to share Jesus' salvation with others. Do not be silent about the enormous treasure God has placed in your heart!

G. Vergara

Do not be afraid to share the salvation of Christ.

Tagalog - United Arab Emirates

Population: 301,000
The Tagalog are originally from the Philippines. They have heard about Jesus and it is estimated 12% have responded to the Gospel. They have the complete Bible and several other resources for evangelism in their language, Tagalog.

Pray: For God to continue to strengthen their faith and for the Tagalog Christians to be a witness for Christ to the whole nation.

Under Authority

> { *Now when David had served God's purpose in his own generation...*
> *Acts 13:36*

The people used by God, throughout the history of time, had one common denominator: They understood what it meant to live under the authority of God. The Scriptures tell of King David being a man after God's own heart. After God removed Saul as king, He placed David in his position and said, "I have found David son of Jesse, a man after my own heart; he will do everything I want him to do" (Acts 13:22).

God longs to use people who are willing to live under His authority. Part of living under the authority of God means responding when He "calls." David (Psalm 78:70-72), Abraham (Genesis 22:11), Moses (Exodus 3:4), and Gideon (Judges 6:14-16) all responded to the call of God. They are examples of what it means to live under God's authority!

God still calls people today. He calls them by extending an invitation to start an obedient relationship with His son Jesus. Having a relationship with Jesus involves deep commitments and lifestyle changes. God is calling you into a relationship with Christ, but you need to respond to the call! Are you willing to be under God's authority? Standing under the authority of God means receiving the promise for a great future!

C. Scott

Are you after God's own heart?

Paĩ Tavytera – Paraguay

Population: 13,132

They Paĩ Tavytera have the Bible in their native Guarani language. Missionaries are currently serving to develop leaders, teachers, and the church. Although missionaries are serving, they are in need of more help. Many Paĩ Tavytera have not understood the Gospel and have mixed their animistic beliefs with the truth of God.

Pray: For believers to understand Biblical truth.

Continually Transformed

> This is how we know what love is: Jesus Christ laid down his life for us. And we ought to lay down our lives for our brothers and sisters. 1 John 3:16

An active relationship with Jesus is marked by continual transformation. When you look at the disciples, what do you see? Do you see a group of holy, perfect people? Or do you see a group of sinners, transformed by God, to do His work?

When Jesus named the Apostle John, He called him a "son of thunder" (Mark 3:17). This was because John was known for being a violent and angry man. On one occasion, Jesus was walking toward Jerusalem and was falsely treated. This enraged John so much that he asked, "Lord, do you want me to call fire down from heaven to destroy them?" (Luke 9:51-56). John's response was so over-the-top, Jesus rebuked him. On another occasion (Mark 10:35-37), Jesus asked John, "What do you want me to do for you?" John responded with the selfish answer, "Let me sit at your right hand in your glory."

John was selfish, violent, angry, and opinionated for the three years he walked with Jesus on earth.

When we look at John's life in the future, we see a different man. We see a man who was patient, loving, caring, and God-honoring. We see a man who writes, "This is how we know what love is: Jesus Christ laid down his life for us. And we ought to lay down our lives for our brothers and sisters" (1 John 3:16).

Do you see a difference in John's character? As John continued to live in faith, the Holy Spirit continued to transform him. If you are walking with Jesus, your spiritual walk should be marked by transformation. The Holy Spirit comes into your life to transform you into a new creation. Can you think of concrete ways God has transformed you? Are you allowing the Holy Spirit to transform your life?

S. Langemeier

Be transformed!

Silesian - Poland

Population: 12,000
The Silesians live in a territory divided by Germany, Poland, and the Czech Republic. They are heavily influenced by these three cultures. Many can understand Polish or German, but no translation of the Bible exists in their native language, Silesian. The majority of Silesians are Roman Catholic. Due to a religious crisis, few have persevered their faith.

Pray: For the Gospel to be born in the hearts of the Silesians.

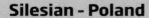

Transforming Adversity Into Opportunity

{ *All authority in heaven and on earth has been given to me. Therefore go and make disciples of all nations... Matthew 28:18-19*

Christians often think the Great Commission begins with the command: "Go and make disciples of all nations." The Great Commission actually begins with the Lord Jesus' statement: "All authority in heaven and on earth has been given to me." We live in an increasingly complex, violent, indifferent, and unbelieving world. Christians sometimes believe because the world is hopeless there is not a reason to actively evangelize. But God, in His power, makes all things possible in even the worst situations.

One of the world's fastest growing churches is in China, a country where it is not allowed to freely preach the Gospel. Although the Chinese church faces extreme barriers, they continue to risk their lives by meeting in secret. They often sing in sign language so no one can hear. The meeting places have no sound equipment, musical instruments, seats, heating, or air conditioning. It is almost impossible for Chinese believers to invite a friend to their underground meeting. But with the power of God, our Chinese brothers have transformed adversity into opportunity. Although they do not have flashy equipment, the presence of God is with them. Be a witness for the Lord! In His power you can transform your obstacles into opportunities! W. Altare

Do it!

Regeibat - Morocco

Population: 35,000
Regeibats live in the high mountains and farm for a living. They are passionate Muslims. They speak Moroccan Arabic, which has several audiovisual resources for evangelism. Christians are typically not public about their faith.

Pray: For missionaries to bring the message of salvation to the Regeibats.

Mary And Martha

> "Martha, Martha," the Lord answered, "you are worried and upset about many things." Luke 10:41

Recently, God taught me a very valuable lesson in an area of my life that I find difficult to understand. I am very active person. I love being busy, just like Martha from the book of Luke. Martha was a woman who believed if she was not constantly busy and striving to make everything perfect, then people would see her as uncaring. Martha desperately wanted to appear busy because she found her identity in what she could do.

I can identify with Martha's feelings. I often feel I have to be busy to have significance. Although I find being idle difficult to understand, God has begun to show me a stark reality. Recently, I felt God asking me the question, "Can you be still?" When I thought of this question, I felt defensive and told God, "But Lord, your Word says to go and make disciples, why would you ask me to do nothing?" I struggled to believe it was God asking me the question, but then I read Psalm 37:7: "Be still before the LORD and wait patiently for him." When I read the word "still", it felt as though the verse applied directly to my life.

As God was teaching me what it meant to be still, I was in the middle of recovering from a surgery. I felt like God was leading me to live like Mary, at the feet of Jesus. Do you find it difficult to be still? Do not be afraid to be inactive. God uses the stillness to renew your strength and to bring your relationship with Him to a deeper level. God looks for workers to serve in His Kingdom, but He expects those workers to also be worshipers!

L. Ashmore

When you are inactive, enjoy God.

Saep - Papua New Guinea

Population: 700

They do not have a translation of the Bible in their native language, Saep. An established church has been planted and it has a 7 members. The majority of Saeps are dictated by "shamans". "Shamans" decide leadership, tribal medicine, religion, and education. Saeps are in need of a stronger testimony of the Gospel.

Pray: For missionaries and people to translate the Bible.

The Love Of God

> *I have loved you with an everlasting love; I have drawn you with unfailing kindness. Jeremiah 31:3*

It is extremely important for ethnic groups who are living in a postmodern society to properly understand the Gospel and faith in Christ so they have strong foundation. The best thing for them is to be taught the basics of the Gospel in their native language so it can really reach the heart. We shouldn't assume everyone understands Spanish or English perfectly in our churches. An Indian couple faithfully attended our evangelical church for year where the sermons were in Spanish. They really seemed to be strong in their faith as Christians because they did what Christians do. They attended church whenever it was offered. The husband didn't drink and he was faithful to his wife. The wife was very quiet, pleasant, and seemingly dedicated to the Christian lifestyle and the church. Unfortunately, this couple is now completely against the church. There could be many reasons for this, but in this case, they most likely copied all the external customs of the church without ever fully understanding the Gospel. Therefore, they couldn't fully understand who Christ was and why He did what He did.

It's sad to see where this couple is now. He's an alcoholic and an adulterer. She voluntarily had an abortion and seems disconnected from her husband. This is just a taste of what can happen in a situation where we teach the Gospel to people in a language they don't fully understand. It is vital to speak the eternal love of God in a language that pierces directly into the heart. This takes time and effort, but ultimately worth it. We hope this couple, like many others, one day understands God loves us unconditionally despite our sin. At the same time, we need to make every effort connect with people in their native language!

G. Rivas

Go and preach the gospel in their language!

Sanusi - Libya

Population: 618,000
This group of Bedouins live in villages. Their herds of goats and sheep roam the desert, and the orchards they cultivate usually have poor production. The Liberian people are Muslim and speak Arabic, which has numerous Biblical resources.

Pray: For a good distribution of the existing Word of God.

Ant Or Elephant??

{ *But you will receive power when the Holy Spirit comes upon you; and you will be my witnesses in Jerusalem, and in all Judea and Samaria, and to the ends of the earth. Acts 1:8*

One day, a herd of elephants decided to stampede and destroy everything that stood in their path. Before the herd took off, a small ant listened in on their plan and decided to join them. In just a few minutes, the elephants destroyed an entire village with their overwhelming strength and speed. All the while, the ant ran alongside them, watching as the elephants left no structure standing. After the long day of terrorizing the people and city, the elephants, along with the ant, decided to rest on the bank of a river. After a while, the elephants spotted the tiny ant laying on the leg one of the elephants. They heard it say, "WOW! We destroyed a lot of stuff!" Although funny, this story is a wake up call to our behavior regarding the Great Commission. Many times, Christians are like the ant and do nothing for the Kingdom of Jesus but brag how much they support missions. Our church needs to be a radical evangelizing church. We pray for missionaries, give offerings for missions, visit jails and hospitals, ect... but my question for you today is: Are you one of the elephants who are using the God-given gifts and strengths to make things happen and advance the Kingdom of Jesus? Or are you simply the tag along ant who celebrates victories without every joining in the work?

W. Núñez

Are you the elephant or the ant?

Sirionó - Bolivia

Population: 830
Living in the Beni, the main activities of the Sirionó are hunting, fishing, and gathering honey. They have embraced the Gospel, but they try to mix it with their indigenous culture. They have some portions of the Bible in their language.

Pray: For discipleship that will help them understand the truths of the Gospel.

November 13

According To The Heart Of God

> *Who can discern their own errors? Forgive my hidden faults.*
> *Psalm 19:12*

A heart after the desires of God is formed through tests and trials. Many times, we think God is trying to punish us with trials and problems, but most of the time, He is only purifying us in the process of making us strong warriors for Him. This is exactly what David experienced. He realized there was no value in having a proud heart or being arrogant. We can see what he wrote in Psalms, "Search me, O God, and know my heart; test me and know my anxious thoughts. See if there is any offensive way in me, and lead me in the way everlasting." (Psalm 139:23-24) We do not know our own hearts. However, we can ask God to make us after His own heart.

David was broken as he suffered from zeal and jealousy of Saul. Saul's army tried repeatedly tried to kill him and he felt cheated when Saul's daughter wasn't given to him as promised. With the military always after him, he had to hide in caves in the desert. Even after being anointed king of Israel, he was misunderstood and ridiculed by people over and over. They mocked him, saying, "Aren't you the one who they say killed ten thousand?" But when the time came for his strength to be tested, he didn't fail. When asked, "What do you mean you cannot kill Saul?" he boldly replied, "I will not touch the anointed one of God."

Love God and submit to His purpose. Brokenness through trials will lead you to a new level of maturity and faith.

C. Scott

How do you react when you are tested?

Siwa – Egypt

Population: 32,000
The Siwa are found in the Siwa Oasis and are well known in the Egyptian desert. They grow dates and olives and travel by donkey to market their products. They speak Siwi Islamic, which no Bible translation.

Pray: For the Siwa to receive the Gospel and take it to heart.

In The Eye Of The Hurricane

{ *The Lord is good, a refuge in time of trouble. He cares for those who trust in Him. Nahum 1:7*

As I watched the weather news anxiously, I saw a deadly storm was about to hit the town where my brother lived. When I called him and asked about the storm, he said they were in the eye of the hurricane. At that moment, I thought the hurricane would end the life of my brother and his life. However, despite knowing the circumstances, he spoke very calmly and told me they were having some normal family time.

Our lives have become so busy that we often seem to have no time to sit down and talk about how each of our days went. Our time is so valuable to us. Yet God, in His perfect love, allows us to get closer to each other, even in the middle of a storm. It is in times like these when families need to come together. When tragedies or disasters happen, cities around the world come to a standstill for a moment to find time to share life with each other.

Have you ever been in the eye of a storm? Have you noticed that God sometimes lets us go through a storm so we can come together and love each other?

G. Galindo

> Hopefully, we will not have to be in the eye of a hurricane to value what God has given us.

Tapeba - Brazil

Population: 6,519
The Tapeba live near the Rio Ceará. They were expelled from their territory, so they now rent land and are now fruit cultivators. Their religion is animistic. They speak Portuguese, as their original language is already extinct.

Pray: For God to heal their wounds and show them the way of salvation.

Preaching With The Power of God

> My message and my preaching were not with wise and persuasive words, but with a demonstration of the Spirit's power. 1 Corinthians 2:4

Unfortunately, there can be many distractions while the Word of God is preached. One particular distraction the world continues to fall into is the attention put on the speaker rather than the Word of God. Public speaking isn't a bad thing and God has given many the gift of preaching. However, the danger lies in the emphasis on how effective or entertaining a speaker is. Spiritual effectiveness can only be expected from clear exposition of the Word of God. However, many preachers and those listening will focus more on brilliant phrasing and eloquent wording rather than the accuracy of delivering the Word. Unfortunately, for some well-known speakers, the Bible was just a springboard to a world-renown public speaking career.

It is extremely important that preachers KNOW the Bible. Knowing the Bible and believing it holds life will only help a preacher better glorify God with the gift of preaching. A preacher's goal should be to help his flock better understand the Gospel and God's power through His Word. A preacher's goal should NOT be to entertain, sound wise, or gather a huge following. The great preacher Charles Spurgeon once said, "I fear our pulpits are not exempt from these sellers of the Wholesale Word."

Paul appeared to the Corinthians with a demonstration of God's power through His Word, not with wise-sounding and persuasive words.

O. Simar

Your preaching should depend on the Word and not your wisdom!

Tigrai - Yemen

Population: 10,000

This group of Semitic origin traces their history to the Queen of Sheba who adopted Judaism. Christianity came to them from the work of Copts missionaries. They have the whole Bible in their language, Tigrigna.

Pray: For the Christians to be a real light in the midst of the people of Yemen.

Divine Plans

{ *Forget the former things; do not dwell on the past. See, I am doing a new thing! Now it springs up; do you not perceive it? I am making a way in the wilderness and streams in the wasteland. Isaiah 43:18-19*

During my teen years, someone gave me these words from Isaiah that become put engrained my mind and heart. I was not always brave; during my childhood I was very shy and was easily embarrassed. Every time I was put in front of people, especially in college, I would blush and couldn't find the words to speak. Unfortunately, I didn't quite understand them until just recently. Remembering the story of my birth and the faith of my mother during a difficult time helped me understand just what these words mean.

God had a purpose for my life, even when I lay in my mother's womb. When I was six months old, I was diagnosed with a life-threatening disease with no cure available. The doctor actually told my parents at that time to take me home to die. My mother desperately sought God. My mother said she had prayed secretly in her heart, "God, if you heal my daughter, I will serve you and give her to you." God heard her prayer and miraculously healed me very quickly. My mother kept her promise, and from then on, she influenced me to walk in the way of God. He has prepared me and molded me throughout my whole life for the work I do now. God has plans for your life, too, and is preparing you for something great as you walk with Him.

I. Santander

Do you realize it?

Swedish - Sweden

Population: 8,156,000
Family values and traditional celebrations of the Swedes are deeply rooted in Christianity. However, most are Christian in name only, and the teaching they are getting from the media is far from Biblical truth.

Pray: For the doctrine of the Bible to again capture the hearts of the Swedes.

An Encounter With God

> In the past God overlooked such ignorance, but now he commands all people everywhere to repent. Acts 17:30

My friends call me Chuz. I am a former Muslim, but God intervened in my life in a very special way. Would you like to read my testimony?

On a trip far from the village I lived in, God gave me a dream. I had this particular dream three times and the message given to me through it seemed imperative. I shared the dream with a friend, but he could not help me with the interpretation. In each of the three similar dreams, there were African foreigners. My friend recommended I ask a foreigner to help interpret my dream. However, at the time, I didn't really know any foreigners and had no idea what to do.

Much to my surprise, when I returned to my village, a group of Africans foreigners had initiated a community development program to alleviate poverty in the area. I searched among the staff for somebody I could talk to about my dream. I was only able to find one who knew my language. So, I explained my dream and he encouraged me to follow the example of the men who received the Word of God long before the Qur'an was written (referring to Abraham). He said without understanding Abraham's faith, it was impossible to get out of the darkness in which I lived and to be saved.

After talking with the man and hearing about his faith and the faith of Abraham, I understand the glorious message of Jesus! It was such good news for me. I remember being completely overwhelmed with joy and gladness in that moment.

I needed someone to interpret the dream for me and guide me to the right path. God spoke through my dreams, but God speaks in many different ways to non-Christians today. Look around at how God is talking to people and working in their lives. If given the opportunity to help a non-Christian understand the sweet message of Jesus, take it! Pescador

Watch and help!

Taushiro- Peru

Population: 30
Living near the Tiger and Aucuyacu rivers, this small group holds animist beliefs. They speak their own unique language, Taushiro, and have no translation of the Bible. Contact was recently made with this small group.

Pray: For Christian researchers to gather more knowledge about this ethnic group and bring them the Gospel.

Proclaim The Wonderful Works Of The Lord

> But you are a chosen people, a royal priesthood, a holy nation, God's special possession, that you may declare the praises of him who called you out of darkness into his wonderful light. Once you were not a people, but now you are the people of God; once you had not received mercy, but now you have received mercy. 1 Peter 2:9-10

These encouraging verses tell of MY (and your) deliverance and status before the Lord of the universe. My position in Christ is as safe as the position of Christ before the God the Father. I was chosen! God didn't have to chose me but He did out of His abundant love. As a blood-bought child of God, I belong in His family. I am holy because Jesus, who died for my sins, is holy. This is my status before the Creator, Redeemer, and King of heaven and earth. Peter confirmed we are to "... declare the praises of him who called you out of darkness into his wonderful light." My identity is in Him and because so, I have an endless supply of His mercy!

Knowing who we are in Christ should give us undeniable motivation to share it with the rest of the world and carry out the Great Commission! We should want every person in the world to have the opportunity to emerge from the darkness and experience the glory of their Creator and Redeemer.

MyT. Goddard

Proclaim It!

Tsun-Lao – Vietnam

Population: 13,000
The Tsun-Lao people are the largest producers of rice in the country. The Buddhist Wat, or temple, is the center of village life. The Bible has not yet been translated into their language, Tsun-lao; it is urgent that the Word of God comes to this town.

Pray: For Bible translators so the Tsun-Lao would know of Jesus in their own language.

Man Of God

> David took courage and put his trust in the Lord his God ... David inquired of the Lord... 1 Samuel 30:6-8

David knew if his strength came from anything or anybody but God, he would fail. When faced with adversity, he sought out and consulted God. Constantly finding himself running from Saul or his enemies, there were many times David must have felt like quitting was the best option. However, when Saul died in battle, David had this to say about him, "The mighty fallen on Mount Gilboa, the beauty of Israel has perished. My friend Jonathan. Saul and Jonathan, noble people! They were swifter than eagles, stronger than lions, united in their life and in their death, the beauty of Israel has fallen." (2 Samuel 1:17-27) Simply put, David was a man of God. God calls us to serve our own generation regardless of how people treat us. Sometimes, God purifies us and shapes us through grief. He accomplishes His purpose even if it seems as though everything is going wrong. David thought, "Saul will kill me," often forgetting he had be anointed as the next king of Israel. But God fulfilled His purpose in David because David lived under His authority.

Do you know God's purpose for your life and our generation? How are you serving despite your circumstances? What does it mean to live under God's authority?

C. Scott

Keep going!

Samoans - Samoa

Population: 162,000

The vast majority of young Samoans have moved to New Zealand, looking to attend universities and find better opportunities. Although they profess to be Christian, they are predominantly Roman Catholic. They have the whole Bible available in Samoan.

18% are evangelical Christians.

Pray: For the maturity of the established church, and that they can reach out to the rest of their ethnic group.

Bible in a year: 1 Peter 2 / Jeremiah 33-34 / Psalm 135

The Two Sides Of The Coin

> *It is a dreadful thing to fall into the hands of the living God.*
> *Hebrews 10:31*

We are usually always open to hearing the message of "God is love (1 John 4:8), "God loves you" (John 3:16), or that He is "slow to anger and abundant in loving kindness" (Psalm 86:15). However, often times, we forget the other side of the coin. We forget the Bible says, "It is a dreadful thing to fall into the hands of the living God" (Hebrews 10:31), which explains the judgment and justice that will be brought to those who turn away or abandon Him.

When we take a look at the life of Solomon, we find God was angry with him for turning his back and disobeying His commands. Solomon had increased his chariots, horses, and women after God had deliberately gave him the instruction not to. As Solomon's heart turned away from God, he built altars and worshiped the gods of his numerous foreign women. As a result, his son's kingdom was divided in two, and he lost the privilege of the promise made to his father David.

Even though we see numerous blessings of obedience throughout the Bible (i.e. Deuteronomy 28), we cannot ignore the consequences of disobedience. Obey and be blesses, or disobey and be cursed and persecuted by the hand of God. We will always reap what he sow.

So "choose for yourselves this day whom you will serve" (Joshua 24:15). In the same verse, Joshua reminds everybody with a strong statement, "as for me and my household, we will serve the Lord." There is nothing better in life than to follow and serve the God of heaven.
F. Chinatti

Do not forget this!

Tila Chol - Mexico

Population: 51,200
They live mainly in the State of Chiapas. When the Spanish arrived in Mexico, they adopted Catholicism, but it is very mixed with their indigenous religion. They have had the New Testament in their language since 1976. 5% have accepted Christ.

Pray: For the indigenous church to reach their ethnicity for Christ.

The Anchor Of Our Souls

> We have this hope as an anchor for the soul, firm and secure. It enters the inner sanctuary behind the curtain, where our forerunner, Jesus, has entered on our behalf. Hebrews 6:19-20

When my wife, Sharon, and I sat down to schedule our wedding, we chose a verse together we knew would sustain and encourage us through marriage:

"May the God of hope fill you with all joy and peace as you trust in him, so that you may overflow with hope by the power of the Holy Spirit." (Romans 15:13)

During the last 33 years of marriage, God has filled us many times His joy and peace, and has renewed the firm hope we have in Christ and His Word. I love how the writer of Hebrews describes hope as "an anchor of the soul, firm and secure." What could be more tremendous? Oh, how we need it!

Nevertheless, we sometimes go through stages in life when it seems this incredible hope runs from us. We can feel this way especially when we don't see the response or changes we desire in our personal lives, in the lives of our families, or in our preparations to be sent to the mission field. Sometimes, we question the strength or safety of the anchor of our souls. If you are going through one of those stages, don't give up!

Beloved Father, we cry: Fill us with all your joy and peace so we will overflow with hope. Renew our strength, break the barriers that hinder our growth and healing and discourage us. Fulfill YOUR purposes in our lives in YOUR time. Thank you! We praise you!

T. Sandvig

Is your soul anchored in Christ?

Tajakant - Algeria

Population: 1,480,000
A branch of the desert dwelling Bedouin, the Tajakant live in tents and travel across the country. They trade copper and livestock. Their language is Algerian Arabic, in which the New Testament has been translated. They profess the Islamic religion.

Pray: For God to bring the Gospel to these desert tribes through travelers.

A Torch

> We also have the prophetic message as something completely reliable, and you will do well to pay attention to it, as to a light shining in a dark place, until the day dawns and the morning star rises in your hearts.
> 2 Peter 1:19

While you live in this world of darkness and sin, you have a divine and powerfully lit torch illuminating your life and your steps. This torch never burns out and is always present. Unfortunately, only those who have put their trust in Christ have this guiding light. Therefore, we must announce the message of Jesus and be a witness of His light to everyone around us wherever we go.

When Jesus prayed for us, He asked God not to take us out of the world, but rather to protect us while we walk and live in this world of darkness. The prophetic message of healing and salvation, which has been given to us, is completely safe because it depends on God, not on man.

How can you bring your light out from under the table so it can give light to others? Are you in the Word of God daily in order to draw strength each day to let your light shine? In the world, there are billions who live in darkness, and for Christ to penetrate their hearts, they need to know the Word because faith comes through His Word. Know the Word, share it, and carry the torch to ends of the earth as you let your light shine before men.

Pescador

Onwards!

Sylhetti - United Kingdom

Population: 114,000

People of Bengali origin, the Sylhetti are heavily involved in trading, tourism, and culinary arts. Marriages are common with the English, but the Islamic religion predominates. They have some scriptures in their language, Sylhetti.

Pray: For Christians to rise up in the UK and share the Gospel with the Bengali Sylhetti.

Bible reading: 1 Peter 5, Jeremiah 39-40, Psalm 133

Don't Worry

> Then Jesus said to his disciples: "Therefore I tell you, do not worry about your life, what you will eat; or about your body, what you will wear. For life is more than food, and the body more than clothes."
> Luke 12:22-31

In this chapter, Jesus is teaching about the distractions that can cause us to worry and hinder us in preaching the Gospel. Earlier, He taught about fear, aggression, and greed. In this particular passage, Jesus is teaching about the distraction of the desire to earn a good living. Food and clothing are basic needs of man. Jesus is referring to luxuries or comfort, which are human instinct to desire.

As you prepare to serve God full-time, you will hear tell you:

"Why are you going to study at a seminary or Bible institute? That's not a profession that brings in money."

"Pastors and their families are starving."

"Why not study a profession that will help you raise your family?"

On the contrary, Jesus says: "seek first the kingdom of God." (Luke 12:31)

Do not let the desires of life be a higher priority than preaching the Good News. Concentrate on how best to serve God and bring salvation to those who need it. God will take care of all the basics needs for you life. The trust is God always gives us more than just food and clothing.

M. de Rodríguez

Depend on Him!

Tlingit - Canada

Population: 1,200
This indigenous group is from the Pacific coast near Alaska. Their language is Tlingit, in which some portions of the Bible have been translated. Although there are not many resources available, 20% of the people are Christian.

Pray: For Tlingit Christians to be a good witness to their people.

The Student And The Painting

> *For you created my inmost being; you knit me together in my mother's womb. I praise you because I am fearfully and wonderfully made.*
> *Psalm 139:13-14*

A young student was looking at a colorful painting in a museum. He had no idea what the painting was about but was suddenly approached by a man who started to explain every little detail about it. His explanation was so descriptive the painting seemed to take on a new form and come to life before the student's eyes. It was no surprise to the student, that the one explaining the painting was its author because he understood perfectly every color and shape of the work.

Psalm 139 says God designed our bodies. He knows every little detail about you and has known you before you were even an embryo in your mother's womb. He knows your every thought and understands every part of you: your spirit, soul and body. Since you are His creation, He knows what is best for you.

Jeremiah 29:11 says, "'For I know the plans I have for you,' declares the LORD, 'plans to prosper you and not to harm you, plans to give you a hope and a future.'" God created you with a purpose: to glorify Him and know Him. Do you want to fulfill God's plan for your life? Put all your trust in God's hands and He will help you do it.

L. Ashmore

Let the adventure begin!

Tihami - Yemen

Population: 4,550,000
The Tihami live scattered across not only the country of Yemen, but also in the countries of Saudi Arabia and the United Arab Emirates. They are faithful to Islam, and there are no known Christians among them. They have the Jesus film in their Arabic Taizzi-Adenine language.

Pray: For the Bible to soon be translated into Arabic Taizzi-Adenine.

In Any Location

{ *As he was scattering the seed, some fell along the path... on rocky ground... among thorns. Matthew 13:1-8*

God has called us to be sowers of the Word of God. To "scatter the seed" means to preach the Gospel of the kingdom of God and the salvation Jesus offers to all people of this world. The field where we must so is the entire world. No matter where you sow, there will be some places with fertile soil and some places with obstacles preventing the seeds from taking root. However, this should not discourage from sowing, nor tempt us to choose the most fertile land. Although there are places with much opposition to the truth, the Word of God can bear fruit everywhere. We are called to have a global vision, whether that means taking the Gospel to your kids, your next-door neighbor, or clear across the world in a foreign country. As the Scriptures says, we are called to be witnesses of Christ in "Jerusalem, and in all Judea and Samaria, and to the ends of the earth." (Acts 1:8)

Where are you thinking about "scattering and watering the seed"? Do you think only about easily accessible locations, where people are waiting for you with open arms? What about the places where torture or even death for the sake of the Gospel is common? Do you think about those places also? If you truly desire to glorify God with your life, will you really only pray for the salvation of the ones you love? Today, think about the places not seen as fertile land, where little seed falls, where there is much opposition to bearing fruit, and consequently, where the workers are few.

M. Gomes

Scatter seed everywhere!

Tamajaq - Mali

Population: 351,000

This Tuareg group are Muslims but are widely criticized of being lukewarm, not even practicing Ramadan. Their religion is rather animistic, very superstitious, and full of magical rites. Their language is Tamajaq, which has some portions of the Bible translated.

Pray: For God to work in their hearts they may open to the Gospel of Christ.

Waiting With Patience And Care

> Commit your way to the Lord; trust also in him and he will do it.
> Read Psalm 37:3-7

One day, hanging out with a group of teenagers in a village in Cameroon, I was asked why I wasn't married yet. In Africa, it is very important and expected for women to marry young and have many children. I took the opportunity to counsel the young group with an illustration. I took a daisy and told them the flower represents our life, alive and full of beautiful colors. However, a beautiful flower will lose its petals, lose its color and die if not properly taken care of (I started to take apart the flower, slowly removing petal by petal). I said, "For example, I like a boy, so I give him my first petal. But then, he leaves because he only wanted a little fun and now is bored with me. Eventually, I like another boy and I give him the second petal, not knowing what I really want besides the immediate attention. This continues through numerous boys until all the petals are gone. Now comes the time when God gives me the man He has prepared for me. But what do I give him? The beautiful flower I could have given him now doesn't even look like a flower."

What will you give to your husband or wife when the time comes? Are you willing to wait for what God has in store?

C. Scott

Trust God's choice.

Sanapaná - Paraguay

Population: 1,942

The Sanapaná live in Boqueron, Presidente Hayes and Alto Paraguay in thirteen different communities. They have strong animistic beliefs and fear the spirits of the dead at night. The New Testament is already in their language, and portions of the Old Testament are being translated by New Tribes Mission Paraguay.

Pray: For a better understanding of the Gospel in every community.

Men Of Valor

> *Therefore, since we are surrounded by such a great cloud of witnesses, let us throw off everything that hinders and the sin that so easily entangles. And let us run with perseverance the race marked out for us, fixing our eyes on Jesus, the pioneer and perfecter of faith. For the joy set before him he endured the cross, scorning its shame, and sat down at the right hand of the throne of God. Hebrews 12:1-2*

We are surrounded by a multitude of witnesses who have already reached the goal. Their lives encourage us to also live a life of faith in Jesus Christ and finish the race well with consistency and perseverance. The only way to do this is to confess the sin and shed the burdens distracting from the gaze of Jesus.

Join us today in making six promises:

1. I will honor Christ through worship, prayer and obedience to the Word God through the power of the Holy Spirit

2. I will live a spiritually, morally, and sexually pure life.

3. I will invest my commitment and loyalty not only to Christ but also to my family. I know the stability of marriage and family depends on the delivery of love, protection, and applying Biblical values.

4. I will actively participate in the fulfillment of the mission and work of my local church by honoring and praying for my leaders and joyfully giving my economic contribution to the growth of the kingdom of God.

5. I will break the boundaries of race and denomination to reflect the unity of the body of Christ.

6. I will change my lifestyle in order to be accessible to live out the Great Commandment (Mark 12:30) and the Great Commission (Matthew 28:19-20).

Today, focus on Hebrews 12:1-2 while fulfilling your promises to the Lord. Come and count those who are here to encourage you!

H. Ziefle

Keep your promises!

Tuvinian - Mongolia

Population: 5,020

This tribe of nomadic shepherds live in leather tents called gers. Their origin is Russian, but their lifestyle and their native language have been absorbed by the Mongolian culture. They have the entire Bible in their language, and 1% are Christian.

Pray: For God to strengthen the small, but flourishing church among the Tuvinian.

Bible in a year: Galatians 2 / Jeremiah 49-50 / Psalm 143

The Purpose Of God

> { By faith Abraham, when called to go to a place he would later receive as his inheritance, obeyed and went, even though he did not know where he was going. By faith he made his home in the Promised Land like a stranger in a foreign country; he lived in tents. Hebrews 11:8-9

Many times, Abraham was faced with leaving a place he had gotten to know and traveling without knowing the next place he'd end up. All the while, God encouraged Abraham through promises: "Through you all the families of the earth shall be blessed!" (Genesis 12:3b) and "I will make you a light for the nations so that you may bring my salvation to the ends of the earth." (Isaiah 49:6b) However, I'm sure Abraham was left with a few questions: Whom should I serve? When? Doing what? Where?

Abraham's questions are fairly similar to the questions we, as Christians, frequently ask God today: What is the path I must take? What is your will for my life, Lord?

The first thing we can say for sure is Jesus Christ is defined as in John 14:6 as "the Way, the Truth, and the Life." This implies we are called to live our lives following in His footsteps and example (1 Peter 2:21). Learn to walk in the Spirit and be determined to leave when God wants you to go some place totally new to you. Jesus is challenging you and says, "Come and see." (John 1:39) You may have uncertainty, fears, and doubts. Setting our own plans often doesn't work because God calls us to have faith in Him and wants our confidence to grow as a result of follow Him.

C. Scott

It is God's purpose!

Sasak - Indonesia

Population: 2,784,000

Originally from the island of Lombok, the Sasak are farmers and fishermen who are normally very friendly and open. Their religion is Islam, but they also worship their ancestors, the forests, rivers, and mountains. They have some audio versions of the Bible in their language, Sasak.

Pray: For the Word of God to be available to all people in this ethnic group.

We Are All Called

> Therefore, holy brothers and sisters, who share in the heavenly calling, fix your thoughts on Jesus, whom we acknowledge as our apostle and high priest. *Hebrews 3:1*

Often times, Christians are under the false impression that only a chosen few are called for ministry and missions. I am frequently asked by fellow Christian brothers, "When did you get the call into missions?" I honestly answer: I never received a special call other than the point when I realized God wants everybody in the world to be an ambassador committed to Him.

This passage in Hebrews reveals to all who are sanctified by His blood, there is a heavenly call to glorify God by bringing the message of Jesus to the world. We are His ministers, representatives, and spokesmen here on earth. This job is not for a select few; the entire Church has a calling to share the Good News with everyone.

For this reason, all the sanctified must be a part, in one way or another, of this heavenly calling. Otherwise, we are not doing that for which Christ left us on earth to do. It troubles me to think how different the world would be if every Christian would begin to respond to the heavenly calling to share Jesus with the world. Since you are sanctified, will you respond to the heavenly calling today?

G. Vergara

Do you share the salvation Christ offers?

Tojolabal - Mexico

Population: 38,000

Living in the State of Chiapas, the Tojolabal have strong roots in Catholicism while retaining their indigenous beliefs. Amid much opposition, 20% of the people are believers in Christ. The New Testament has been translated into their language. Pray: For the protection and strengthening of the church.

Are You A Sheep?

> My sheep listen to my voice; I know them, and they follow me.
> John 10:27

We can draw a few truths from this very revealing passage:

1. The sheep know their master. They spend time with Him and have heard Him many times. This means they can differentiate the Master's voice from other voices trying to distract them. Sheep are naturally scared, but because the voice of the shepherd is familiar, they are not afraid and are confident. Do you pay attention to the voice of God? Do you recognize it clearly? God speaks to us through His Word, the Bible.

2. He knows us. What a privilege! He doesn't say who we are, or how we are. He says he knows us! He knows where you come from, how you're doing today, what you've been through, your deepest dreams, your fears, your pain, your strengths, and your struggles. Rest assured, what Jesus tells you will be the truth.

3. "Follow me" involves continuous decisions and actions. When we hear Him, we must listen, trust, and follow Him with confidence. With ears extremely in-tune with the voice of God, other voices around you will start to disappear. Never mind the tendencies and ways of this world; we live under the precepts of God and His Word.

Are you practicing spiritual truth? Are you being led by the Good Shepherd? Remember: He gave His life for you and the rest of His sheep.

L. Ashmore

You can trust Him.

Tamezret - Tunisia

Population: 3,600

The Tamezret are original inhabitants of the island of Jerba in the Mediterranean Sea. They are mostly fishermen and farmers. They know only of the Islamic faith and practice it with much fervor. No portion of the Bible has been translated into their Nafusi language.

Pray: For missionaries who want to share the message in this part of the World.

DECEMBER

Keep The Word!

{ *How can a young person stay on the path of purity? By living according to your word. Read Psalm 119:9-16*

I will never forget this passage because of the important role it has played in my life. When I was young, every time I would read this Psalm, I would try to live out the words written on the page. I had a great fear of God and also a fear of failing or straying from His ways. One day, I said to Him, "Please take my hand and never let it go, and I will never let go of you." Before saying these words, God already had a purpose for my life, but at the time I could not understand it. All I knew was I wanted to serve Him and know Him more.

In our world today, we are surrounded by challenges. This generation is bombarded with new opportunities and technology. The Internet, cell phones, and globalization cause temptations and problems other generations never had to confront. In the past, people were happy taking advantage of opportunities like playing a guitar, taking a group of young people to the beach, or sharing His Word with those willing to listen. But times have changed. Each year brings new challenges and opportunities to serve God. These opportunities and challenges can either be a distraction from God, or an occasion to serve Him.

How can you remain true to God? The Psalmist says, "By living according to His Word." Do not be entangled with the things of this world. Meditate on the Word, and through His strength, you can face all challenges. Surrender!

I. Santander

Keep strong and go!

Umbundu - Czech Republic

Population: 100
They have adopted a culture with Russian traits. Recently they have begun to adopt Christianity, but their faith and understanding is shallow. It is estimated 40% are Protestant and 60% are Roman Catholic.

Pray: The Umbunus will have access to the Bible and will find salvation.

Apostles Needed

> Paul, an apostle of Christ Jesus by the will of God, to God's holy people in Ephesus, the faithful in Christ Jesus... Ephesians 1:1

When Paul wrote a letter, he used the title "apostle". It was important for Paul to be introduced with this title because it indicated his purpose. It said that he was a messenger, one sent with authority, an ambassador, a spokesperson, a delegate, or in short, a missionary! We know Paul was not part of the first twelve apostles chosen by Jesus, but he was an apostle in a special category. Paul was called and sent by the risen Jesus while he was on the road to Damascus. This category of apostles and prophets, in its primary sense, refers to a limited group of historical messengers who God used during the history of salvation to write the Scriptures and establish His church.

The title of apostle, in a secondary sense, is still applicable to the church today. Apostles and missionaries today are cross-cultural. They are individuals who carry the Gospel to new horizons, crossing geographic, cultural, and linguistic barriers. Today there is a need for missionaries and apostles to be sent by churches. They are needed to bring the message of salvation to new places.

A. Neufeld

Do you want to be an apostle?

Toba Maskoy - Paraguay

Population: 2,650
They have heard the Gospel, but their core belief remains animistic. The New Testament is currently being translated by "Letra Paraguay." They work with farmland and livestock. They are adapting into Paraguayan life.

Pray: For the translation of the Bible and the existing literacy programs for the Toba Maskoy.

Bible in a year: Galatians 5:16-26 / Ezekiel 1 / Psalm 148

Deny Yourself And Obey

{ *Then he said to them all: "Whoever wants to be my disciple must deny themselves and take up their cross daily and follow me." Luke 9:23*

The Chinese Church is growing like never before. Over 30,000 people are converted every day. In Guatemala, there are more than five churches with over 4,000 members. Each week, there are more than 3,500 churches established around the world. This is what God is doing! But the question is: what are you doing?

While we try to improve our standard of living and deepen our "communion" with friends in the church, there are more than 11,000 unreached people groups who haven't heard the Gospel! While you argue about what the best version of the Bible is, there are 2,200 people groups sitting idle, with no version of the Bible in their own language. If you change your priorities, you can change these realities!

Why is the Gospel advancing so slowly when the command to "go" is so clear? The reason is because we are disobedient! Obedience cannot be bought at the mall or be achieved by going on a "better" diet. Obedience is achieved by giving God the right to change our desires. Be a blessing, without the goal of being blessed. The cost of being part of God's plan is denying yourself!

T. Vögelin

Do you deny yourself?

Vafsi - Iran

Population: 20,000
They are Shiite Muslims. There are no known Christians or missionaries serving among them. The government monitors each person to ensure they faithfully follow their religion. Bible translation is desperately needed.

Pray: For Iran's doors to be opened for the Gospel.

A Great Example

> Truly I tell you, wherever the gospel is preached throughout the world, what she has done will also be told, in memory of her. Read Mark 14:1-9

This passage captures some of the last moments of Jesus' earthly life. As He said these words, He was staying at the house of one of His friends, when suddenly a woman appeared with a bottle of expensive perfume. Without a word, she broke the flask and poured its contents upon the head of Jesus. As Jesus' friends observed her action, they were upset because they thought it was wasteful.

Instead of scolding the woman, Jesus drew attention to the narrow perspective of His disciples. Jesus knew the woman was preparing His body for burial. The disciples could not understand this was an act of love and worship. They had not yet learned to love Jesus as this woman loved Him. The woman had experienced God's forgiving grace and therefore responded in love and worship of her Savior. Her response of love was so touching that Jesus said the action would be remembered everywhere the Gospel is preached.

God calls us to go and teach His Word to the world, but above all, He wants us to learn to be worshipers. We need to continually offer our own lives as an offering and sacrifice to God. This is the first thing God expects from our lives.

A. Betancur

Be a worshiper!

Tokelauan - Tokelau

Population: 1,000
They occupy the three islands of Tokelau. They make up 100% of the population. Approximately 8,000 have emigrated to Australia and New Zealand in search of education and employment opportunities. They are fishermen. It is estimated 3% have believed the Gospel.

Pray: The Gospel would be understood and more missionaries would invest in their lives.

Practical Discipleship

{ *Therefore go and make disciples of all nations, ...teaching them to obey everything I have commanded you. Matthew 28:19-20*

A lot of people think discipleship refers to Christians studying important doctrines, taking lessons on baptism, or meeting one hour a week with a brother in Christ. These examples are all good things, but Matthew 28:20 says discipleship is "teaching them to obey" and not teaching them what they MUST obey. These two expressions are very similar, but also very different. It is important for new Christians to know they should be praying every day, but discipleship teaches them how to pray. A good disciple learns that it is important to read the Bible, but we must teach him how. It's good and important to encourage new believers to evangelize, but it is better to teach them how to evangelize. Discipleship must be practical and not just theoretical.

The one who disciples, teaches with his life. Paul tells Timothy, "To set an example for the believers" (1 Timothy 4:12). He says, "Whatever you have learned or received or heard from me, or seen in me - put into practice" (Philippians 4:9). True discipleship is a lifestyle. We must be an example that disciples can imitate.

F. Rodríguez

Are you discipling with your life or just with your words?

Trinity - Bolivia

Population: 6,900
They live in the Beni. They work mainly with agriculture. Their religion is animistic. There is a small Christian church, but they need help to reach the rest of their people.

Pray: For missionaries to be willing to bring the Word of God and resources for evangelism.

True Faith

{ *...Considered him faithful who had made the promise." Hebrews 11:11*

When we follow Jesus Christ, walking in faith can often be difficult. God shakes us, moves us, and He may not always allow us to know where we are being led. Faith is difficult because God puts us to the test (Hebrews 11:17-19). Faith is not easy, but a comfortable faith that costs nothing is empty. Following Christ and having faith is more than just having a theology that appeals to your selfish nature. True faith is risky and costly. Having this kind of faith is what led Jesus to the cross.

Like Jesus, our walk of faith could be costly and difficult because we are called to be witnesses to the ends of the earth. On our journey of faith, we are to remain in the heart of the battle, not to settle into a comfortable journey, as we are often tempted to do. We have to be willing to go wherever God may send us. This means we are not owners of a particular place. We are constantly in progress and we must move forward. We should be continually looking for new horizons where we can bring the Gospel message.

C. Scott

Do you walk in faith?

Yoron - Japan

Population: 900
They are natives on the Yoron Island, near Okinawa. Buddhism is practiced by 99% of the population. The rest of the population has no religion or are Catholic. Their native language is Yoron, but Japanese is the most spoken language. They have the opportunity to read the Bible in Japanese.

Pray: They recognize the void in their hearts and realize they need Jesus.

Overcoming Prejudice

> And should I not have concern for the great city of Nineveh, in which there are more than a hundred and twenty thousand people who cannot tell their right hand from their left—and also many animals? Jonah 4:11

Jonah exemplifies a Christian who is reluctant to go as a missionary to another land. God sent Jonah to preach to Nineveh, but the prophet had a deep hatred for the people. Jonah's hatred toward the city of Nineveh was understandable because the cruel and bloodthirsty Assyrian empire governed the city. This empire conquered Israel, destroyed its capital, Samaria, and took the people into exile and captivity. Experiencing these things would cause anyone to have negative feelings! Jonah did not want to bring the Word of God to the Assyrians. He wanted them to be consumed by God's judgment.

We all have our prejudices against people. We tend to generalize our thinking and say that all people of a particular race, religion, nationality, or ethnic group fit into a specific category. This error is the result of ignorance. Generalizing does nothing more than disrespect people and feed a sense of superiority. We need to see people with the same perspective as God, with love and compassion. We need to see everyone as human beings in need of love, hope, peace, and eternal salvation for their lost souls. God might not physically move you from your neighborhood to another country, but He still wants you to put aside all prejudice, pride, racism, arrogance, and stereotypes. He wants your heart to love every human being, regardless of their race, creed, sexual orientation, social class, tribe, or country.

G. Vergara

What prejudices should you give up to God?

Tasawaq - Niger

Population: 13,000

They are located in the center of the country. Their language, Tasawaq, has no translation of the Bible. They profess Islam. There are no known Christians among them. They need to hear the Gospel in their language.

Pray: For Bible translators and missionaries willing to boldly speak the word of God.

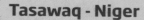

The Burning Light

{ *Be dressed ready for service and keep your lamps burning. . . Read Luke 12:35-40*

In this passage, Jesus is teaching His disciples how to be effective ministers of the Gospel. He uses the example of a servant watching and waiting for the coming of his master. The servant is not laying in bed, but instead dressed and ready for service. He keeps his light burning as if he were waiting for his master to return.

Often we live in disbelief thinking Jesus will not return. We get easily distracted by the cares of life and neglect our role as servants of God. We turn our "lights off" and live in darkness. Light symbolizes our connection with God; when the light is burning, we know the Holy Spirit is in our lives. How is our light turned out? It can be turned out by neglecting to read the Bible or forgetting to take time for personal prayer. Our light also grows dimmer as we give into the desires of the flesh, rather than the desires of the Holy Spirit. Our laziness or failure to be obedient to God can also hinder our light from burning brightly.

Jesus wants us to be prepared for His return. He desires us to "preach the word; be prepared in season and out of season; correct, rebuke and encourage—with great patience and careful instruction" (2 Timothy 4:2). We need to be serving with our light brightly burning for Him! Be watchful and prepared so you are not surprised by His return! Jesus concludes by saying it is good for the servants who are ready and watching when he returns (v.37)!

M. de Rodríguez

How are you awaiting the coming of the Lord?

Tongan - New Zealand

Population: 47,000
They are from the island of Tonga. They are a very educated people group. They speak Tongan and English. There are numerous campus ministries working among them. Some ministries have experienced success sharing the Gospel.

Pray: For the maturity of the Tongan believers and for a willingness to return to their island and share Christ.

Bible in a year: Ephesians 4:17-32 / Ezekiel 12-13 / Isaiah 43

God's Provision

> So do not worry, saying, 'What shall we eat?' Or 'What shall we drink?' Or 'What shall we wear?' For the pagans run after all these things, and your heavenly Father knows that you need them. Matthew 6:31-32

One Saturday night, my family and I were visiting friends to say goodbye because we were leaving to be missionaries in another country. At that moment, I decided I should go to church the next morning, despite the fact we had already said our goodbyes to our church family the previous week. When I got to the church, I sat on a bench and a lady came and sat next to me. She looked at me and wanted to know if I was the missionary the church had said goodbye to last week. I told her I was. She told me we needed to chat after the service. At the end of the service, she met me with a smile and said it is amazing how God works. The women told me that God had spoke to her and encouraged her to give my family an offering. She did not think it was possible because she had thought my family and I had already left, but because of God's power we were standing there side by side. She gave me an envelope and I went on my way. When I got home, I opened the envelope and found a generous offering that exceeded my expectations. The amount was just what we needed for our trip and the next few weeks. The Lord knew and supplied for our needs in time!

J. Segnitz

Trust in the Lord!

Vlax Romanies - Romania

Population: 510,000
They have very high morals. Sexual purity and fidelity are very important values in their society. They are traders by profession. They believe in curses, ghosts, and supernatural powers.

Pray: For them to be led out of the spiritual darkness and into the light of God.

A Closer Look

> *As you sent me into the world, I have sent them into the world. John 17:18*

As we study this verse, we see Jesus sends us into the world in the same way His father sent Him. In order to know how we are sent, we must understand Jesus' purpose on earth. What did Jesus do on earth? He healed, restored, delivered, taught, discipled, died and ultimately conquered the grave. What an example our God has given us! For God, nothing is more important than people. That is why, as children of God, we are called to love our neighbors. As believers, our hearts must break for the same things that break the heart of God.

Luke 10 tells of a man who was laying on the ground, wounded and needy. Those who passed by were not bad people, but were too busy to stop and help. They knew it would require time and effort to assist him, but a Samaritan, "saw him, took pity on him," and went to bandage his wounds. In this story, the Samaritan took time out of his schedule to do what the others weren't willing to do. Accomplishing the Father's purpose begins by investing our time and denying our personal schedules.

Jesus left Heaven, came to earth, and provided a way for us to have a personal relationship with Him. Where are you today? Are you on your way to your next event or meeting? Are you willing to leave your schedule to fulfill God's desires?

L. Ashmore

Come and do His will.

Trumai - Brazil

Population: 200
They live in Mato Grosso. They wear western attire and sleep in hammocks. They trade crafts and paintings. They are animIstic and speak Portuguese. Currently, no one is known to be reaching out to this people group.

Pray: God is revealed and they receive a desire for salvation.

Faith with Purpose

{ *All peoples on the earth will be blessed through you. Genesis 12:3*

God sends His children throughout the world because He desires His Kingdom to extend to all people. God's goal is to reach every person on the planet with the Gospel. When you begin actively pursing God's goal, you will face challenges. Challenges occur because reaching people requires interaction with unchartered territories and new environments.

Walking in faith, while participating in God's goal, can be dangerous because it means being exposed to new situations, difficulties, delays, and discomfort. Following Jesus involves making choices and decisions to have courage during times of suffering and waiting. Abraham had faith as he walked to the Promised Land. When he arrived, he was only a foreigner who lived in a tent. He woke up each day trusting God and His plans. Abraham was not guided by feelings of safety or happiness, but was guided by knowing God was with him.

Faith is an adventure because it means putting your complete trust in God without knowing His exact plans. Faith is fundamental when pursing God's goals to reach the nations!
C. Scott

Are you walking in faith?

Regeibat - Western Sahara

Population: 74,000
Regeibats live in the desert and travel the country with their herds of goats and sheep. Their language is Arabic Hassaniya. They have the "Jesus film" and an audio Bible in their language. They are Muslims with very little Christian influence.

Pray: For doors to be opened so the Gospel may be shared!

Great Commission

> *Therefore go and make disciples of all nations... Matthew 28:19*

The Great Commission is a beautiful task Jesus entrusted to His disciples and church. It is a continual task assigned to all generations and it is the reason why the Church is on earth. I like to call the Great Commission the "Great Responsibility" because it is so essential to our faith. Throughout history, many people have understood their responsibility and made huge sacrifices in response to it.

It is interesting the meaning of the word "commission," can be drastically changed by removing the letter "C." In the world today, many people have removed the letter "C" and caused the Great Commission to become the "Great Omission." The word "omission," means failure to fulfill an obligation or required action. Treating the Great Commission like the "Great Omission" shows our negative attitude toward this positive responsibility.

When we neglect to share about the love of Jesus, we fail to do what is required of us. However, when we act in obedience, we fulfill the responsibilities required of us. When Jesus spoke of the Great Commission He was very clear, "... all power and authority has been given to me, therefore go..." Do not make excuses and remove the letter "C" from God's Great Commission!
W. Núñez

Take Part in the Great Commission!

Turoyo - United States

Population: 5,300

Turoyos originally come from Syria, but have a small population living in the United States. They live in New York, New Jersey, and Massachusetts. They have heard the Gospel in English, but it is estimated only 2% believe it to be true.

Pray: For the Gospel to make an impact within this ethnic group.

Authority To Forgive And Heal

> Which is easier: to say, "Your sins are forgiven,"'or to say, "Get up and walk"? But I want you to know that the Son of Man has authority on earth to forgive sins. So he said to the paralyzed man, "Get up, take your mat and go home."
> Matthew 9:5-6

Within this passage, Jesus reveals His authority to forgive sins. He authenticates the power of His authority by healing a paralyzed man. By authenticating His authority, people could not contend His ability to forgive sins.

The Father sent Jesus with power and authority and Jesus sends His disciples in the same way. At the end of the Gospel of Matthew, Jesus tells His disciples, "all authority in Heaven and Earth has been given to me." This means if Jesus has all authority, the devil has none. Jesus sends us to the world to share the Gospel of forgiveness and preach eternal life. In Jesus, we have been given everything we need for the world to be transformed. He gives us the power to do things we are not capable of doing alone!

Are you serving in our Father's business? Are you bringing the Gospel to the ends of the earth with His authority?

D. Travis

Use your authority!

Yahudic - Iraq

Population: 200
Yahudics are also known as Iraqi Jews. They practice Judaism mixed with moral beliefs. Their language is a dialect of Iraqi Arabic. They have a great need to hear the truth of the Gospel.

Pray: For God to break every chain preventing evangelism to the Yahudics.

Preaching To Save

> When I came to you, I did not come with eloquence or human wisdom as I proclaimed to you the testimony about God. For I resolved to know nothing while I was with you except Jesus Christ and him crucified. 1 Corinthians 2:1-2

The Word of God is what saves souls. Our ability to captivate an audience with jokes or funny one-liners is not the deciding factor in salvation, nor is salvation dependent on illustrations or the number of hours spent on preparing for a sermon. Salvation is dependent on the power of the Word of God. Being a polished speaker is important, but it is God alone who saves. Our preparation and ideas should never replace the overall message of the Word of God.

A sermon filled only with imagination and interesting stories is not worthy to be called preaching. A sermon that only uses Biblical texts to support the preacher's personal opinion is not preaching as God intended. Illustrations can help catch a listener's attention, but illustrations are subservient when compared to Biblical text. To place a higher importance on illustrations than the word of God is to betray the Gospel. The truth of the Word of God cannot be replaced by a passionate ending plea at the end of a sermon. If preaching is not focused on unpacking Biblical truth, then we can no longer consider it preaching. Talking only with eloquent words will not save a soul; only the Word of God brings salvation!

O. Simari

Evangelization begins with the Bible!

Yurak Samoyed - Russia

Population: 42,000
Yurak Samoyeds are one of the largest groups living in Siberia. They breed reindeer. They believe in Shamanism and in the power of spells, curses, demons, and spirits. Their language, Nenets, has some portions of the Bible translated. It is estimated only 0.5% are Christians.

Pray: For the Christians to grow in faith and for more believers to be added to their numbers.

More Workers

> { *Ask the Lord of the harvest, therefore, to send out workers into his harvest field. Read Matthew 9:35-38*

Within this passage, we are encouraged to pray for more laborers to be sent into God's harvest field. When a large number of workers are serving together and unified with a common goal, the assigned task is easier to fulfill. Working together lightens the overall load for all who are involved.

It is interesting, the passage does not ask us to pray for lost people to come to salvation. This does not mean God is indifferent about lost souls, but rather, God recognizes the size of the task and knows the workload demands more workers. It is crucial to understand spreading God's Word requires laborers!

Praying for workers results in more workers being called to serve! Our prayers will enable ministers, teachers, and missionaries to take part in the Lord's harvest!

When we pray for one lost soul, one is saved. When we pray for a worker to be added to the harvest field, hundreds or thousands can come to know Jesus through the one worker's labor! God desires all people to be saved, but reaching this goal is only possible when enough workers are mobilized to serve. We must pray for more workers! Pray more believers would be trained to go into the harvest field.

D. Travis

Are you praying for more laborers?

Uspanteco - Guatemala

Population: 4,300
Uspantecos live in Uspantán. They strongly oppose mining and the construction of a hydroelectric dam on their territory. Mining and construction has influenced them to reject all foreign things, including the message of Jesus. It is estimated 8% are Christian.

Pray: Believers would share the Gospel with power.

December 16

Speak Lord!

{ *The Lord came and stood there, calling as at the other times, "Samuel! Samuel!" Then Samuel said, "Speak, for your servant is listening." Read 1 Samuel 3:3-11*

Do you ever wonder if God can speak to you? In this passage, God spoke directly with Samuel. Although this took place during ancient times, God is the same today as He was yesterday! This means God can still speak with you today!

God is a God of communication. He always has a desire to talk with you, but communication requires two parties. God wants you to listen to Him, just as much as you want God to listen to you. God is always ready to share His heart with you!

How can you listen to God? Listening to God begins with having a personal relationship with Him. This occurs through reading His Word and by spending time in prayer. It is in our quiet time, alone with the Lord, when the Bible begins to speak into our lives. Through his holy Word, He will speak to your heart. This can often mean giving clear and specific directions for what He desires.

Have the attitude of Samuel. "Speak, for your servant is listening." Be willing to listen to everything God has to say. Have an open heart that receives both the joyful and difficult messages.

Hearing the voice of God can be a challenge, but it's a beautiful adventure. Begin your adventure today by spending time in the Bible!

I. Santander

Keep your Bible and ears open!

Temne Banta - Sierra Leone

Population: 55,000
Temne Bantas have experienced many wars, which has caused them to flee into other countries. In the last decade, they have begun to return to their land. Their main religion is Islam and Animism. They have the New Testament in their language. It is estimated only 4% are Christian.

Pray: God would strengthen the church and Christians would be witnesses to their people.

Bible in a year: Philippians 3 / Ezekiel 23 / Isaiah 51

A Superior Concept

> { *... because God's love has been poured out into our hearts through the Holy Spirit, who has been given to us. Romans 5:5*

In our postmodern society, Christians are not always understood. I live in Argentina, a country where two people of the same sex can marry freely and also have the ability to adopt children. If any citizen is dissatisfied with their sexual identity, they can receive a sex change and can adopt a new name. Argentines are confident abortion and private consumption of drugs will soon be legalized.

Often when we, the church, emphasize Biblical truth as the basis of our faith, we are accused of being intolerant. Today, tolerance has become a fashionable term. In the past, "tolerate" meant to permit wrong actions. Today, "tolerate'" means respecting people's actions regardless if they are healthy or unhealthy.

When people are tolerant, they are often admired, but when people are intolerant, they are quickly categorized as being cruel. The danger of tolerance is it allows unrestricted actions despite consequences. I could be a tolerant father, but if my child is going to walk off a cliff I cannot remain tolerant. Instead of being tolerant, we need to love! Loving is the superior concept! As children of God, He has poured out His love into our hearts so we can freely love others. Love is the action of a great missionary!

W. Altare

> **Many people are tolerant, but Christians love without limits!**

Tuvaluan - Tuvalu

Population: 9,500
Tuvaluans make up 98% of the population of Tuvalu. They have the entire Bible translated into their language and 17% have accepted the Gospel. The church is still dependent on missionaries. They are in need of spiritual maturity.

Pray: For the maturity of the established church. Pray they will become capable of reaching the rest of their ethnic group.

Follow His Footsteps

{ *Jesus replied, "Let us go somewhere else- to the nearby villages- so I can preach there also. That is why I have come." Mark 1:38*

Jesus encourages us to walk in faith as we look into a future that is often full of risk. When looking to the future we must understand the urgency needed to fulfill God's mission. Taking part in God's mission means facing unknown circumstances, but it is worth the risk! It was once said, "The biggest risk is always that of taking the steps, not just talking about them." When we take part in Gods mission, to reach the world with the Gospel, we are being obedient to Biblical truth: "Enlarge the place of your tent, stretch your tent curtains wide, do not hold back! Lengthen your cords and strengthen your stakes. For you will spread out to the right and to the left... " (Isaiah 54:2-3). This passage encourages you to spread out your tent and strengthen the stakes. This is a metaphor to show God's desire to reach new people with the Gospel. God does not want anyone to perish, but rather wants everyone to repent. We have to understand God desires for us to "spread out" and be a "blessing to all ethnic groups." Although the future of Jesus was full of risk, He never stopped walking in faith. Jesus took part in God's mission by preaching in new houses, towns, and cities. Follow in His footsteps! Stretch out and reach new people with the Gospel!

C. Scott

Are you reaching new people?

Walser - Switzerland

Population: 16,400
Walsers live in several Swiss Cantons (Valais, Bern, St. Gallen, Graubünden and Ticino). They profess Christianity, but mainly only by name. Secularism and materialism dominate their lives.

Pray: For a spiritual awakening in the lives.

December 19

Disruptors

> But they did not find them, they dragged Jason and some other believers before the city officials, shouting: "These men who have caused trouble all over the world have now come here." Acts 17:6

In this verse, Paul and Silas are accused of causing trouble all over the world. In other translations of the Bible, they are accusing of disrupting the world. To disrupt something means to alter or destroy the structure. Synonyms of disrupt are: upset, confuse, distress, bother, or disturb. Paul and Silas were seen as a disruption because they were preaching a message of transformation to a group of people who were unwilling to be changed. Paul and Silas preached the message of a risen Christ and this angered many. Their boldness in preaching the Gospel was so powerful it resulted in disrupting other parts of the world!

God wants you to be a radical. He wants you to be someone who is not satisfied until His message of salvation is proclaimed to the ends of the earth. God wants to use you to disrupt this world! Are you ready? Will you be a trendsetter? Will you share the message of salvation to others?!

A. Gulard

The Gospel can disrupt an entire nation!

Yurupí - Brazil

Population: 350
Yurupís live on the border of Colombia, in Vaupés. They are fruit growers. Their main food is cassava. They are animists and believe the moon, sun, and stars are people. They teach values through fables.

Pray: For missionaries to be bold and preach the Gospel.

Godly Leadership

{ *The Lord answered, "Who then is the faithful and wise manager, whom the master puts in charge of his servants to give them their food allowance at the proper time?" Read Luke 12:42-46*

Becoming a leader is something most young people desire. It is temptation to believe leadership is only a position of power, but leadership also involves responsibility. In this passage, Jesus speaks to his disciples as leaders of servants. The responsibilities the leaders have are to give food allowances at the proper time.

In this passage, Jesus warns of the temptations a leader may face. In verse 45, Jesus says it is a temptation for a leader to lose respect for the Lord, the true Master of the house. He warns it is a temptation to abuse authority and abuse those the leader is responsible for. Selfishness and greed are a couple other temptations leaders face. Leaders cannot succumb to the temptation of fulfilling only their personal interests or indulging in their selfish pleasures. If a leader acts so carelessly, Jesus says a day will come when the Lord will return and deliver a severe punishment (v. 46).

Are you being a good steward of the roles God has given you? Are you serving those God has placed in your care? Are you caring for them or mistreating them? Do you look out for the needs of others before your own? Jesus desires for you to be a good servant and leader!
M. de Rodríguez

Lead with integrity.

Uuld - Mongolia

Population: 7,700
Uulds are Buddhists who live in the northwest of Mongolia, near the border with Russia. They speak Mongolia's national language, Mongolian Halh. They have the Bible in their langauge, but there are still no known Christians.

Pray: Uulds would have a desire to read the Bible and know Jesus.

Philip's Mission

{ *Then he got up and went. Read Acts 8:26-40*

Philip received the missionary task of personally presenting the Gospel to a eunuch. A "eunuch" is a person who has been castrated. By Jewish law, eunuchs were not allowed to enter the temple (Deuteronomy 23:1). The eunuch Philip spoke with was a religious man, but needed to be born again. Philip's testimony was the instrument God used to give the eunuch hope and salvation.

When you are serving outside of the Church, you have a special mission: to faithfully give a testimony of God's grace to those who do not believe.

In giving your testimony it should reflect the story of Philip and the eunuch. In this story, four crucial points desire your attention.

1. Be obedient to Gods calling (v.26-27).
2. Have hope in God's faithfulness (v.27).
3. Salvation is given by God (v.28).
4. Live in dependence on the Holy Spirit (v.29).

Take full advantage of the opportunities God gives you. Pray daily for the salvation of your friends, or distribute Bibles to people on the streets. Tell others what Christ means in your life! Keep you eyes open for opportunities God gives you to reach the world!

L. Díaz

Stay alert!

Tubu Tedas - Niger

Population: 17,000

The majority of Tubu Tedas are Muslim, but they perform many rituals of their native animistic religion. There are some Christians, but they have been removed from the group. Their language, Tedaga, has some audio stories of the Bible.

Pray: For the protection of Tubu Tedas believers and for a strengthening of their faith.

Serve Where God Has Called You

> In the spring, at the time when kings go off to war, David sent Joab out with the king's men and the whole Israelite army. They destroyed the Ammonites and besieged Rabbah. But David remained in Jerusalem. 2 Samuel 11:1

David the King of Israel, the commander in chief of an army, was on the balcony of his palace when he should have been on the battlefield. Sitting on the balcony shows how David was overlooking his responsibilities and leaving his duties to be fulfilled by others. What is the role God has called you to fulfill? Do not fall victim to the common saying: "Don't worry, someone else will do it."

David was not fulfilling his responsibilities as king. Not fulfilling his responsibilities led to one of the biggest mistakes of his life. While David was sitting on the balcony, he saw a woman bathing. As he saw her, he sent his servants to retrieve her. When the woman appeared before him, he gave into his weakness and committed adultery with her.

The story of David is a warning for our lives. God has given us responsibilities and we should not neglect them. David's sin of adultery was not the greatest sin of his life. His greatest sin was his disobedience to God. David failed to comply with the responsibilities God had entrusted to him.

How about you, has God given you a responsibility in His kingdom? Did you know if you neglect your responsibility you become vulnerable to falling into a series of sins?

L. Ashmore

Stand firm where God has called you.

Toba Qom - Paraguay

Population: 1,020
Toba Qoms have a translation of the New Testament. Some churches are established, but they need education and native leaders. Some young people are responding to the Gospel.

Pray: For the missionaries who are serving with them and for the Toba Qom believers.

God Has Spoken To Us...

> *The heavens declare the glory of God; the skies proclaim the work of his hands.*
> *Psalm 19:1*

God speaks to us through His creation, His faithfulness, His glory, His wisdom and His interest in our lives! God communicates with us through His Word and has shown us the importance of knowing and obeying His commands (1 Peter 1:23, Proverbs 22:10).

Psalm 19:7-10 says, "The law of the Lord is perfect, refreshing the soul. The statutes of the Lord are trustworthy, making wise the simple. The precepts of the Lord are right, giving joy to the heart. The commands of the Lord are radiant, giving light to the eyes. The fear of the Lord is pure, enduring forever. The decrees of the Lord are firm, and all of them are righteous. They are more precious than gold, than much pure gold; they are sweeter than honey, than honey from the honeycomb. "

Today God speaks through His Son, Jesus.

Hebrews 1:1-2 says, "In the past, God spoke to our ancestors through the prophets at many times and in various ways, but in these last days he has spoken to us by his Son, whom he appointed heir of all things, and through whom also he made the universe."

God is a God of communication. He is creative and speaks to us in many ways. Follow the example of God and do everything possible to allow God's message to be understood in the language of peoples' hearts!

MyT. Goddard

Let's let them know!

Tekna - Western Sahara

Population: 113,000
Teknas come from Egypt. Their religion is Islam and they follow it faithfully. Having another religion can be punished by death. Their language is Tachelhit, which has a translation of the New Testament.

Pray: God would have mercy on the Teknas. Pray they would have a desire to know Jesus!

The Meaning Of Christmas

> When they reached the house they saw the child with Mary his mother, and fell down and worshiped him. Then they opened their treasures and presented him with gifts of gold, frankincense and myrrh. Matthew 2:11

By this time in the year, we have decorated the house with colorful lights, put out a tree, made a list of gifts we want, and got out the Santa Claus suit! Christmas is coming, but these holiday traditions are not the true meaning of Christmas.

This time of the year is full of joyful people, but how can you take advantage of the season? Here are a few suggestions:

1. Write a letter to your friends telling them the true meaning of Christmas.
2. Watch a video with your friends about how people around the world celebrate Christmas.
3. Deliver gifts for children in the nearest orphanage.
4. Raise money for an offering to be sent to missionaries so they are able to buy gifts for their family.
5. Organize a garage sale and send the money to children who are in need.

This is a short list of ideas, but you can create a list specific to your situation. Christmas is not about what we give. Christmas is about the gift God has given us! Share His gift with the world.

A. Corrales

Are you sharing the gift God gave you?

Yonaguni - Japan

Population: 800

Yonagunis are natives of the Yonaguni Island, located near Taiwan. They are Buddhists. Yonagunis believe worshiping ancestors is very important. Today, they speak predominantly Japanese, which has a translation of the Bible.

Pray: For the Word of God to change their culture and religion.

The Gift Of God

> For to us a child is born, to us a son is given, and the government will be on his shoulders. And he will be called Wonderful Counselor, Mighty God, Everlasting Father, Prince of Peace. Isaiah 9:6

This time of the year, families and friends gather together to celebrate Christmas. When people are gathering, it is a temptation to forget the true meaning of the season. Christmas is a remembrance of when God provided the greatest gift ever given. The greatest gift ever given was Jesus. Jesus came, was born in a manger, grew up as a child obedient to his earthly parents, and as an adult gave His life as a sacrifice for sinners. Through Jesus, we received gifts that we can freely share with others.

Through Christ we have received PEACE. John 14:27

Through Christ we have received COMFORT. John 14:26

Through Christ we have received STRENGTH in times of conflict. John 16:33

Through Christ we have received ETERNAL SALVATION. John 3:16

Through Christ we have received TRUE JOY. John 17:13

The child who was born in a stable is the one who gives us peace, comfort, strength, eternal life and joy. Today remember with gratitude these priceless gifts.

Share with others the truth God has given. Be a witness to His beautiful gift for all mankind.

D. Duk

Experience the meaning of Christmas!

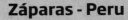

Záparas - Peru

Population: 200

Záparas live near the border of Ecuador. Their language is beginning to die because of rapid globalization. They trade and exchange goods. They are Animists and believe salvation is achieved by pleasing their spirits. They can read the Bible in Spanish.

Pray: Their eyes would be opened to their need for Jesus.

Bible in a year: Luke 2:1-20 / Ezekiel 37 / Isaiah 60

The Call Of God

> Then the Lord said, "Rise and anoint him; this is the one." So Samuel took the horn of oil and anointed him in the presence of his brothers. 1 Samuel 16:12-13

Although David lived many centuries ago, you can still learn from his life. David was a man who was not worried about having power or being elected king. David's main concern was to be responsible for the work entrusted to him. David was content being a shepherd, writing poems, and singing songs to the Lord.

David wrote in times of joy, sorrow, danger and refuge. He was always in contact with his Creator and was responsible for caring for his sheep. God knew the heart of David better than David's own father did. David had a personal relationship with God, which is why David was considered a man after God's own heart. God chose David to be king because He knew the heart of David!

David's life was not easy. He fought a giant, was almost killed by Saul, and fought in many intense battles. David was faithful to God's call on his life and God was faithful to fulfill the call He placed on David.

How about you? Is there something God has called you to do? Are you actively pursing your calling? Follow the steps God has given you to achieve your mission!

I. Santander

Follow your calling!

Yazidi - Syria

Population: 14,000
Yazidi's live in an Arab mountain village. Their language is a dialect of Levantine Arabic. Portions of the Bible have been translated. They are animistic and very superstitious.

Pray: Yazidi's would recognize the emptiness in their lives and would surrender to Christ.

Ideal Candidate

> But God chose the foolish things of the world to shame the wise; God chose the weak things of the world to shame the strong. God chose the lowly things of this world and the despised things—and the things that are not—to nullify the things that are, so that no one may boast before him. 1 Corinthians 1:27-29

Many people feel unworthy to serve God full time. They have a sincere desire to be a pastor or missionary, but do not dare follow their call. Often people feel unworthy when they do not have an education, come from poor families, or are new believers. If you can identify with feelings of unworthiness, I have great news. You are the perfect candidate to serve God! Why? God desires to be glorified, recognized, and praised. When you are a humble servant, you maximize the glory God receives. The "success" of a Christian worker is not dependent on education or economic resources. When people become dependent on education and finances, the glory of God is minimized.

To serve God, you do not have to be rich or poor. Being an old believer or a new believer is irrelevant for your calling. Having a degree from a University or only a basic education is not what qualifies you for service. The most important characteristic of serving God is the condition of your heart. If you have a sincere and willing heart, God will prepare you for what He has called you to do.

F. Rodríguez

Are you ready for God to use you as you are?

Watchi - Benin

Population: 53,000
Watchis live in the province of Mono. Their economy is based on agriculture. Their language has some audio Bible stories. Their religion is animistic. It is estimated only 2% are Christians.

Pray: For spiritual strengthening of Christians. Pray they will have an impact on other Watchis.

The Mission And Purpose Of The Church

{ *According to his eternal purpose that he accomplished in Christ Jesus our Lord. Ephesians 3:11*

Within the last few years, the meaning of "missions" has begun to be more clearly defined. Twentieth century theologians Rick Warren and Christian Schwarz have played a significant role in defining missions within the global church. Their books, *A Purpose Drive Church* and *Eight Characteristics of a Healthy Church* emphasize the importance of the church being defined by its purpose or "mission".

We can see Paul took the same approach as Warren and Schwarz in his letter to the church of Ephesus. Paul emphasized that the purpose of the church should dominate the minds of pastors and leaders when making decisions. When pastors fail to do this, churches end up in traditionalism, denominationalism, socialism and other "isms" that oppose the "riches both of the wisdom and knowledge of God." The global church has received a mission from God. The mission is "to proclaim the praises of Him who called us out of darkness to light," and not just in our own county, but to "all nations." Any church that wanders from this God-given mission ceases to be a church that loves and desires God.

A. Neufeld

What is the mission of your church?

Viti Levu - Fiji

Population: 23,000
They live scattered in the smaller islands of Archipelago. They are famers and fishermen. The entire Bible has been translated into their language, Fijian. It is estimated 20% have responded to the Gospel, but the church is still weak and lacks education.

Pray: For teachers trained in the Word of God to engage with these people.

Bible in a year: Luke 3:21-38 / Ezekiel 42-43 / Isaiah 63

Caretakers

> { Sir, the man replied, "leave it for another year, so that I can dig around it and fertilize it. So perhaps it bears fruit, if not, cut it down." Read Luke 13:6-9

Luke 13 begins by Jesus talking about the importance of repentance and the forgiveness of sin. To illustrate His point, Jesus tells a parable about a fig tree in a vineyard. He discusses how the owner of the vineyard instructs the vineyard caretaker to cut down the tree because no fruit had been received in three years. The vineyard caretaker interceded on behalf of the tree and vowed to carefully tend it for one year. The caretaker said if nothing changes after his service then the tree can be cut down.

The stark reality is every human is under the condemnation of sin. God does not desire their destruction, but rather repentance of sin. Similar to the vineyard caretaker, Jesus is interceding for us. He desires us to come to salvation and bear fruit.

Jesus is a beautiful example of a caretaker! Do you have love for the lost? Are you prayerfully interceding for their salvation? Are you trying different things so the message can be received?

M. de Rodríguez

Be a noble gardener in His vineyard!

Tamasheq - Mali

Population: 462,000
They live in leather tents. The majority are Muslims, but they are considered passive in their faith. Their language, Tamasheq, has a translation of the New Testament.

Pray: For missionaries to be willing to serve and reach Tamasheqs with the Gospel of Christ.

Good Reputation

> Hezekiah trusted in the Lord, God of Israel. There was no one like him among all the kings of Judah, either before him or after him. 2 Kings 18:5

The story of Hezekiah is very motivating for young people. Hezekiah was 25 when he began his reign in Jerusalem. He was recognized as the one who "put his trust in the Lord." He had the incredible reputation of having no one like him among all the kings of Judah.

Why was Hezekiah so prosperous?

1. "He did what was right in the eyes of the Lord" (2 Kings 18:3). How can you know what pleases God? You can know by reading His Word, the Bible.

2. "He removed the high places" (2 Kings 18:4). Removing the high places refers to destroying pagan alters. It is often difficult to repent from sin, but you need to remove any sin that is taking the place of God in your life.

3. "He put his trust in the Lord" (2 Kings 18:5). Often we use God as the last resort in difficult circumstances. We act like He is not capable of supplying everything we need. Put your trust in Him. He is faithful!

Do you want to have a testimony like Hezekiah? Do what pleases God, turn from sin, and trust Jesus. Doing these three things will change your life dramatically.

L. Ashmore

You can do it!

Yeniche - Austria

Population: 1,700
They are of German decent. They are known to be nomads. They are predominantly Catholic. Their native language is Yenish, but most speak German.

Pray: The Gospel would bring life to the Yeniche.

Bible in a year: Luke 4:31-44 / Ezekiel 46-47 / Isaiah 65

Do Not Live In The Past

> Elijah said to Elisha, "Stay here; the Lord has sent me to Bethel." But Elisha said, "As surely as the Lord lives and as you live, I will not leave you." So they went down to Bethel. 2 Kings 2:2

Elijah was instructed to leave the town of Gilgal, so he ordered Elisha to stay in the town while he departed. Gilgal was a historic city. It was the city the Israelites reached when they crossed the Jordan. Gilgal was the city where Joshua placed the twelve stones in the Jordan and where the Passover was celebrated for the first time. The city of Gilgal was a place of memories and blessings of the past. In human eyes, Gilgal was the ideal place to stay, but Elisha had different plans.

Elisha wanted to push forward with Elijah, so together they went to Bethel. In Bethel, Elisha was told again to stay. Bethel was another attractive destination because it was the city where Abraham built an altar to God and was renamed "Israel". Although he was told to stay, Elisha's response was persistent. "I want to go with you across the river."

The next place they traveled to was Jericho. When they reached Jericho, Elisha was instructed to stay. Jericho was another appealing place with significant history. Jericho was the city the Lord conquered by crumbling the city walls. Jericho was also the place Rahab hid the spies, but Elisha was still not satisfied because he wanted to go on.

God desires to show you new horizons! He wants you to overcome new challenges and lift you into a "supra-life"! To reach new horizons with the Lord, you cannot live in the accomplishments of the past! Press forward!

T. Vögelin

> Are you willing to go where the Lord desires to take you?

Worodougou - Sierra Leone

Population: 101,000

They live in 213 separate villages. They grow rice, corn, yams, cashews and cotton. 95% profess Islam. A small group of Christians exist, but they are often persecuted. They do not have the Bible in their native language Worodougou.

Pray: For the Gospel to powerfully work in the lives of the Worodougous.

Authors

Altare, Walter: Pastor and lecturer, from Argentina. Board member of the "Council of Pastors of the City."

Ashmore, Laura Anne: Teacher, writer, and artist, from South Africa. Director of "Paraguay De Pie y Mujeres de Pie", author of various plays for children and youth. Lives in Paraguay.

Bascur, Hebert: Civil Engineer and Specialist in Strategic Management, from Chile. Youth pastor and Director of MOVIDA Latin America South-Region, based in Argentina.

Bello, Wendy: Translator, author, and teacher, from Cuba. Has a blog ministry that helps women in their faith. Lives in Florida.

Betancur, Adolfo: Missionary and Social Communicator, from Peru.

Chinatti, Fabián: Master in Missiology, from Argentina. Pastor in Chile.

Chiquie, Munir: Pastor, from Bolivia. Leader of a monthly pastors' meeting in the city of Cochabamba.

Corrales, Andrés: Missionary, from Uruguay. Director of "SIM" (Serving in Mission) and Director of "Youth Specialties in Uruguay." Mobilization Coordinator for Latin America of SIM Ocla.

De Rodríguez, María: Accountant and graphic designer, from Chile. Degree in Pastoral Theology. Missionary at MOVIDA Paraguay. Coordinator of the devotional book "Explorer".

Diaz, Luis: Pastor, from Paraguay.

Duk, Delia: Accountant, from Argentina. Worked for 14 years with MOVIDA in the area of Accounting and Finances. Has edited books and devotionals.

Eitzen, Martin: Pastor and missionary, from Paraguay. Has Doctorate in Missiology. Works for the National Pastoral Development.

Galindo, Ginny: Finance Manager and Legal Representative of the company TARGUET SRL, from Bolivia.

Goddard, Mike and Trisha: Counselors and mobilizers, from the United States. Mike has a Bachelor of Arts and Trisha a Bachelor of Science in Intercultural Ministries from New Tribes Mission. Coordinators of Amazon & Lowlands Tribal Empowerment Coalition (ALTECO) in Paraguay.

Gomes, Marcos: Pastor and profesor, from Brazil.

Gulard, Alex: Pastor, from Uruguay.

House, Geoff: From Nebraska in the United States.

Inciarte, Maria: Lawyer, from Venezuela. Has Doctorate of Law.

Langemeier, Scott: Missionary, from Nebraska in the United States. Founder and president of MOVIDA USA.

Nacif, Munir Chiquíe: Pastor and educator, from Bolivia. Bachelor of Theology - Church Resources Management. PhD Candidate in Theology and Science Education. "Precept Ministries" national director of Bolivia.

Neufeld, Alfred: Pastor, from Paraguay. Has Doctorate of Theology. Member of MOVIDA Paraguay.

Núñez, Warry: Movida missionary and youth pastor, from Costa Rica. Founder of MOVIDA Costa Rica.

Pescador, Jero and Adri: Jero - missionary in Costa Rica among West African Sooninke. Has Bachelor Degree in French Language and Literature (UCR) and Theology (IBCA). Currently working on Master of Science of Religion with Missions emphasis. Adri - professor of music and business entrepreneur, from Brazil. Founding member of LAGRAM.

Rivas, Gilmar and Noemi: Missionaries, from Peru, serving in the Peruvian Amazon among the Mastanawa.

Rodríguez, Félix: Pastor and missionary, from Paraguay. Director of MOVIDA Paraguay. Member of CONAMI. Professor at the Evangelical University of Paraguay. Representative of COMIBAM in Paraguay.

Sandvig, Tim: Missionary, from the United States. Serving with SIM in Chile. Personnel Director of ProVisión.

Santander, Ivette: Cross-cultural missionary, from Chile. Served with YWAM (Youth With A Mission) for 21 years. Currently living in England and supports missions work in Africa.

Scott, Carlos: Pastor, from Argentina. Facilitator and Mentor for the mission initiative GloCal. member of the Missions Commission "World Evangelical Alliance" (WEA).

Segnitz, Jörg: MOVIDA missionary, from Germany, currently serving at the MOVIDA international headquarters in Weingarten, Germany.

Simari, Osvaldo: Pastor, from Argentina.

Travis, Drake: Pastor, from the United States. Has Master Degree in Literature of the New Testament. Worked in missions for over 30 years. Promoter of public relations of the dental health ministry "Good Samaritan."

Vergara, Gonzalo: Pastor and missionary, from Uruguay. Director of MOVIDA Argentina.

Vögelin, Thomas: Missionary, from Switzerland. Founder and director of MOVIDA International. Served in South American for 25 years, but now serves at the MOVIDA international headquarters in Weingarten, Germany.

Ziefle, Hans: Pastor and missionary, from Germany. Serving with SIM in Chile. Director and founder of SAMI, SalGlobal, and co-founder of the "Vallenar Filadelphia NGO". Director of "ProVisión." Member of COMIBAM Chile.

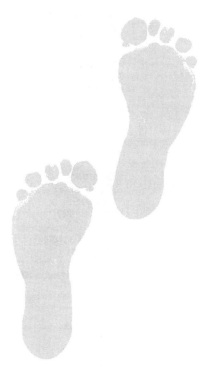

Index of People Groups

Eka 141
Ersu 240
Kemei 197
Laba 65
Menia 245

Colombia:
Achagua 12
Andoque 53
Awa Cuaiquer 61
Barasana 82
Betoyes 95
Cabiyaris 106
Chimilas 132
Chiricoa 160
Coconucos 147
Guanacas 191
Hitnu 202
Inga 218
Letuamas 252
Matapi 273
Nunkak Macu 294

Costa Rica:
Cabecar 86

Croatia:
Friulano 181

Czech Republic:
Czech 97
Boii 215
Umbundu 355

Denmark:
Danish 115
Faroese 150

Dominican Republic:
Dominicans 170

Egypt:
Fur 169
Oromo 324
Siwa 336

Eritrea:
Nialetic 318
Rashaida 326

Estonia:
Estonians 129

Ethiopia:
Anfillo 27
Hamer Banna 182

Fiji:
Bhojpuri 94
Viti Levu 382

Finland:
Finnish 164
Karelians 231

France:
Alsatian 13
Auvergne 38
Brittany 72
Giay 189

Gabon:
Arab 42

Gambia:
Khasonke 241

Ghana:
Chakali 98
Mamprusi 282

Greenland:
Eskimo 179

Guatemala:
Chortis 142
Uspanteco 369

Guinea:
Lele 274

Guinea Bissau:
Kobiana 255

Guyana:
Akawaios 30
Pemon 322

Haiti:
Haitian 194

India:
Agaria 18
Ahar 26
Baiga 69
Baori 81
Dhavad 316
Kurmi 24
Lodha 67

Indonesia:
Aghu 17
Aji 34
Alas 44
Ambelau 52
Ambonese 21
Ampanang 62
Anus 68
Asilulu 74
Bakumpai 79
Baliaga 87
Dampelas 123
Daya 134
Diuwe 138
Earn 159
Gaius 167
Gorontalo 172
Java Banten 185
Java Banyumasan 203
Java Mancanegari 211
Java Osing 217
Java Pesisir Lor 222
Javanese 226
Kaili Unde 238
Kikim 247
Korowai 253
Lubu 265
Masama 284
Sasak 351

Iran:
Galeshi 158
Herki 186
Koroshi 223
Lasgerdi 242
Vafsi 357

Iraq:
Bajelani 93
Shabak 298
Yahudic 367

Ireland:
Shelta 325

Israel:
Arbil 75
Cochin 140
Dzhidi 149
Domari Gypsy 177
Maghrebi 251

Ivory Cost:
Neho 314

Jamaica:
Jamaicans 210

Japan:
Amami Oshima 40
Kikai 204
Okinawan 268
Toku-no-shima 310
Yonaguni 378
Yoron 360

Kenya:
Aweer 50
Ilchamus 201
Kachchi 236
Mijikenda 303

Kosovo:
Gorani 207

Kuwait:
Khoja 214
Sorani Kurdos 233

Laos:
Alak 31
Bit 100
Halang 145
Jeh 176
Pacoh 283

Latvia:
Latvians 246
Livonian 264

Liberia:
Manya 287

Libya:
Awjilah 60
Jofra 230
Sanusi 334

Lithuania:
Lithuanians 254

Malaysia:
Abai Sungai 11
Bawean 85
Illanon 162
Kanarese 180

Mali:
Bozo-Sorogama 146
Bozo Tie 92
Bozo Tiema Ciewe 111
Tamajaq 348
Tamasheq 383

Mauritania:
Duaish 143
Masna 293
Moor 305

Mexico:
Chiapanecos 124
Chocholtecas 137
Cocopa 152
Mocho 285
O'odham 308
Tila Chol 343
Tojolabal 352

Mongolia:
Bayad 91
Khotogoid 200
Khoton 216
Tuvinian 350
Uuld 374

Morocco:
Haratines 188
Jebala 219
Regeibat 332

Mozambique:
Koti 259
Makwe 278
Mwani 311

Myanmar:
Chak 113
Chakma 131
Kiorr 220
Orisi 275

Nauru:
Marshalle 276

Nepal:
Ath Pahariya Rai 51
Bahelia 64
Halwai 148
Kyerung 234
Mugali 250

Netherlands:
Ambonese 21
Dutch 289
Friesian 173

New Caledonia:
New Caledonia Javanese 313

New Zealand:
New Zealand 306
Tongan 362

Nicaragua:
Matagalpa 266

Niger:
Daza 136
Tasawaq 361
Tubu Tedas 375

Nigeria:
Afade 23
Cineni 119

Somalia:
Dabarre 125
Jiiddo 224

South Korea:
Koreans 153

Spain:
Aragon 29
Catalan 88
Extremadura 139
Fala 156

Sudan:
Acheron 14
Fezara 166

Suriname:
Kwinti 244

Sweden:
Izhorians 221
Swedish 339

Switzerland:
Walser 372

Syria:
Adyghe 10
Ossete 279
Yazidi 380

Taiwan:
Tayal 302

Thailand:
Bisu 96
Huay 157
Samtaos 292

Togo:
Anufo 36

Tokelau:
Tokelauan 358

Tunisia:
Duwinna 154
Matmata 297

Tamezret 353

Tuvalu:
Tuvaluano 371

Ukraine:
Ruthenes 315

United Arab Emirates:
Bedouin 121
Malayali 261
Tagalog 329

United Kingdom:
Cornish 120
Goanese 199
Mandaean 272
Sylhetti 345

United States:
Adyghe 20
Amish 45
Baggara 78
Cherokee 118
Turoyo 366
Western Cham 110

Vanuatu:
Fortsenal 144
Letemboi 258

Venezuela:
Japrería 213

Vietnam:
Alu 35
Arem 43
Brao 105
Cao Lan 109
Churu 122
Nung 263
Ta'oih 296
Trieng 320
Tsun-Lao 341

Wallis and Futuna:
Futuanes 151

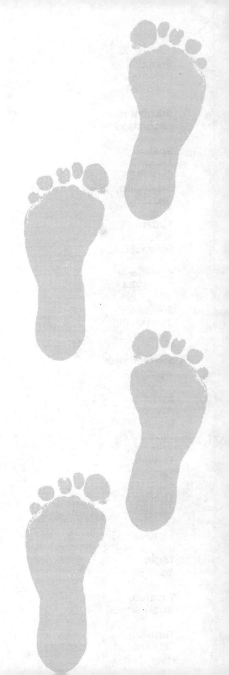